Putting the Psychoanalytic Frame to Work

Psychoanalysis is not just about what happens in the room – it is also about the structure that holds it all together. In *Putting the Psychoanalytic Frame to Work*, Allannah Furlong rethinks one of the traditional approaches to the analytic frame, arguing that disruptions – missed sessions, consent complexities, and third-party demands – are not necessarily obstacles but can be essential moments for deepening therapeutic insight.

The book argues for a benevolent expectation of "trouble" as an inherent part of the therapeutic couple getting to know each other more deeply, and as an aspect which distinguishes the psychoanalytic frame from that usually taught by professional regulatory bodies. Furlong proposes that the analyst or psychoanalytic therapist welcome framework glitches as opportunities to "put the framework to work" rather than simply disposing of them as acting out or error. In so doing, the book invites clinicians to critically examine different theoretical approaches to the framework and its inevitable breaches.

A why-to rather than a how-to book, *Putting the Psychoanalytic Frame to Work* aims to invigorate the practice of analysts everywhere – both seasoned and in training.

Allannah Furlong is a psychoanalyst based in Canada. She is a member of the Société psychanalytique de Montréal, and is coeditor of previous books including *Confidentiality: Ethical Perspectives and Clinical Dilemmas* (Routledge). She has authored numerous articles treating individual aspects of the classical framework and was awarded the JAPA Prize for excellence in psychoanalytic scholarship.

"The frame 'groans,' observes Furlong, as she explores it in fresh and frank detail, with special appreciation of its dynamic quality, a breathing skin more than a locked, invariant container, an attitude, an offer, that both insists on the frame while remaining astutely poised to examine its inevitable breaches and revisions. As she plumbs the framework of the treatment, Furlong provides a clear rationale for psychoanalysis itself. This is an enriching must-read for students and experienced analysts alike."

Dr Arthur Leonoff, *Ph.D., Supervising and Training Analyst, Canadian Psychoanalytic Society; Chair of the International New Groups Committee of the IPA*

"Any psychoanalytic practitioner whose own work leads them to serious reflection on the frame/setting will find Dr Furlong's discussion illuminating, original, thought-provoking, refreshing, and helpful. Describing it as a 'why-to' rather than a 'how-to' book, she combines clear theoretical considerations with close attention to clinical details. Examined in particular depth are problems of consent and assent, the special character of the initial encounter and analytic offer, the meanings of missed sessions, and psychoanalytic confidentiality. A book not to be missed."

John Churcher, *British Psychoanalytical Society*

Putting the Psychoanalytic Frame to Work

Why it Matters

Allannah Furlong

Routledge
Taylor & Francis Group

LONDON AND NEW YORK

Designed cover image: Getty Images

First published 2026
by Routledge
4 Park Square, Milton Park, Abingdon, Oxon OX14 4RN

and by Routledge
605 Third Avenue, New York, NY 10158

Routledge is an imprint of the Taylor & Francis Group, an informa business

© 2026 Allannah Furlong

British Library Cataloguing-in-Publication Data
A catalogue record for this book is available from the British Library

ISBN: 9781032864204 (hbk)
ISBN: 9781032864198 (pbk)
ISBN: 9781003527459 (ebk)

DOI: 10.4324/9781003527459

Typeset in Times New Roman
by KnowledgeWorks Global Ltd.

My gratitude to my colleagues Gilles Fauvel, who read and critiqued each chapter as it was written, and to Deborah Zack who made valuable suggestions. I also thank my husband, Thomas Milroy, for his patience with my devoting so much time to this project.

Contents

Acknowledgements

The author wishes to acknowledge the encouragement and support of Susannah Frearson, Publisher at Routledge, Taylor & Francis Group in the writing stages of the manuscript and to production staff who guided me through the equally crucial editing and indexing preparations of transforming it into a real book.

We thank Craig Myles, Rights Permission, at Sage Publications for permission to reuse an article originally published in 2020 in the Journal of the American Psychoanalytic Association, 64:583–613, and which appears with minor editorial corrections in Chapter 3.

Introduction

The impetus for this monograph

It is perhaps disheartening to realize that most books bought are scarcely read, though often because people just do not have the time. The Japanese have invented a word for it: *Tsudonku*, for leaving a book unread after buying it, typically piled up together with other unread books (Popova, 2023). It is hoped that this volume can be useful and thought-provoking while remaining relatively compact. The author has written many times about different aspects of the framework for psychoanalytically oriented treatments, attempting to work through the why and wherefore of challenges to it, precipitated in equal portions by her personal inhibitions and by patients' pushback. At the beginning, a preoccupation with money matters, especially the role of the patient's "gesture of payment" in private practice and the lack of it in institutional settings, led to experimentation with symbolic payments in work as a hospital psychologist (Furlong 1993, 1998a). It did not take long to learn how fraught the missed session can be (Furlong 1994, 1992). Then Bollas and Sundelson's disturbing 1996 critique of the erosion of confidentiality in psychoanalytic practice, *The New Informants: The Betrayal of Confidentiality in Psychoanalysis and Psychotherapy*, sparked a decades long concern about the matter, on several fronts, clinical, legal, and ethical (Furlong 1996, 1997a, 1997b, 2003a, 2003b, 2005a, 2005b, 2013a). Eventually, the issue of informed consent appeared on the horizon both as a controversial aspect of clinical writing about patients and as an exigency of professional regulatory bodies before commencing treatment (Furlong 2020, 2006, 2003c, 1998b, 1998–1999). Throughout these years, especially in exchanges with colleagues (cf. the IPA Confidentiality Report of 2018, Section 2.7 on Institutional and Individual Responsibilities), the necessary participation of psychoanalytic institutions and peers in protecting the unique configurations of psychoanalytic work became obvious as an additional crucial thread (Furlong 1995). The collation of this thinking in one monograph may be of service to other analysts, and particularly to younger colleagues: those who are training to become analysts and those psychotherapists who find psychoanalysis an inspiring reference theory.

Psychoanalysis remains less ideological and normative than many critics have asserted. As we have learnt many times, revolutions tend to be less progressive over

DOI: 10.4324/9781003527459-1

time than they first appeared to be because the original rallying cries for change overlooked treating the unruly and unpleasant complexity of human inner life, individual and collective, and ended up as self-serving, self-deceiving, and grossly unfair to the common person as the regimes they overthrew. At the same time, we will not forget that criticism both within and without the profession remains necessary. Psychoanalysis, as the "science of unconscious knowledge", needs to evolve with as much humility and excitement as any other science. Freud's discovery of the mechanisms by which individuals and groups delude themselves about their motives and aims, and distort their histories and their relationships to others, applies equally to practicing psychoanalysts and the institutions to which they belong. Laplanche loved saying that he was not a "Freudian"; he preferred to say that he liked to put Freud's writings "to work" even if it meant making them "groan", by carefully studying the inconsistencies, regressions, and revisions contained therein. Laplanche was applying the psychoanalytic method to Freud's corpus itself. The reader is invited in this book to assess the value of applying a similar method to our frameworks.

The present monograph will gather thoughts on four aspects of the framework in psychoanalytically oriented work where the author, some colleagues, and many supervisees have struggled and stumbled: setting up a working configuration at the beginning of treatment, thinking psychoanalytically about informed consent, handling the always prickly matter of missed sessions, and managing potential intrusions into the dyad of third-party requests for accountability and information. Take note, however: the aim has not been to create a *how-to book*, but rather a *why-to book*. The framework is psychoanalytically meaningless without a theory to explain it and without an appropriate method of listening to bring the proper "empirical" data to light (or more correctly to "representation in the patient's voice"). In attending to the derivatives of the patient's unconscious in what he says and does, our data has its own form of "materiality" or "empiricism". And our discipline is not alone in its curiosity for what appears in the "gaps", in the intangible pressure of something else seeking expression in and around the manifest perception of an object, in our case, words (or signifying gestures). One will find a few concrete suggestions in these pages; it will be interesting to compare mine with those other clinicians have derived from theoretical backgrounds and clinical contexts dissimilar – or perhaps even similar – to mine.

The internal *why-to* informs the *how-to* of implementing a specific framework, both registers in constant motion and evolution, as we shall see, depending upon the individual analyst's knowledge, background, savoir-faire, and personality. Ambrosiano (2005) refers to this internal amalgamation as the analyst's "professional novel". This does not mean that the framework (and the technique pertaining to it) are professional free-for-alls; rather – as we shall see in subsequent chapters – they can be ongoing objects of study. *We hope for congruence between what the analyst does and what the analyst thinks. The framework entails, therefore, periodic pieces of psychic work on the part of both parties to it, patient and psychoanalyst.*

The benevolent expectation of trouble

The reader will notice that *psychoanalysis "proper" will not be set apart from psychoanalytically oriented psychotherapy.* That structural change is possible in both types of work, especially if undertaken by fully trained psychoanalysts, is now taken for granted by many (for example: André Green, Raymond Cahn, Manzano et al., François Richard, Robert Wallerstein, D. W. Winnicott). Without equating outcomes, one can still claim that in both settings, the classic challenge is to divine the elusive and avoided thinking which has undercut the psychic "emancipation" (Tessier, 2020) of individuals. Short or extended fragments of this kind of work can occur in a face-to-face setting or on the couch, as well as in periodic or punctual consultations à la Winnicott, à la Roussillon, or à la Ferro. Certain insights, certain words, certain signifying exchanges, alter the psychic functioning of patients over and above the necessary supportive comfort to the ego of being in a relationship with a concerned professional. This book is not the place to revisit the already abundant literature examining the numerous valuable variations from the "classical" framework that a full psychoanalytic training can enhance (see Stern, 2009). *The focus here is on sharing thoughts on a few – perhaps relatively neglected – points regarding the framework as an intrinsic feature of the analytic offer in the consulting rooms of psychoanalysts and psychoanalytically oriented psychotherapists.* Bear in mind that each thread of the current study of creating a frame and putting it to work is just that: a thread in a bountiful, never mastered field of study, that of unconscious human experience.

In the traditional pedagogy of psychoanalysis, the framework or setting is habitually presented as the constant part of treatment. The patient and analyst, once they have agreed to work together in a certain way, are supposed to settle in against this stable, *silent*, background. Yet the "invariant" details of this background can and do become dynamic in every analytically oriented treatment, where their "variance" can become sustainably meaningful only when conjoined with the analyst's *internal framework*. The imbrication of internal framework with the analytic offer of the clinician will be the subject of Chapter 4. There are inevitable breaches in the setting/framework, in fact triggered by the analyst or psychotherapist just as often as by the patient, which need reflective attention, not because they are distractions but rather as precious openings into unintegrated features of the relationship (see Manzano, Palacio-Espasa, & Abella, 2016). As Bleger puts it "sometimes permanently and at other times sporadically, the setting is transformed from the background of a *Gestalt* into a figure, that is, into a process" (1967/2012, 229). In our lingo, "process" means an analytically meaningful exchange. In this manner, particularly when considered in conjunction with the method of free association, the setting can usefully "groan", thereby providing the analytic couple with useful "empirical" data about not yet understood aspects of their relationship. Bleger wrote that the framework or setting can "cry" (1967/2013, 230), a more dramatic and even traumatic occurrence. This can be true. Nonetheless, the evocation of "groaning" as in the sound of wood responding to changes in air pressure or load, is more consonant with the view of occasional strain as an integral – and not only dramatic – part of the wood's (the setting's) ongoing being. Once the framework has been set up, it can be expected to groan sooner or later.[1]

As we shall see in later sections, *it is in this benevolent expectation of "trouble" as an inherent part of the therapeutic couple's getting to more deeply know each other that starkly distinguishes the psychoanalytic frame from that taught by professional regulatory bodies.* Though analysts do – often legitimately – speak of patients "attacking the frame", it is perfectly consonant with a psychoanalytic perspective to treat mistakes, confusions, memory lapses, and even outright criticisms on the part of patients of our way of working as inescapable expressions of themselves which a guilty or punitive response on our part may block from more nuanced elaboration. Bleger thought it rash to speak in terms of an "attack" on the setting when the patient does not comply with it. "The patient brings 'what he has' and this is not always an 'attack' but the patient's own organisation (even though it is disorganised)" (1967, 242).

Consequently, this book will not aspire to be comprehensive, and the review of the literature will be succinct and narrow, bearing the stamp of the author's unusual anglophone membership in a French-speaking North American psychoanalytic society which has led to a preference for certain authors more than others. Already in 1973, Roy Schafer ventured that "at this point in the history of our discipline, there may no longer be much sense in the goal of a definitive, unitary treatment of any major psychoanalytic topic as it stands at any one time" (260). Soon after Freud had discovered a new theory of unconscious thinking and a novel method of access to it, he took pains to sketch out the details of the framework he had found useful, returning periodically for the rest of his life to reexamine its specificity. After his death, on both sides of the Atlantic, critics of the hegemony of the ego psychological interpretation of the frame, seen as "classic" at the time, produced many valuable insights into what is essential and specific about the frame as a working tool. The frame has been studied with respect to treatment of different age categories, with groups, with institutions, with psychosomatic conditions, with delinquents, and now with racially heterogeneous subjects. Recently, attention has been drawn to the impact on the frame of extreme environmental conditions, such as war or economic hardship, as well as the massive migration to distance work during and after the pandemic. Fifty years after Schafer's observation, the goal of an encyclopedic treatise of the frame would either require a decade of one individual's lifetime devoted to the subject, or an erudite team working intently over a shorter period of time (such as the ongoing work of the *International Psychoanalytical Association's (IPA) Inter-Regional Encyclopedic Dictionary of Psychoanalysis* which indeed contains a comprehensive entry on the "Setting". See Schachter et al, 2024). One struggles with the realization that granting oneself the right to speak before achieving a far-reaching grasp of the literature entails accepting relative ignorance and the associated risk of eclipsing alternative approaches to the topic.

Definitions

Which brings us to the term itself of frame, framework, setup, psychoanalytic situation, or analysing situation which are all designations used in the psychoanalytic literature with useful distinctions (see, for example, Tabakin, 2017). For instance, while Faimberg (2019) and Manzano, Palacio-Espasa, and Abella (2016) stick with the "frame", Bleger (1967/2013) refers to the "setting" (*encuadre*), to the "frame" (*marco*), and to the "psychoanalytic situation",[2] Green (1975) to the analytic setting/situation, Donnet to the "analysing site" and the "analysing situation", Winnicott (1956), Cooper (2019), and Ferro (2002/2021) to the "setting".[3] The different nomenclatures are not synonymous, with each author wishing to carve out areas of the analyst's arrangement and personal disposition with patients for separate study. Whereas Winnicott's reference to the setting as "the summation of all the details of management" (Winnicott, 1956, 297) seems similar to Bleger's use of the Spanish word "encuadre", Donnet's notion of the analytic site is broader. For the purpose at hand, these terms will be used synonymously, unless indicated otherwise, because I find that the various authors' reflections amalgamate well in separate scrutiny of details of a global "analytic offer". These authors have all had in mind the agreed-to analytic "contract" with its formal elements of reciprocal exchange (time and money) and complementary and/or asymmetrical disposition regarding other elements of their work together (couch or chair, missed sessions, the method of free association, relative silence on the part of the analyst, and a listening understood as including non-manifest content), which once agreed upon, continue as relatively "constant" aspects of the work. The author's personal preference is for the term "framework" precisely because it contains the word "work".[4] The object of this book, and my use of frame and framework, is closer to Bleger's definition of the psychoanalytic setting as "comprised of an analytic process and a 'non-process'" (1967, 228) "within what we have characterised as the process (that which is 'in motion', as opposed to that which isn't: the setting)" (234).

None of these writers view the "contract" between an analyst and a patient as simply pragmatic and operating in splendid isolation. They acknowledge in one way or another that the contract is always informed by a theory of mind (or the "soul/ âme" as Laplanche's team has offered as a new translation of Freud's "*seelischer/ psychischer*") – the analyst's and the patient's – and a theory of psychoanalytic action. They recognize that any alteration of the analytic contract on the part of either party is bound to call for a re-examination of some part of analytic theory and experience. In clinical practice, as will be illustrated in more detail as the book progresses, the contract is part of a whole setting informed by psychoanalytic theory, clinical experience, personal background, and the analyst's personality and necessarily *carried within the analyst's mind*, as internal counterpart. It would be unconscionable to expect less experienced psychoanalytic clinicians to meet their new patients "without memory or desire", if that iconic Bionian advice is taken at face value. In the following pages, it will be argued that a unique preparedness in the clinician's mind and manner is conducive to eliciting the patient's cooperation in the setup. Alongside the "evenly hovering attention" counselled by Freud (1912), the "analytic offer" benefits from an equally "floating theorization" (de Mijolla-Mellor, 1998, attributed to Piera Aulagnier) to thicken and anchor that listening. In this book, I seek to pursue what Cooper (2019) calls "a paradoxical thread regarding the setting as not just a set of rules of engagement that facilitate the analytic process but something that is itself incorporated into that process" (1441).

Not every psychoanalyst or even psychoanalytically oriented psychotherapist will agree with the framework gradually fashioned by the author, and in fact we should expect this to be the case. Our frameworks (the pluralization is crucial) inevitably carry a personal stamp but they cannot be mere projections of our inner worlds. Most analysts would agree with Aulagnier (1984/2016) in observing that: "each analyst – their writings confirm it – will favour those elements in their theoretical contributions and clinical experience which aid in fathoming their own "fundamental questions" (author's translation,[5] location 49 in Kindle Edition). Much more recently, Donnel S. Stern (2024, 648) has claimed that "[w]e still appreciate too little how much our theoretical convictions are anchored in our preferred theory's capacity to speak to us, to address what matters to each of us in our particular lives". Though most analysts would broadly agree, D. B. Stern's formulation slides into territory more classically minded analysts would be reluctant to enter. Like other interpersonal/relational practitioners, Stern not only recognizes the "analyst's presence and subjectivity" (658) but apparently skirting or minimizing self-analytic investigation, embraces this subjectivity as contribution to a "relational unconscious" (659) co-created with each patient. As we shall see in Chapter 2, an article of Bass (2007) marked an early view of the psychoanalytic enterprise as a mutual benefitting "partnership". In a similar vein, Ogden (2024) has recently lauded the co-creation of dreams with his patients. In contrast, Aulagnier's view was more self-restrained. She suggested that attentively reading the works of others can partially offset the ineluctably selective nature of our interests which might "amputate the theoretical capital at our disposal as well as reducing the pertinence of our clinical work" (1984/2016, location 54). *Opening a personal vision of the framework to the critique of peers is precisely the goal of the current publication. I have the impression that relational writers are unusually generous in this regard.*

Since the hope is that others can benefit from the author's mistakes, struggles to repair them, and efforts to theorize them, not all possible aspects or distortions of the framework will be covered in this volume. Targeted will be the research and psychic work undertaken by the author to navigate specific challenges she and (usually junior) colleagues kept meeting. The tribulations in creating and maintaining an adequate "analysing situation" (Donnet, 2001) in individual psychoanalysis and psychoanalytic psychotherapy, seem to occur in one form or another in most analytic practice. Clinicians struggle with making the best use of their limited knowledge, with their tendency in favour of some theorical orientations more than others, and with the funnel of their personal psychosocial history. Since more rides on the "personal equation" (Freud, 1926) in our field than in other health professions, a universal and manualized framework becomes an impossibility.

Every framework derives necessarily from a personal distillation of theory and experience though one should resist relativism or eclecticism as rationalizations to feeling overwhelmed. Consequently, our "scientific" method needs to include the personal distillation of theory and experience in sharable, rational, form so that others can empathize as well as critique. In asserting as Faimberg has done, that "the logic of the method can 'capture' the logic of the unconscious" (2019, 447), we also need recognize that the illogical, and indeterminate nature of both "method" and "unconscious" in any given clinical situation means we may not all agree on what we are observing.

A note should be made as to the handling of clinical material in this monograph. Since it seems to me unbearably intrusive, I am personally allergic to asking patients for permission to use their clinical material in a project of publication (see Stimmel, 2013, 2024, for a similar view). Though I have been thinking about it for years, I am not close to overcoming this inhibition. No doubt this is related to narcissistic issues in my personality that I see no way to resolve. Given the risk in the current technological environment of patients discovering use of their material without permission, a severe curtailing of recourse to my own practice for clinical illustrations is rendered necessary. The most recent guideline of anonymization of clinical examples (see Barrett & Miller, 2024; Grier, 2023) would give up the exquisite detail of ingenious unconscious expression. Previous studies have found that former or actual patients are more likely to come across clinical material published without their permission by cross-referencing the name of their analysts, something which is becoming easy to do via internet archives. Publishing anonymously or referencing someone else's clinical work are two ways to make it less likely that patients will either identify themselves in clinical writings or be identified by others. For the most part, I have chosen the latter option in these pages by borrowing material from unidentified supervisees or from the published record. In some cases, I have taken advantage of vignettes only available in French, imagining[6] that they will be less identifiable as well as providing a fresh feel for readers lacking access to the literature in that language. In these ways, I have tried to make theoretical assertions come alive for readers while reducing the potential "harm" to patients (and therapists) of using their experiences for teaching purposes. In Chapter 6, the reader will find a summary of the controversies in the literature about the ethics of using clinical material for professional purposes.

An analyzing situation does not emerge spontaneously; it must be actively forged and maintained against temptations from within the consulting room and from clamouring outside of it. In trying to rectify and theorize her mistakes, the author reached a gratifying appreciation which others, as we shall see, have also reached: *the framework itself can be a tremendous asset in insight-oriented work. Nevertheless, to be useful, it must first clearly exist. Then, with an agile mind and a forgiving superego, the analyst or psychoanalytic therapist can welcome framework glitches as opportunities to "put the framework to work" rather than as viewing them as errors needing to be put to "rest".* At these moments the framework, the free associative method, and the analyst's mindset and technique can fertilely intertwine, becoming the very place and expression of a new cycle of psychic growth, where we can join our patients in greeting its inevitable complications as openings to yet unknown aspects of the therapeutic relationship. It helps to bear in mind that as analysts we are neither servants nor masters in our house: we are participant observers (Glick, 2024), a more productive – though occasionally precarious – vantage point, as will be seen in the following example taken from Paulette Letarte's untranslated book, *Entendre*[7] *la folie* (Hearing/Understanding Madness). This vignette illustrates several of the points we will come back to in later chapters as we will elucidate the unavoidable challenge in most psychoanalytic treatments of putting the frame to work and why it matters.

The psychoanalytic setting is not a place of zero tolerance

A poorly integrated, impulse-driven woman sought analysis after reading a book on the "marvelous victories of psychoanalysis". Mme X, with an awful history of violent experiences at the hands of her parents and an older brother, asked for help regarding her disturbed relationship with her little daughter in which raw loving and hateful elements were being played out in frantic alternance. Based on her history and psychic structure, Letarte would have preferred to undertake a psychotherapy face-to-face, but the mother's narcissistic investment of the couch in the wake of the manic illusions promoted by the book was such that Letarte felt constrained to accept Mme X's wish to lie down. An initial attempt to make an interpretation of the patient's repetition of her own childhood abuse with her daughter failed. The patient did not "hear" the interpretation as an interpretation, instead feeling narcissistically supported by the confirmation of the analyst's attentive "listening to her", a reaction not uncommon among borderline patients. According to Reid (1999), in these cases the surface positive effusion of patients to the therapist's intervention is a symptom of their flight from a subjection appropriation of their anguish. Instead, these patients experience anguish in sessions as triggered by their uncertainty about their therapist's "approval". This discomfort can then be counteracted by alienating themselves in what they imagine to be the desire of the therapist, revealed by the fact that she or he has "spoken". Their "acceptance" of the interpretation does not favour the analytic process since the content of the therapist's intervention is not heard, only the fact that he or she has been kind enough to "respond". And so it was with Letarte's Mme X: though she continued to speak freely, Letarte noticed an undeniable pathological turn. Comforted by the regularity of her sessions and Letarte's listening, Mme X was using the analysis as an essentially cathartic magic wand, that is, as a confessional where one confesses to wrongdoing in the expectation of official forgiveness and internal appeasement. The explosions with her daughter persisted, recounted in excruciating detail to the analyst, the latter becoming increasingly concerned about the long-term effects on the child of this deeply unhealthy pattern. In the meantime, Mme X no longer expressed remorse, seemingly at peace with her confessions and an expectation of miraculous absolution. As Letarte noted, a reversal had taken place: the "analysis" was soothing the patient while worrying the analyst. The framework was no longer serving its function of the promotion of symbolization.

> It was necessary to find a way for the analysis to become the place of conflict and for the battles of Mme X to become concentrated within the analytic framework rather than in their narration. In these situations where the patient uses the analysis to re-establish a disturbing behavioural equilibrium, the analyst realizes that he must intervene very actively... we were forming, Mme X and myself, a psychic apparatus à deux.... [W]hen Mme X was striking her child, it was I who was bearing the marks just like her daughter because I was equally a victim of being forced to watch the spectacle, tied down by my impotence as an analyst.... I decided to use my revolt to force a conflict into the heart of the analytic situation.
>
> (2018, 94)

After a particularly "disgusting" description of another debacle with the daughter, Letarte brusquely interrupted:

> Now, it is I who is going to speak! You will grant me the pleasure of never again hitting this child! Your daughter is not your brother, nor is she your analyst! If you have something to say to me, say it then!" I used my indignation as a hostile trampoline to assume the role of a tempered superego, one which conserves the object rather than destroying it. So that hate can be harnessed by love, as Freud would have said. Some would speak here of the containing function of the mother.
>
> (2018, 95)

Mme X reacted to Letarte's ultimatum with white hot rage: "What! Is this what your benevolent neutrality amounts to? I was told you were a good analyst, but I realise I was misinformed. Dr X [of the 'marvelous victories' claim] says that the analyst never intervenes" (2018, 95). For several sessions, Letarte was treated to an onslaught of insults, many according to her, chosen with art and intelligence and precision, reaching sensitive spots. But she wrote: "What a strange vocation it is to be an analyst: something in me was reveling in these attacks... Didn't they have the merit of verbal form, at last targeting the analyst, while not leaving any bruises ... visible ones at least!" (95). Letarte gives several justifications for her *punctual* departure from the usual analytic stance of neutrality as central to the psychoanalytic setting. Here we will only mention one: whereas forbidding a neurotic from doing something would likely lead to bolstering the Superego and repression, the injunction to Mme X favoured, Letarte believed, the installation of a more evolved superego, one that expresses a link with a loved, internalized object as well as releasing aggression. Laying down the law with Mme X had the advantage of diminishing the sadism of her archaic superego, since if she had become aware of the irreparable damage she was inflicting, Letarte feared that she would not have been able to forgive herself. Letarte was perfectly aware of the role of the aggressor, of the smack delivered to the patient's self-esteem, assumed in the analyst's intervention. Yet it also contained hope, according to Letarte, because for the first time in her life Mme X was being offered a method of treating aggressive feelings without blows and tears, where impulses of love and hate can be combined in the tie to the object. *The symbolizing capacities of the analytic situation were thus paradoxically restored through the analyst's momentary twisting of the frame.*

Notes

1 Since writing this, I have come across a similar image of "creaking" in Reith et al. (2018).
2 See Churcher and Bleger's editorial discussions in their translation of *Symbiosis and Ambiguity*.
3 When Klein and Joseph refer to the "total situation", they are not designating the framework but "everything that the patient brings into the relationship" (Joseph, 1985, 447).
4 Like the German "arbeit" which appears so frequently in Freud's oeuvre, such as in *Traumarbeit, Trauerarbeit, Durcharbeitung, Verarbeitung, Bearbeitung, Ausarbeitung, Aufarbeitung.*
5 The author assumes responsibility for all translations of previously untranslated French literature.
6 Cautions John Churcher, "the operative word here is 'imagining'. In an age of machine translation, this may be naive. The risk of de-anonymisation does not come principally from psychoanalytic readers but from algorithms" (January 24, 2025, personal communication).
7 In French, « entendre » can mean both "understanding" and "hearing".

References

Ambrosiano, L. 2005. The Analyst: His Professional Novel. Translated by H. Graham. *International Journal of Psychoanalysis* 86:1611–1626.
Aulagnier, P. 1984. *L'apprenti-historien et le maître-sorcier: Du discours identifiant au discours délirant* (Le fil rouge) (French Edition). Paris: Presses Universitaires de France, 2004. Kindle Edition, 2016.
Barrett, D. G. & Miller, J. M. 2024. Cultivating a Culture of Concern Regarding Confidentiality in Writing about Child and Adolescent Psychoanalysis. *The Psychoanalytic Study of the Child* 77(1):1–6. https://doi.org/10.1080/00797308.2024.2307867
Bass, A. 2007. When the frame doesn't fit the picture. *Psychoanalytic Dialogues* 17:1–27.
Bleger, J. 1967. Psycho-analysis of the psychoanalytic frame. In *Symbiosis and Ambiguity: A Psychoanalytic Study*, edited by J. Churcher & L. Bleger, 2013. London: Routledge. Kindle version.
Bollas, C. & Sundelson, D. 1996. *The New Informants: The Betrayal of Confidentiality in Psychoanalysis and Psychotherapy*. Northvale, New Jersey: Jason Aronson.
Cooper, S. H. 2019. A Theory of the Setting: The Transformation of Unrepresented Experience and Play. *International Journal of Psychoanalysis* 100:1439–1454.
Donnet, J.-L. 2001. From the Fundamental Rule to the Analysing Situation. *International Journal of Psychoanalysis* 82:129–140.

Faimberg, H. 2019. Basic Theoretical Assumptions Underpinning Faimberg's Method: "Listening to Listening". *International Journal of Psychoanalysis* 100:447–462.

Ferro, A. 2002. *In the Analyst's Consulting Room.* Translated by P. Slotkin. Hove, UK: Routledge. Kindle Edition, 2013.

Freud, S. 1912. Recommendations to Physicians Practising Psycho-Analysis. *Standard Edition* 12:109–120.

Freud, S. 1926. The Question of Lay Analysis. *Standard Edition* 20:177–258.

Furlong, A. 1992. Some Technical and Theoretical Considerations Regarding the Missed Session. *International Journal of Psychoanalysis* 73:701–718.

Furlong, A. 1993. Le paiement symbolique: une solution imaginaire au dilemme réel de la gratuité d'une psychothérapie d'orientation psychanalytique? *Filigrane* 2:42–55.

Furlong, A. 1994. A propos des séances manquées: considérations théoriques et techniques. *Trans Printemps*, 55–72.

Furlong, A. 1995. Encadrer le cadre: Pour une cure moins infernale. In *La Cure Infernale*, edited by F. Gauthier, 9–26. Association des psychothérapeutes psychanalytiques de Québec.

Furlong, A. 1996. The Conflict of Interest between Treatment and Expertise. *The Psychoanalytic Psychotherapy Review* 7:45–47.

Furlong, A. 1997a. The Treatment vs. Expertise Tightrope. *Canadian Underwriter* 64:52–54.

Furlong, A. & Lefebre, M. 1997b. La confidentialité des dossiers et la Cour Suprême. *Psychologie Québec* 14:30–31.

Furlong, A. 1998a. The Symbolization of Absence Under Third Party Payment: Symbolic Markers With Adults. *Canadian Journal of Psychoanalysis* 6:75–98.

Furlong, A. 1998-1999. Histoire de cas: histoire de qui? *Trans* 10:105–118.

Furlong, A. 1998b. Should We or shouldn't We? Some Aspects of the Confidentiality of Clinical Reporting and Dossier Access. *International Journal of Psychoanalysis* 79:727–739.

Furlong, A. 2003a. The why of sharing and not the what: Confidentiality and psychoanalytic purpose. In *Confidentiality: Ethical Perspectives and Clinical Dilemmas*, 39–49. Hillsdale, N.J: Analytic Press.

Furlong, A. 2003b. The questionable contribution of psychotherapeutic and psychoanalytic records to the truth-seeking process. In *Confidential Relationships. Psychoanalytic, Ethical, and Legal Contexts*, edited by C. Levin, A. Furlong, & M. K. O'Neil, 13–29. Amsterdam/New York: Editions Rodopi.

Furlong, A. 2003c. Negotiating Consent in Psychotherapy. *Canadian Journal of Psychoanalysis* 11:567–576.

Furlong, A. 2005a. Cadre et confidentialité. *Filigrane* 14:62–76.

Furlong, A. 2005b. Confidentiality With Respect to Third Parties: A Psychoanalytic Perspective. *International Journal of Psychoanalysis* 86:375–394.

Furlong, A. 2006. Further Reflections on the Impact of Clinical Writing on Patients. *International Journal of Psychoanalysis* 87:747–768.

Furlong, A. 2013a. Record Keeping and Professional Autonomy: Commentary on Bemister and Dobson (2011, 2012) and Mills (2012). *Canadian Psychology* 54(1):80–82.

Furlong, A. 2020. Consenting and Assenting to Psychoanalytic Work. *Journal of the American Psychoanalytic Association* 64:583–613.

Furlong, A. & Lefebvre, M. 1997b. La confidentialité des dossiers et la Cour Suprême. *Psychologie Québec* 14:30–31.

Glick, Y. 2024. Parallel processes and the circulation of desire. *Presentation made to the Canadian Psychoanalytic Society, Quebec English Branch, on January 18, 2024.*

Green, A. 1975. The Analyst, Symbolization and Absence in the Analytic Setting (On Changes in Analytic Practice and Analytic Experience)—In Memory of D. W. Winnicott. *International Journal of Psychoanalysis* 56:1–22.

Grier, F. 2023. Anonymisation. *International Journal of Psychoanalysis* 104(6):981–985. doi:10.1080/00207578.2023.2286763.

International Psychoanalytic Association. 2018. *Report of the IPA Confidentiality Committee*. November 1. https://www.ipa.world/IPA_DOCS/Report%20of%20the%20IPA%20Confidentiality%20Committee%20(English).pdf

Joseph, B. 1985. Transference: The Total Situation. *International Journal of Psychoanalysis* 66:447–454.

Letarte, P. 2018. *Entendre la folie*. Paris: Presses Universitaires de France. Kindle Edition.

Manzano, J., Palacio-Espasa, F., & Abella, A., 2016. *Précis de technique psychanalytique avec son application à la psychothérapie*. Collection: Le fil rouge. : Presses Universitaires de France. https://doi.org/10.3917/puf.manza.2016.03

Mijolla-Mellor, D. 1998. *Penser la psychose. Une lecture de l'œuvre de Piera Aulagnier*. Paris: Dunod.

Ogden, T. H. 2024. Ontological Psychoanalysis in Clinical Practice. *The Psychoanalytic Quarterly* 93(1):13–31. https://doi.org/10.1080/00332828.2024.2314776

Popova, M. 2023. Umberto Eco's Antilibrary: Why Unread Books Are More Valuable to Our Lives than Read Ones. In *The Marginalian*, consulted January 17, 2023. https://www.themarginalian.org/2015/03/24/umberto-eco-antilibrary/

Reid, W. 1999. Le cadre analytique revisité. *Filigrane* 8:33–48.

Reith, B., Møller, M., Boots, J., Crick, P., Gibeault, A., Jaffè, R., Lagerlöf, S., & Vermote, R. 2018. *Beginning Analysis: On the Process of Initiating Psychoanalysis*. London & New York: Routledge.

Schachter, J., Tabakin, J. T., Blucher, T., & Jemstedt., A. 2024. The Psychoanalytic Setting. *International Psychoanalytical Association Inter-Regional Encyclopedic Dictionary of Psychoanalysis*, 817–836. https://online.flippingbook.com/view/544664/816/ Accessed November 28, 2024.

Schafer, R. 1973. The Idea of Resistance. *International Journal of Psychoanalysis* 54:259–285.

Schafer, R. 1983. *The Analytic Attitude*. London: Hogarth Press.

Stern, D. B. 2024. Beginning the Treatment on a Personal Note: Creating Emotional Connection. *The Psychoanalytic Quarterly* 93(4):647–674. https://doi.org/10.1080/00332828.2024.2398590

Stern, S. 2009. Session Frequency and the Definition of Psychoanalysis. *Psychoanalytic Dialogues* 19:639–655.

Stimmel, B. 2013. The Conundrum of Confidentiality. *Canadian Journal of Psychoanalysis* 21:84–106

Stimmel, B. 2024. Episode 163: Secrets kept and secrets told: The analyst's responsibility with Barbara Stimmel. *IPA Off the Couch*. July 14. https://ipaoffthecouch.org/2024/07/14/episode-163-secrets-kept-and-secrets-told-the-analysts-responsibility-with-barbara-stimmel-phd-new-york/

Tabakin, J. 2017. The setting and the frame: Subjectivity and objectivity in the psychoanalytic relationship. In *Reconsidering the Moveable Frame in Psychoanalysis*, edited by I. Tylim & A. Harris, 72–91. London: Routledge.

Tessier, H. 2020. *Rationalism and Emancipation in Psychoanalysis: The Work of Jean Laplanche*. New York: Unconscious in Translation.

Winnicott, D. W. 1956. On Transference. *International Journal of Psychoanalysis* 37:386–388.

Chapter 1

Why it matters

Having a good psychoanalysis is like buying a good house, though the benefit long outlasts the time you are actually inside it. This is because the psyche is not only an imaginary space; it is also a very real – tangible to self and often to others – structure, which can be strengthened, loosened up, or partially reconfigured by the insight wrought in analytic work. Unfortunately, the pace and organization of contemporary culture have conspired to make psychoanalysis out of reach for a great number, though, luckily, there are numerous alternative therapies available now, which can bring relief to many. Nevertheless, psychoanalysis remains relevant in modern life because it is more self-reflective and intersubjectively curious than other approaches. It steadfastly investigates – at least in the psychoanalytic theories that have influenced me – the repudiated otherness within which makes all of us divided subjects. And in lending an ear to everything the patient has to say, it picks up threads from all time zones, as it were, though they may no longer be recognized as such, leading eventually to a more integrated wholeness of the personality. Alan Bass makes a wonderful comment in an interview in 2020 with Jeremy Bloomfield (available on You-Tube) which is worth quoting in full:

> Psychoanalytic thinking about people is the most complex, but I also think it is the most realistic… It's a scientific fact that the human brain is the most complex object in the known universe because of all the trillions and trillions of neuronal connections. Well, if that's the case, there is every reason to think that the mind, however brain produces mind, that the mind would be equally complex. And people's problems are expressions of the incredible complexities of their minds. So that's why I think … while psychoanalysis is the most complex way of thinking about people, and trying to help people, that's why I also say it's the most realistic… It has the most objective view of the mind, how it functions, of how people think, which is not always the prettiest view.
>
> (Bloomfield, 2020. 0.21 to 1.44)

DOI: 10.4324/9781003527459-2

Thinking of the framework as more than a contractual relationship

Milner (1952) is often credited with making the first explicit references to the "frame" which she described in analogy to art, specifically the traditional presentation of a painting within a separately constructed frame. The frame here distinguishes the illusion of the image from the more tangible surrounding world. The frame was seen as separating treatment from "real life", a viewpoint I accepted for many years. Nowadays, however, *it seems to me more accurate to view the frame as empowering the dyad to sense phenomena which could otherwise easily slip by unperceived in 'real' life. The metaphor is that of sensor more than picture frame.* In the consulting room, inadvertently and unexpectedly, overdetermined investment of aspects of the setup can emerge "ultra-clearly", as in the perceptually enhanced quality of dream elements which Freud unravelled as nodal points for multiple lines of latent thinking (for example, Freud, 1898, 1899).

Whether one is operating in a classic psychoanalytic framework using the couch or in the face-to-face setting of psychoanalytic psychotherapy, one hopes over time to facilitate a psychological climate in which observations can be made (by either the analyst or the patient) of signs of unconscious activity stirring the surface of words and gestures in the session. As proposed in the introduction, the therapist's analytic stance with respect to individual patients, based on an initial apprehension of their relational impasses and psychic structure, is intimately intertwined with the material, contractual aspects of the frame to be offered to them. Consequently "some of the most complex and fateful analytic work can take place in the early stages of treatment before an analytic process has fully deepened or matured" (S. Stern, 2009, 647). This observation helps us to understand *what a strain on both parties the beginning of treatment can be,* a fact to be explored in Chapter 3 when we look at the patient's capacity for informed consent.

For the moment, we are continuing our study of why a clear framework matters. For many patients, *the analysing situation is not a given; and for all patients, the analysing situation is not natural.* There is a certain *construction* involved. To call this construction artificial is true in the sense that any observational instrument is artificial, art – i – ficial (art made by human hands): it has been fabricated via human knowledge to perform a certain function, usually a function that extends natural human observational abilities (telescope and microscope for eyes, megaphones and microphones for the ears) but just as often the instrument allows humans to observe phenomena completely outside their natural ken, a *new* perceptual system. Pioneers in the study of X-ray and gamma-ray radiation did not realize the danger of exposure, in part because these wavelengths are not perceptible to the human sensory system. Special measures had to be devised to allow scientists to "see" these wavelengths and conduct themselves accordingly. Marie Curie, her husband, and others experimenting with purified radioactive ores had no idea, to begin with, that they were exposing themselves to deadly doses. For similar reasons, in our own time, carbon monoxide detectors are recommended in buildings and artificial aroma is added to the natural gas used in domestic appliances. Freud claimed that the method of free association was at the heart of psychoanalytic treatment, its most essential ingredient since it gives access to experience otherwise eclipsed. Yet absent an adequate "analysing situation" free association, says Jean-Luc Donnet, will not "be practicable, interpretable and beneficial" (2001, 129). On this premise, analysts of various theoretical allegiances will agree.

The central idea in this book goes a step further in believing that the framework, once properly constructed, or sometimes as a symptom that it has not yet been properly constructed, will eventually "groan" and in so doing will provide an opportunity to extend the detection work and the working-through reach of the dyad. A powerful antecedent in the literature for this view is Bleger's insight into the function of the framework as hidden repository of the more regressed aspects of the ego, its undifferentiation. He felt this to be true of every type of patient. "The knowledge of something arises only in the absence of that something, until it is organised as an internal object" (1967/2013, 23). He goes on "The function of the setting is the same: it is a support and a framework, but it can only be seen – for now – when it changes or is broken. The most persistent, tenacious and unnoticeable 'bastion' is the one deposited in the setting" (24). It is only when the setting is disturbed that the hidden bastion becomes "ultra-clear".

> Thus, we are better able now to acknowledge the catastrophic situation that the analyst's disruption of the setting (holidays, or cancelled, missed or incomplete sessions, etc.) always entails to a variable degree, since in these disruptions (disruptions that are part of the setting) a 'crack' is created through which reality is introduced, which is catastrophic for the patient. 'His' setting and his 'phantom world' lose their depositary and it becomes evident that 'his' setting is not the psychoanalytic setting.
>
> (1967/2013, 27)

As we shall see in Chapter 3, the framework cannot perform as a sensor for conflictual zones of the dyadic relationship unless it has been *clearly stated, consented to, and maintained.* If, as Ferro put forward, "transformational operations are to be possible, the setting must be a container with properties of elasticity and absorbency" (2002/2021, 121). The beauty of Ferro's formulation is the nod it gives to the structure's tolerance to both movement and shock. We have already had occasion in the Introduction to turn to the work of Paulette Letarte where the analyst's momentary infringement on a sacrosanct aspect of the frame, her neutrality, was used to facilitate the creation of a protective barrier in her patient's corroded superego operation. Another dramatic sequence from Letarte (2018, 79–82) comes to mind about the framework's potential for absorbing a patient's temporary breakdown and symbolically transforming it. Letarte had recently started seeing "Nathalie", a desperately unhappy and rebellious adolescent, who did not yet share the goal of self-inquiry through talking with an analyst, having consulted merely to please her parents and openly contemptuous of the whole enterprise. For several

months, Letarte tolerated Nathalie's shenanigans: pushing furniture about, ciga-
rette butts on the floor, an expulsive discourse recriminating everyone, including
herself; outside of sessions, promiscuous sexual activity and drug use. A turning
point occurred when Letarte delivered a well-timed but "brutal" interpretation to
the effect that Nathalie was acting out her fantasy about her origin as having occurred in a one-night stand, without love and without relationship, between her
biological parents. Despite the acknowledged roughness with which the interpretation was delivered, Letarte viewed its efficacy as having stemmed from the fact that
for the first time the patient was sharing the analyst's worry about the risks she was
taking. Letarte added in her defense that via her rough enunciation "the object of
interpretation was not insinuated into the patient; on the contrary, it was thrown on
the table in the intermediary space created by the violence of separation" (76–77).[1]

The turmoil of Nathalie's analysis was far from over. On the day of the cata-
clysm I am using as illustration of putting the frame to work, Nathalie arrived absolutely disgusted with life after hearing of two news items: the death of a famous
singer, known for his humanity and criticism of authority, and the assassination of
a political figure she admired. Nathalie raged around the office, crying, kicking the
furniture, scandalized with the injustice of these events before stopping before a
large, heavy table which she proceeded to shake. Though far too ponderous to turn
over, Nathalie was able to move the table enough to destabilize a large opal glass
lamp poised on it. Boom, the lamp burst into "a thousand pieces"! Nathalie tried
to flee but could not in her state of shock manage the door; instead, she wrapped
herself in a wall hanging and collapsed on the floor. Letarte came over, calling her
by name, and stretching out her hand to the prostrate young woman, opined: "A
broken lamp is not the death of a person!" As soon as Nathalie was back on her
feet, Letarte withdrew her hand. Letarte wrote that this detail was important to
her: when Nathalie was curled up on the floor, she was a little girl. Back on her
feet, Nathalie had resumed her position of adulthood. Letarte returned to her armchair, allowing Nathalie to decide whether to leave or return to the session. Then
she waited while her patient wept in shame, promising to "pay for" the breakage.
"Don't worry", Letarte retorted, "I will be giving you the bill". However, Letarte
offered the patient another appointment that very day, so that they could "talk qui-
etly about what had happened between them". Astonishingly, Letarte was able to
go out and buy another lamp before the patient's return in the afternoon (oh Paris,
how wonderful thou art!), along with a bill for the patient.

In Letarte's work, as in this example, we see a sensitivity to the narcissistic
integrity of even her most disturbed patients. The patient's right to a position of
equality permitted by the possibility and the acceptance of reparation is recognized
in straightforward fashion. The breach of the traditional framework in this session
with Nathalie incarnates Winnicott's concept of the "use of an object" (1969), in
which the object's lack of retaliation allows the patient to integrate and tame aggressivity. Letarte shared Winnicott's belief in the positive value of destructiveness
as an "unconscious backcloth for love of a real object, i.e., an object outside the
area of the subject's omnipotent control" (Winnicott 1969, 715). It follows that

the psychoanalytic setting cannot be a place of zero tolerance. Letarte's setting was impressively imbued by the "elasticity and absorbency" counselled by Fero. Yet her description of the incident is dense in preconscious theoretical elaboration; as we shall see later in this chapter, Letarte's framework was only capable of such flexibility and utility by its incarnation as part of her psychoanalytic offer and her moment-to-moment psychoanalytic understanding of the patient. Even Winnicott himself had to learn, as Margaret Little's (1985) account of her analysis with him has shown and his subsequent insights imbued the theorization he was able to pass on to other analysts. If he had not fled the consulting room when Little stomped on a vase of lilacs and returned at the end of the session to notice her cleaning the mess up, would Letarte have been able to stay in the room with Nathalie and help her up out of her mess? If Winnicott had not replaced the vase while never again referring to the incident, would Letarte have been able to replace the lamp, permit the patient to make reparation, and set aside time to think about it together? In what we know of Winnicott's exceptional framework concessions with challenging patients, there are ironic echoes of the hands-on pre-analytic physical interventions (spa treatments, hypnosis, messages, cold baths, laying on of hands, etc.) used by Freud and medical colleagues of his generation before he and Breuer "discovered" the analytic method. Winnicott extended the length of Little's analytic sessions, held her hands while she covered herself with a blanket, hospitalized her, and sent her postcards during his holidays. Letarte's tolerance for Nathalie's fragile narcissism and boundary testing, her capacity to be "used", was derived from a third generational "leaning": first on Freud who learnt from his mistakes, then on Winnicott who learnt from his own to come to the extraordinary notion of the use of an object.

After Freud, there was Winnicott thinking about his frame; and after Winnicott, there was Letarte thinking about hers. These new "savoirs" (additions to psychoanalytic knowledge) transmitted from one generation of analysts to the next are what allowed such "absorbency" in Letarte's frame. Because of this transmission, there was value, in Letarte's mind, for creating a place where hate and frustration can be safely expressed, or at least with minimum damage. We can suspect that it was a lot harder for Winnicott for whom the broken vase had sentimental value, as he confided to Little years later (Little, op. cit.), and because the vase had been broken as a direct representative of himself in Little's deranged mental state at the time. Without the concept of the use of the object already integrated in his understanding of his role, Winnicott was more vulnerable to feeling directly damaged, whereas Letarte clearly appreciated the displacement of her patient's rage as a sign of psychic resources, which allowed her to value the progressive elements in her patient's agitation.

I am hoping that the present monograph motivates beginners in *constructing* (and for more experienced therapists, in *tinkering with*) a workable frame without recourse to a one-size-fits-all. *But, as mentioned in the Introduction, this will not be a how-to book; it will be a why-too book.* No psychoanalytically oriented practice is possible without a great deal of theory. When practitioners claim to be "eclectic", they are basically confessing to not knowing what to do. In perplexing circumstances, they rely on their instincts, which is better than being paralyzed but hardly a prescription others can follow. Not knowing what to do or say with a patient happens to everyone, probably at least once a day, if not once a session. But, unless there is post-hoc reflection on the analyst's part regarding "what happened between us", there is no advance in the therapeutic couple's knowledge. It will also be easier to listen to patients when one has reached an internal rationale for the kind of listening one is offering. And that is precisely why theory is so important to our management of the framework. Though we cannot anticipate every conundrum – and if we could, we would no longer be acknowledging an individual but offering a manualized treatment implemented by category – the psychoanalytic literature constitutes a huge resource for thinking about unconscious life. *The ultimate usefulness of theory is its generation of new psychic receptors for the thoughtful clinician.*

The out-of-ordinariness of the setting

What astonishes people most is that meeting a psychoanalyst is like no other relationship in life (see D. B. 2024, for a remarkably different take on the similarity or not of the psychoanalytic encounter with other aspects of the analyst's life). For starters, the psychoanalytic encounter is not at all an ordinary conversation since its aim is not – at the beginning at least – to achieve understanding. Rather, its aim, argues Laurence Kahn, is "to summon the unexpected psychic event, the emergence of the unknown, the manifestation of the psychic 'stowaway' which, for Freud, first took the form of an internal 'foreign body'" (2021, 1). Thomas Ogden concurs: "All that has been most obvious to the patient will no longer be treated as self-evident; rather, the familiar is to be wondered about, to be puzzled over, to be newly created in the analytic setting" (2012, 173–174). Though these psychic events are happening all the time, they are like the elusive Higgs boson elementary particle physicists had been trying to "capture" for decades after it was first theorized.[2] The supposition is that stars, planets, and finally life can only have emerged because particles of light gained their mass from a fundamental field named after Higgs. The existence of this mass-giving field was finally confirmed in 2012, when the Higgs boson particle was "observed" by CERN (European Organization for Nuclear Research) at the world's largest particle physics laboratory. It took almost fifty years to "prove" the existence of the Higgs boson because it cannot be directly observed by scientists, breaking down at mind-boggling speed into other particles. Currently the only place scientists can generate, and study Higgs bosons is in CERN's Swiss laboratory, thanks to the special "container" of the highest-energy particle collider in the world and to an incredible number of experimental repetitions (Office of Science, 2024). Even then, its existence can only be demonstrated from monitoring its decay into other elements. We can draw an analogy with the psychic stowaways of human beings that similarly remain invisible or overlooked in ordinary life and can only be inferred from their conscious or behavioural offshoots in the specialized setting created by Freud. These "offshoots", like the products of decay at CERN, allow the dyad to "suppose" psychic motions beyond direct apprehension.

There are other ways in which the psychoanalytic framework, compared to the setting cultivated by other psychotherapeutic approaches, is counterintuitive. For instance, it is not by making the patient feel "comfortable" and "understood" when he or she first meets the analyst that the conditions for observation are propitious. In contrast to alternate approaches to psychological distress, the psychoanalytic situation puts the patient somewhat off kilter, a delicate operation which takes training and experience to optimally manage. If things go well, both parties to the initial interviews submit to a certain duress as unconscious anxiety is mobilized which it may take time to figure out. In fact, we owe to Bion (1979) the insight that the psychoanalytic situation sets off an "emotional storm" though – weirdly – this event can easily be overlooked or defended against by both parties. Lack of aware-ness of this initial storm can lead to the patient's premature flight from treatment or to the unconscious creation by the clinical pair of an ongoing blind spot in their work together. Though Freud warned of the panic and confusion that the "fire" of unconscious transference can bring to an ongoing "theatre" of analytic treatment (Freud 1914), I do not know of a passage in his work wherein he addresses the invisible storm which may break out right at the beginning of treatment.

Patients often arrive late to their first appointment, out of breath or exasperated by having missed their subway stop, or by having taken the wrong highway exit. They think they are worked up by their mistake and the limited time they have left to talk to us, little realizing that their disconcertment, at the unconscious level, had preceded rather than followed their bewilderment. There will be an uncon-scious pull within analyst and patient to undo or smooth over this chaotic start-ing position. Yet, the unconscious anxieties stirred up in the two protagonists at the inception of their relationship are not accidental, nor are they something to be avoided. *Implausible though it may seem, this state of disequilibrium is the vital hallmark of a psychoanalytic framework and methodology.* Laplanche (2006/2011) drew attention to their "destructuring" objective where hidden features are sought where they are least expected. Undermined are "the coherent unities upon which an entire life might have been organized … in order to identify their separated components" (280). Odgen concurs in recommending "sustaining psychological strain in the analytic setting" (2012, 175), whereas Michel de M'Uzan (2019) has encouraged psychoanalysts to preserve a state of "permanent disquiet" in their work! Laplanche had used the metaphor of the accelerator somewhat differently as depiction of the intensity of unbound drive unleased in the analytic situation. Caper (1992) shared that in his experience, "painful emotions are reliable clinical indicators that the work of analysis is progressing. If these indicators are consist-ently absent from what is supposed to be an analysis, the analyst should consider the possibility that a pseudo-analysis has taken over" (287).

The difficulty of managing this paradox in a helping profession such as ours may account for the trouble analysts can have putting the framework into place as well as keeping it in mind as the work continues. This has been true, in my experience, for both beginning and experienced clinicians, myself included. And it is especially true of psychoanalytically-oriented psychotherapists, who though admiring aspects of psychoanalytic theory, have not been able to grant themselves the luxury of full psychoanalytic training, and are thus less "equipped" to withstand this type of extended emotional turbulence. Caper (op. cit., 287) circumscribes the "emotional difficulty for the analyst" in the following way:

> [It] stems from the fact that psychoanalysis is a very peculiar activity and even, in a certain way, an unnatural one: one is unable to do the natural thing, which is to offer immediate solace, support or reassurance in the presence of obvious suffering. One can offer only support for the patient's attempts to integrate his mind, and the solace that comes from that .... to refrain from offering the more immediate (if less profound) forms of relief is one of the most difficult injunctions of the rule of abstinence. However, if the analyst is to do his job, he must accept the fact that, by withholding immediate solace, he is in a way 'causing' real suffering in the short run for the sake of the greater long-term relief that comes from psychological integration.
>
> (287)

Viewed in this light, Caper goes on to say, the analytic rule of abstinence – that the relationship between patient and analyst cannot really be that of friends – is not simply a procedural rule

> and in fact not a procedural rule at all, but a consequence of the fact that analysis as an activity must necessarily exclude too many of the elements that are vital to any ordinary, natural human relationship. Its power stems from its intense, exclusive and dispassionate focus on the passions of the unconscious.
>
> (288)

The problem with psychic stowaways is that we do not realize that they are there, with a *motivation and agency separate from ours*. In French psychoanalytic thinking, stress has been laid on appreciating the unconscious as a "thing presentation", going back to distinctions made by Freud (1915). Without words to represent it, the unconscious *springs forth* outside of the ego or the self. These appearances are felt to be alien, not "subjective", which is why French authors can be critical of English and American conceptualizations of counter-transference as conscious experience an analyst can gather up and use to understand the patient. An example comes to mind from my own practice of the "non-subjectivity" of counter-transference (or simply transference). In a session in which a patient was speaking about doubts about whether to continue her relationship with a young man, I stopped the session ahead of time, completely oblivious to my error. The sensation was deeply unsettling when I realized my mistake. Not knowing why, I had to ponder what dynamics were being mobilized from my personal life. My shock was emblematic of the non-subjective nature of the unconscious intrusion, which appeared *as an unmentalized "thing", in the form of something I did*. Abruptly, the term psychic stowaway no longer appeared metaphorical but concretely foreign: how could that have been me? And yet it most assuredly was me, or at least it "came out" of me, as Freud (1925) would have said.[3] "This is due to the fact" writes Laplanche "that the repressed Id is not constituted of meaningful sequences, but instead of elements which have escaped the original conferring-of-meaning" (1997/2024, 5). An ordinary conversation, or even an empathetic inquiry into what I was feeling, would have been of no assistance in dissipating my confusion.[4]

For these reasons, psychoanalysts tend to agree that Freud invented a hitherto never experienced human relationship (see D. B. Stern, 2024, for a contrasting, relational analyst's opinion). This invention did not happen all at once. It required several informative but unsatisfactory attempts at relating to his patients in other ways (hypnosis, post-hypnotic instructions, laying his hands on the patient's forehead suggesting she would remember, cold packs, etc.) before Freud eventually settled upon what has been called the "classic" framework: use of the couch with the analyst sitting out of sight for sessions 6 days a week. Over time, the post-Freudians realized that the frame's configuration is optimally determined both by the therapeutic aim of analysis and the psychic structure and resources of the patient. You do not need a billion-dollar particle collider to study the visual part of the light spectrum where a properly polished and shaped piece of glass will do. Nor is a lapsus interpretable if the patient cannot view it as expressing anything about himself other than a meaningless glitch.

Some therapists strive to help their patients feel accepted in their current identities and sexual strivings where conflict is mainly experienced between self and others\society; their frameworks are naturally more flexible and emotionally symmetrical. The psychoanalytic aim is very different: in constructing a space where the psychic stowaway can be detected, it seeks to disentangle the conflict within by teasing out the soldered together layers of environmental excitations and unconscious reactions past and present which inform adult identifications and longings. In treatment with more impoverished or handicapped psychic constellations, the mindset of the therapist may need adjustment without losing sight of the same goal. In subsequent chapters, we will have occasion to mention related efforts (such as those of Bass, Cahn, de M'Uzan, Letarte, Odgen, Reid, Roussillon, and both Stern) to generate technically new settings, often face-to-face, which bolster the patient's pleasure in his or her own mind so that more of unconscious experience can come within his purview. Freud's familiar image of the ego as a rider astride the unruly horse of the id, or pinned between id and superego, is more pertinent today than ever in psychoanalytic theorizing and technique. To my way of thinking, the framework should perform like a saddle stiff enough to allow the therapeutic couple to feel the movements of resistance within the treatment and not as a cushy blanket which softens disjunction between them.

The framework as part of the analyst's theory

Michael Parsons introduced the phrase "internal analytic setting" in 2007, believing that "[t]he idea does not seem to have been articulated and developed, at least in English, as a specific concept" (2007, 1443). Yet, it is clear from the way they have described their work that many analysts before him were aware of the conceptual distinction. Manzano et al. (2016) do not even cite Parsons in declaring: "These two aspects of the framework, called respectively 'internal framework' (the mental attitude of the analyst) and 'external framework' (the practical rules of functioning) are mutually interdependent and of one piece (*solidaire* in French)" (5). Instead, Manzano et al. reference Donnet (2005) and Caper (1992) with regard to a "state of mind" already present in the analyst. Churcher (2022, 45) counts a dozen authors describing similar notions, apparently, at least partially, independently of each other. Leo Bleger (2022, 33) has even complained that the whole notion "seems to be somewhat redundant with the classical idea of 'analytical attitude' (Schafer, 1983)".

As early as 1977, Lipton had argued using Freud's work with the Rat Man as illustration, that neutrality is not a matter of a particular behaviour on an analyst's part but of the attitude with which he conducts the analysis. Merton Gills' (1984a) separation of "extrinsic" from "intrinsic" aspects of psychoanalysis has been mentioned sometimes as if it foreshadows Parson's concept. This is not strictly speaking true. Gills was using these terms to break down the way postwar American theorists were differentiating psychoanalysis from psychotherapy, that is, what was being claimed as "intrinsic" to "true" psychoanalysis and what were considered inconsequential "extrinsic" features. In so doing, nevertheless, his questioning of conventional notions about what constitutes the analytic framework, such as indeterminate length, use of the couch, and limited goals – bring Gill close to the notion of internal frame. He writes: "In practice the difficulty in maintaining analytic technique in the *vis-à-vis* position seems to be at least as much a *matter of the analyst's psychology* as the patient's. The technique requires a *stance on the therapist's* as well as the patient's part which is significantly different from the give and take of most human relationships" (added emphasis, 175). He goes on to refer to the adoption of a particular "frame of mind" which could be "integrated and consistent" in a "combined psychoanalytic and psychotherapeutic practice".

Gill's insistence on including all aspects of the setting, the analyst's handling of it, and other gestures and communications as possible factors inadvertently impacting the here-and-now of the transference *before* (though not instead of) seeking sources in the patient's history, is very contemporary because it sees the analytic situation as unavoidably influenced by the analyst's presence and behaviour. Ferro (2002/2021) has made the analyst's "mental attitude" one of what he calls the "four quadrants" of the analytic setting, with only the first defined as a "set of formal rules". The analyst's mental attitude avers Ferro is far from invariant, subject to oscillations, that is "*continuously disturbed and continuously refound*" (original emphasis, 122). Though in typically French fashion emphasizing the "paternal" function of the framework, Letarte includes reference to the analyst's "character", a similar nod to the analyst's psychic disposition, as one of four "limits" to the setup, the others being time, place, and speech (Ferro 2002/2021), 72).

Let us look at Parsons' definition: "the internal setting defines and protects an area of the analyst's mind where whatever happens, including what happens to the external setting, can be considered from a psychoanalytic viewpoint" (1444), a position that joins our own in believing that happenings in the framework can "be put to work". Manzano et al., cited above, give their definition as "This attitude is in fact a state of mind characterized by the psychoanalyst's interest in understanding the unconscious psychic functioning, repressed or split off in the patient, with the aim of communicating this and allowing the patient to integrate it. *In this manner, the frame is already present.* It will be expressed explicitly later through a proposition of a "contract" (added emphasis, 5).

Letarte's management of her own anxiety occasioned by Nathalie's dustups (the one described was only one of many) would not have been conceivable without Letarte's internal conviction that:

the framework is to be established, not by virtue of a fixed rule, but rather with respect to the possibilities each patient possesses to tolerate its [the framework's] effects, both excitatory and frustrating. The analytic setup (dispositif) has to take into account the relationship each individual has with his internal world, with his intra-psychic space.

(2018, 88)

Implicit in the fundamental rule of trying to say whatever comes to mind regarding elements of dreams, but also regarding other components of patients' speech, such as words which insist or are repeated, issues coming up at home or at the office, obsessive thoughts, physical symptoms, or any other content of sessions is the notion that words ferry more than a single manifest content. The very notion of associations entails, though it may not dawn on the patient right away, that our minds are more like skeins of interconnected images and memories than computer programmes of either-or choices, more like sliding tectonic plates of fluid meaning than organized cubbyholes of definitions. Words and the thoughts trailing through them always mean more than they seem on the surface to convey. In the consulting room, we decline to "believe that meaning is already unproblematically settled" (Glick, 2024, 8).

It was Winnicott (1951) who put his finger on the monumental step forward in development by the child's acquisition of a transitional object which both is and is not the mother, which is both alive and inert, which is imbued with feeling as well as assumed itself to have feelings without impulses for retaliation. And, it was Winnicott's brilliant insight to realize that these psychic paradoxes, developed by the child and tolerated by the family, constitute the *mental germ cells* of all eventual shared culture, that is the ability to enjoy the representations of things that are not strictly speaking "there". These paradoxes, offering the child new registers of play, are the essence of what Winnicott thought of as "transitional space". Yet, as he pointed out, because facilitating adults are not always available at key moments in development, this psychic capacity is not universal.

The concept of transitional space has allowed post-Winnicottian authors, such as Pontalis, Green, Roussillon, Brusset, Cahn, and Reid, penetrating insights into the forms of compromised representation common in infra-neurotic personalities as well as, though usually less often, in the so-called neurotic-normal range. New theories of technique and framework installation have ensued, with consequent incidence on contemporary practice. Jay Greenberg (2016) put the change this way: "[O]ur analytic target changes accordingly; we become less interested in helping our analysands to find the truths that they have not allowed themselves to know and more interested in helping them to develop the capacities that would make knowing possible" (272). The challenge, however, is to listen in both the ways mentioned by Greenberg: in the way Freud listened which is fading away in certain psychoanalytic communities *and* in the additional ways post-Freudian authors have taught us. Both the support for inhibited thinking and the interpretation of hidden conflicts in thinking are necessary.

The personal framework delineated below is certainly a figment, a personal contrivance, and an elusive beacon, insofar as every clinical session has never happened before and requires yet unaccomplished mental work to absorb, to contain, and to make use of in a helpful way to the patient. Though it describes *how* I have come to practice preliminary interviews, this personal model was gradually developed as a behavioural expression of the evolution of my thinking, of the *why* of introducing patients to a new kind of relationship and a new way of experiencing themselves.

One framework *proposal*

When I was in psychoanalytic training, I had difficulty retaining "cases". I must have lost two or three who gave up after only a few weeks or months. The truth was that although I was deeply committed to my personal analysis, I had no idea how to make patients comfortable with a relatively unobtrusive presence, the main reason being that neither they nor I knew how "simply talking" was going to lead to change. When Lacan compared the analyst to the position of "dummy" in a game of bridge, one needs to remember that the other players know the rules of the game and enjoy the challenge. But when patients feel that they are talking to a "wall", the muteness of the dummy takes on a persecutory cast. It took me quite a while before I learnt to convey listening imbued with interest and mental activity on my part without either leading the conversation or intruding on the patient's capacity to find his own way. *There are ways of waiting that convey a holding which a flurry of words might fail to offer.* As Green, Roussillon, and Winnicott have shown us, there are ways to be (relatively) silent that are supportive and encouraging. I credit in my case the work of three authors in particular with imbuing my quiet listening with analytic purpose and receptive power: practically everything I have read of Jean Laplanche's work, André Green's seminal article of 1975, and a series of articles and lectures by a Montreal colleague, Wilfrid Reid (1994, 1998a, 1998b, 1999). All of these thinkers were post-Winnicottian and were developing versions of what the French call a "third model" of psychic structure. The third model is a term used to designate the work of post-Freudian authors across the psychoanalytic literature who have tried to think about how the Freudian relatively autonomous mind comes into existence. These thinkers have been attempting to theorize an earlier moment in the development of the psychic life of the individual by including the adult care-taker's mind as part of the model.

In "The Analyst, Symbolization and Absence in the Analytic Setting", Green elaborates on Lacan's insistence on language as representation of something "absent", a key stumbling block for certain patients whose deficits in symbolization transform the analyst's "absence" (the relative reserve of his presence, the relative silence of her listening) in the setting into emptiness (that proverbial sensation of "talking to a wall" or of "being alone in the session"). Representation is absence insofar as it designates a *presence no longer there* whereas emptiness, blankness, and some halts in associations imply deficits in symbolization, where the object has been lost or decathected. It is incumbent on the analyst to sense the difference in the quality of the analysand's discourse since it makes a difference in what can become meaningful as an intervention. Awareness of this distinction was not enough, in my case, to reduce my puzzlement with the inability of certain patients to use what appeared to me as perfectly obvious interpretative openings or connections. I had been insensitive to a confusion of tongues in these cases, where words were not endowed with the same communicational density for one speaker as compared to the other. Before I read Reid's work, diagnostic differences were hardly more than names for me, as though the issue were one of individuals with different symptoms leading to classification into particular categories. The fact that *minds actually operate in distinct ways* was a revelation. For instance, Reid (1994) describes the register of neurotic functioning as that of one holding "an infantile theory of limited psychic space" versus the "infantile theory of unlimited space" held in the minds of individuals functioning at the limits of the analysable. Mention of these influences can only be made in passing since my goal is merely to give the reader a sense of qualitatively separate modes of listening associated with psychoanalytic theories of the framework which imbue our potential response to breaches in it.

Not losing sight of the fact, therefore, that in its essence though it has material extensions, the framework is a state of mind in the analyst or psychoanalytically-oriented psychotherapist, what follows is a description of the setting I usually offer in the initial stages of working with a new patient. Though the details are prosaic, even apparently trivial, and probably familiar to most analysts, I have found substance in their accumulation. To begin with, I have always practiced in an office outside of my home, a choice made jointly with family members to protect their privacy and freedom. This contrasts with the widespread convention of home offices in our field with letters of nobility going back to Freud. Ronald Langs has repeatedly and vehemently criticized the home office setting which he claimed "is universally seen deep unconsciously as a harmful frame modification that also fails to conform to the ground rule archetypes that pertain to therapists' relative anonymity without deliberate self-revelations and the uncompromised total privacy and total confidentiality of a treatment experience" (2007a, 182). This draconian view has not been shared by other analysts, a situation Langs lamented (2007b, 728), yet he may have inadvertently contributed to his isolation on this matter by referring only to research done by himself in support of his declarations. There is, nevertheless, merit in many of his observations and arguments. He took up a bipersonal field model of the analytic situation long before it became seriously entertained by others in North America. This 'interactional model' allowed him to consistently pursue the possibility that patient material could be read in two directions: not only as unconscious derivative of personal conflict, but also as unconscious 'commentaries' (1978, 508) on the analyst's interventions "in that they contain both unconscious perception and unconscious fantasies". We will have occasion later on to mention a similar view expressed by Sedlak (2003, 2025), without apparent knowledge of Langs' work. In this manner, Langs had his own version of "listening to listening" later introduced as a separate concept by Haydée Faimberg (1996).

Yet the possibility of seduction and boundary slips are not confined to the home setting. As Gerald's (2011) study of psychoanalytic offices showed, analysts can intensely invest office settings as well, thus exhibiting to their patients just as many aspects of their psychic life, without necessarily noticing what their patients make of it. The point to retain is that all details, material and behavioural, of the treatment room, including analysts' bodies and clothing, can produce enigmatic messages for patients, which are ultimately our responsibility. As mentioned earlier, Gills' work (1984a, 1984b) followed Langs in drawing attention to the fact that aspects of the analyst's person, setting, and behaviour can be sources of what appears to be classical transference, but which have unconsciously provoked the patient. Both Langs and Gills might have welcomed Laplanche's concept of "enigmatic message" to describe what patients can experience as a deliberate "address" to them. Moving inquiry even more deeply into this implication of the setting, Jane Kite (2016) added an ethical dimension: "How do we as analysts take (ethical) responsibility for aspects of our own behavior and motivations that inevitably remain unknown to us?" (1153). Though there is not space in this book to pursue this subject further, less experienced clinicians are encouraged to reflect on the potential day to day fallout on patients of their "personal equation" which necessarily insinuates into the analytically-minded frameworks they build.

If the patient has contacted me by phone or by email regarding an appointment, I set up by return email or phone message a time when I can make or receive a call. When the patient is French-speaking, I use the formal "vous" address. In English, I try to convey the same professional attitude in my manner of speaking. The call is usually brief, allowing for the communication of precise details about where my office is and a date we can meet. I discourage discussion – though it is a frequent question – of fees and theoretical orientation over the phone, demurring that we will have time to pursue these matters in person when they become more meaningful. My internal position is that if the patient is dissatisfied with our first meeting and does not want to pay, I would rather lose out on that score than be forced into a negotiation over the phone with a total stranger. My office is in a building consecrated uniquely to medical and paramedical specialists. There is a waiting room across the hallway, and another down the hallway. A small sound-proofed vestibule provides space for outerwear, knapsacks, and shoes.

I usually shake hands in greeting. Like Ogden (2018), I avoid small talk as much as possible upon greeting them in the waiting room, if I can do so without embarrassing them. More effort is required to remain reserved when the patient arrives in a flap, which as noted above, occurs frequently enough at the first meeting, but the aim remains the same. I refer the reader to Odgen's perspicacious observations on the matter which can be summed up in his remark that "One must not deprive him [the patient] of the opportunity of writing the opening lines of his own analytic drama by burdening him with the analyst's unconscious contents before he even sets foot in the consulting room" (177). Implicit in Ogden's words is an interpretation of benevolent neutrality as a certain "hollowing out" out of the analyst's presence, a partial self-effacement, but not distance, to leave space for the patient's spontaneous expression. Cahn (Tisseron & Clément, 2017) refers to the "maintenance [by the analyst] of a [patient's] narcissistic homeostasis without which the distance established in the cure would be intolerable" (39). Letarte felt that the analyst is required to frustrate patients' libidinal strivings but not their narcissistic ones.

Patients unfailingly inquire politely how I am to which I reply with equal courtesy that I am fine without expanding the inquiry in their direction. When new patients invariably ask whether they should remove their shoes, I suggest that they are a better judge than I as to whether their shoes will bring dust into the room. Most decide to remove them. My office has a couple of desks, some bookshelves and filing cabinets, two chairs, a couch, plants, and windows. I gesture to the armchair with an invitation to be seated and place myself in a swivel chair about eight feet away. If the sun is pouring through the window behind my chair, I put down the blind; on hot summer days, I ensure the individual's comfort with the air conditioning blowing from the window somewhat behind them, turning it off if requested. Then I sit and take up a fresh notebook with the invitation to start where they would like. In this note-taking, I remain a lone wolf among my peers, though I came to it early in my career via Lacan's attention to Freud's emphasis on what the patient says in the session and lacking Freud's phenomenal memory. Colleagues insist that they retain more, or associative more freely without notes. All I can say is that this is not true for me, since I find that I can better follow the ebb and flow and the crisscrossing of associations with notebook on my lap. I listen for a good part of the hour I have set aside for the first meeting, longer than my regular 45-minute appointments, and I make provision for a temporal cushion at the anticipated end of the hour, in case the session would benefit going on longer, particularly if the first session has started late. There is no organized history-taking; I encourage the patient to unspool what is foremost in mind, with the odd clarification or encouragement to elaborate.

A major personal reference point is Freud's insistence that "no exception … is to be made to the rule that the first thing that comes into the patient's head is the first thing to be dealt with" (1911, 92). I bear this in mind when I encourage patients to begin the first session with a "Start where you wish" and an inviting way of my hand, a formula I prefer to the less open-ended "What brings you here?" Sometimes, the first thing that comes to mind is a comment on the appearance of my office, or of the error of direction they made in coming, or even "I don't know where to begin". All of these openings are instructive in their own way and can be handled in a similar fashion with an encouraging gesture and a demeanor of curious listening.

When patients express anxiety about what you have understood and whether they are getting anywhere, there is definitely an art in being able to give a reflective answer without dodging the urgency of the question for the patient and without making a theoretical declaration of some sort which is invariably hollow. I cannot over emphasize the importance of continued reading to furnish the analyst or psychotherapist's mind with hypotheses about the current interchange. Many clinicians are caught off guard, having imagined that being a good listener is good enough for all patients, whereas it works well for a time for some patients but is far from satisfying for those whose speech is restricted by mistrust or primary process thinking. These patients feel very much alone without regular prudent commentary and encouragement; they sincerely feel that they are "talking by (not even to) themselves" without some exchange with the therapist; talking is not a way of figuring things out for them, but a mode of discharge quickly spent. It is because of this psychic position that the therapist can feel under pressure to "say something" and the temptation is to blather out a superficial or abstract comment of little use to the patient.

Like most analysts, I am attending first and foremost to indications about how the patient thinks, how comfortable they feel relating to me, what has motivated their request for consultation, what prior therapeutic experience they have had, and what their hopes are for the future. After fifteen years as a PhD clinical psychologist and thirty-five years as an analyst, I have developed intuitions about where to gently probe which I can readily explain after the fact but find difficult to articulate as an anticipatory guideline. I try to comfortably sustain the communication of frightened and inhibited patients without engaging in meaningless reassurance. I take notes, sometimes sip coffee, shift positions as needed to be more comfortable or to add a physical dimension to my occasional intervention. I do not believe I have ever found myself disinterested in pursuing conversation with a potential patient. As the hour closes, I ask whether the patient would like to come again to continue exploring what has brought them to therapy and deliberately pause for a response. In my mind, we are not ready for a conclusion; yet I do not want to hurry the patient into a second meeting. There is an implicit message in this suspension of judgement to the effect that one hour is very little time for the patient to express her problem and its context in her life, as well as to take in a first impression of the therapist and the latter's style of listening and intervening. The invitation to come back again before concluding also suggests that the decision should not be impulsive, that time for reflection is a necessary component of the approach the therapist is taking, and that one is curious about the patient's metabolization of the first meeting when not exposed to the pressure of our presence.

A suspension of judgement without the pressure to either "tidy up" or "settle accounts" will create space for deferred reactions and/or après-coup revisions of the first encounter. The invitation to resume without immediate obligation should be sincere: "I see that we have run out of time for today. Would you like to continue talking next week about your project of getting help for yourself here?" Inquiries about fees, frequency, theoretical approach, or other aspects of the setting can be gently postponed, deflecting (when possible) the patient's anxiety about these matters to when they can be discussed in greater detail in a later meeting "if we decide to go ahead together". Patients are often worried about being manipulated into paying an unexpectedly high fee for the consultation; whereas therapists can be concerned about getting paid for a first visit if the patient decides not to pursue afterwards. The internal framework of the therapist is thus flushed out by a suspension of decision because risk-taking is happening on both sides. The therapist needs to be confident that psychoanalytic listening will eventually bear fruit but equally to believe in the patient's capacity to decant the upheaval of the first meeting and to wish to return to talk about it.

If the patient acquiesces, a second meeting is arranged which usually occurs a week later, or exceptionally, if the situation is urgent, more rapidly. Thus the "contract" is not offered or concluded in the first session which is ended on a note of suspension. When the patient leaves on this occasion and on all subsequent partings, I always extend my hand for another handshake. It is a habit I inherited from my French analyst, a symbolic gesture combining formality, warmth, and equality which seems to me a perfect way to close the as-if world we have been inhabiting.

Most of the time the patient shows up for a second visit, though there have been a few who have called in the interim to cancel, and more rarely still there have been no shows. These non-sequiturs are always occasions for uneasy self-questioning: I know I have missed something in the first meeting which cannot be repaired since the patient, in these cases, has typically closed the door without wishing to explore the reason. The second meeting – if it occurs – allows us to explore in an open-ended fashion the patient's reaction to the first interview and other thoughts that might have come to mind in the interval. I deem it key to communicate in this indirect manner that psychic work can and does occur outside of, as well as within, sessions. While giving the patient free rein for most of the second session, I insert an inquiry somewhere as to the thoughts and feelings the patient might have had during our first meeting or since. I like to make space for the patient's reactions to the couch, to the imagined, ideal, sex of the analyst, to former therapists. I also, if I can, try to make a preliminary link or two between certain events or feelings which the patient has not apparently connected in their thoughts. All the while, I am trying to assess the patient's capacity to reflect, to think in a transitional space, to tolerate my reserve, to react to the thinking I have shared, so as to formulate in my mind a *reasonable "framework offer", one that could reasonably address the patient's conundrums in the light of their psychic functioning.* I do not want to offer too little or too much by way of a framework. Some patients do not seem to have much to say or go on and on about apparently trivial matters. Many a supervisee has complained of being bored and of the (probably defensive) impression that they (the supervisees) are not "doing anything" or that they "must not be doing something right". This attitude constitutes a stumbling block in the supervisee's listening; they do not yet know how to invest "passionately" in such trivia as part if patients' thinking. I was glad to find that Raymond Cahn (1985, 39) noted in an interview that "There is no valid reason for looking down on or considering uninteresting the collection of comments a patient might make about happenings and incidents which occur in his daily life. They sometimes play a fundamental role in the subject's homeostasis, which is a condition for the success of the cure". Over and above this necessary equilibrium, the repetitive details of many "ordinary" stories can convey core conflicts.

In general, it is towards the end of the second hour that I leave enough time to make a proposal of a way of working together. This proposal is detailed: it includes a suggestion about using the couch, or eventually using the couch, about frequency, about the length of a regular session (forty-five minutes), a proffered fee, and a description of my stance as a listener who needs time to think about what the patient brings, who will intervene when she has something to say or ask. It is no longer considered de rigueur by many analysts to announce the funda-mental rule of free association, but I, on the contrary, consider it important. Why should patients not be introduced early to the notion of a new register of talking which values an unexpected, unconventional, and less polished discourse? Just because we know that real associativity can rarely be achieved is no reason for not explicitly enunciating it as part of our specific method. My preference for the couch is made known even for patients coming once a week because I think bet-ter in that disposition but it is not forced upon the dubious. Moreover, there are persons who do not tolerate not being able to see the analyst, due either to projec-tive paranoid structure or to an inability to treat their ideas as transitional entities.

Though I am as inhibited about money matters as many a colleague, since open-ing a private practice rather early in my career, I have become sensitized to the necessity of dealing with them in as open, as benevolently neutral, and as analyti-cally minded way possible. The many aspects of renumeration I have had occasion to reflect upon over the years are reflected in my treatment protocol. I explain my policy about missed sessions in some length, both because it can become a sore point sooner or later, and because many people genuinely have not thought through the concrete commitment which psychoanalytic work entails. The shared suffering of the missed session will be treated in more detail in Chapter 5. For the moment, we need only note the existence of a degree of magical wishing as to how much effort and how long a "cure" might take. My policy has evolved: in recent years, it means expressing the wish for regular hours to which both of us can reasonably commit; that once scheduled, I expect there will be occasions when unforeseen and untoward circumstances will prevent the patient from coming. Nevertheless, they will be responsible for the cost of the missed hour. I continue with a standing offer to find another time for sessions the patient anticipates missing due to a planned commitment elsewhere. However, I state just as clearly that I cannot always, given my own schedule, propose an alternate time suitable for them. If pressed, I will articulate that this way of working has a double function: not only does it provide a balanced income for me: it has proven its worth in our field as a protection for therapeutic work as well. I do not hide my belief that regularity is good both for the treatment and for my best functioning as an analyst. I mention that I usually take 3 weeks of summer holidays, 2 weeks off in the fall, a week at Christmas, and all statutory holidays. If they wish to take holidays during the summer period between July 1st and September 1st, which does not coincide with my own absence, they will not owe for missed sessions. I encourage the reader to bear in mind that I conceive my proposal as an *identificatory project* for a specialized way of working, a clinical posture to be explained in more detail in Chapter 4. The proposal is quite self-consciously *an offer to work psychoanalytically* because I am a psychoanalyst. Naïve patients are not expected to "get it" right away, nor will parts of the frame be forced upon them, but it is infantilizing and misleading to pretend to be like any other contemporary therapist. Nor is it useful for patients to meander into a relationship with a psychoanalyst just because they, the patients, are desperate for some kind of psychological relief. Allowing patients to decline this offer with dignity for a more attractive approach with another kind of therapist is a question of integrity for both parties.

New patients are apprised of my custom of not issuing a bill; rather they will be expected to add up what they owe and render it on their last session of the month. I am happy to produce monthly receipts if useful and, in any case, there will be an annual receipt for income tax purposes, since fees for psychotherapy and psychoanalysis can be included under health expense deductions. I never bring up the "limits" of confidentiality which I consider not only an insult to the patient before he or she has hardly opened their mouth but a contradiction in terms (we will come back to further considerations of confidentiality as part of framework integrity in Chapter 6). Postpandemic, I might include that my framework includes meeting in person. Time is provided for the patient to ask a few questions. I then invite the patient to take a week to think about my offer and to come again before finalizing an agreement. This agreement, if reached after an open discussion in the third session, is then summarized in the formal file I am required as a health professional to keep on the patient.

The professional order in my territorial jurisdiction, the *Order of psychologists of Quebec*, has officially encouraged quite a different payment model, the pay-as-you-go policy because it is "customary", they claim, to do so in commercial transactions (Houde, 2022). This perspective seems to have left aside the numerous occasions on which commercial transactions are conducted differently (such as monthly rentals for apartments and cars, partial payments upfront and the rest upon receipt of product in large orders, reductions if paid in advance, and many other models of payment). Pre-authorized internet transfers are good, the Order opined because "it is a solution which avoids the oversights and tensions connected with the monetary question". I, in contrast, am persuaded by the clinical function of a "gesture of payment" (Aisenstein 1986, Cahn 1985, Guedeney 1985, Halpert 1986, Raney 1986, Weissberg 1989) by the patient in psychoanalysis or psychoanalytic psychotherapy, which is why when I was working on salary in a hospital where patients did not pay for therapy, I experimented with Françoise Dolto's "symbolic payments" (Furlong 1998). Yet, I also feel it more coherent to a method which values optimal psychical "absence", not too close and not too far, to space payment in regular units of time, so that a certain debt is systematically part of the process. Under the circumstances, and given the shortage of space in this monograph, I do not need to summarize the literature as to why very low fees or extended debt beyond one month at a time are unpropitious conditions (see Krueger 1986).

As explained earlier, I expect the framework to eventually "groan" in one way or another and I try to cultivate an open mind about what that might mean to the dyad. The policy of monthly payments and of not handing invoices to patients may need some explanation. I learnt about this from my own analysis but its fecundity as a policy has been proven over and over. Patients (and therapists) make mistakes: either overpaying or underpaying what is owed or believed to be owed, which duly provides fascinating opportunities for exploration. One supervisee managed to hand out an invoice at the same time as complaining that she had not been properly paid, a tour-de-force which led us into a dense post-mortem exchange! Lacanian-inspired analysts seem to prefer being paid at each session, presumably because of the frequent obligation of a "gesture of payment". In a similar mindset, these same analysts also tend to request cash. Interestingly, Anna G.'s diary of her analysis with Freud in 1921 revealed that she was required to pay him monthly (Avakian 2011). My own cultural background makes paying after each session unacceptable: it smacks of payments to dentists, hairdressers, and tradesmen, not professional work. Moreover, I like the gentlemen's agreement implied in being paid for regular blocks of sessions, signifying an ongoing relationship, rather than one which is "settled up" one session at a time. Money is also important as a sublimation, and as a reference to the paternal function as symbolic mediator and third party. It seems accurate to view payment in psychoanalytic treatment as "an affair, not of a contract stipulating the content of an exchange, but an ethical pact organising the exchange itself" (Lew 2005, 37). We are paid not only to make a living (and I do not hide from patients that my sessions with them are my bread-and-butter), but also as a barrier against slipping into other gratifications in lieu of payment. Lew is onto something when he reminds us that "The [Latin and French] etymology brings forth a truth in articulating "paying" with a common origin in the term 'peace'. Peace implies appeasing the (possible) adversary, by fixing an accord with him; it means passing through a 'pact' in an agreement not to kill each other" (37). It was in the Middle Ages that the term began to be used to mean "to pacify one's creditors".

In committing this personal protocol to the page, I worry again about appearing overly concrete. To reiterate: I want to shy away from "how-to" advice and communicate to the reader the "why-to" of my personal opening gambit. In the next chapter, we will pursue the analytically fertile idea of "putting the frame to work" particularly when it seems to have broken down. In Chapter 3, we will turn to the understudied question of informed consent to the framework offered by the analyst, followed in Chapter 4 with the importance of the "analytic offer" implied in the framework "contract", – at least in the clinician's mind – as it pertains to reasons why both its installation and its disruption matter. Rounding out our examination of shaky aspects of the framework within this monograph are the tribulations specific to the missed session and to potential threats to confidentiality which will be studied in Chapters 5 and 6, respectively.

Notes

1 The author assumes responsibility for all translations of previously untranslated French literature.
2 See the Office of Science which I consulted online January 17, 2024. Peter Higgs died in April 2024.
3 Freud (1925, 133) observed in discussing the moral responsibility for dreams: "I shall perhaps learn that what I am disavowing not only 'is' in me but sometimes 'acts' from out of me as well".
4 Coming from another theoretical background, Vic Sedlak makes a similar point in a presentation to the Toronto Psychoanalytic Society April 26, 2025.

References

Aisenstein, M. 1986. D'un singulier usage du don. *Les Cahiers du Centre de Psychanalyse et de Psychothérapie* 12:21–35.
Avakian, D. 2011. Mon analyse avec le professeur Freud d'Anna G., sous la direction d'Anna Koellreuter. *Revue française de psychanalyse* 75:217–224.
Bion, W. R. 1979. Making the best of a bad job. In *Clinical Seminars and Four Papers*, edited by W. R. Bion, 247–257. Abingdon, UK: Fleetwood Press, 1987.
Bleger, J. 1967. Psychoanalysis of the psychoanalytic setting. In *Symbiosis and Ambiguity*, edited by John Churcher & Leopoldo Bleger. Trans. Susan Rogers, Leopoldo Bleger, and John Churcher, 228–242. London: Routledge, 2013.
Bleger, L. 2022. What is the setting after all? In *Psychoanalysis of the Psychoanalytic Frame Revisited: A New Look at José Bleger's Classic Work*, edited by C. Moguillansky & H. B. Levine, 21–37. New York: Taylor & Francis. Kindle Edition. DOI: 10.4324/9781003252252-3
Bloomfield, J. 2020. Alan Bass Ph.D. On psychoanalysis and psychoanalytic training. Video available at: https://www.google.com/search?client=firefox-b-d&q=Alan+Bass+psychoa nalyst#fpstate=ive&vld=cid:4444ee5d,vid:tikFWSpmEv8,st:0
Cahn, D. 1985. Les infortunes d'un destin et la gratuité dans la cure. *Les Cahiers du Centre de Psychanalyse et de Psychothérapie* 11:65.
Caper, R. 1992. Does Psychoanalysis Heal? A Contribution to the Theory of Psychoanalytic Technique. *International Journal of Psychoanalysis* 73:283–292.
Churcher, J. 2022. The psychoanalytic setting, embodiment and presence. Exploring José Bleger's concept of encuadre. In *Psychoanalysis of the Psychoanalytic Frame Revisited: A New Look at José Bleger's Classic Work*, edited by C. Moguillansky & H. B. Levine, 39–56. New York: Taylor & Francis. Kindle Edition. DOI: 10.4324/9781003252252-4
De M'Uzan, M. 2019. *Permanent Disquiet Psychoanalysis and the Transitional Subject*. New York: Routledge.
Donnet, J. 2005. La voie sublimatoire et la situation analysante. *Revue française de psy-chanalyse* 69:1485–1490.
Faimberg, H. 1996. Listening to Listening. *The International Journal of Psychoanalysis* 77(4):667–677.
Ferro, A. 2002. *In the Analyst's Consulting Room*. Translated by P. Slotkin. Hove, UK: Routledge, 2021.
Freud, S. 1898. A Psychical Mechanism of Forgetfulness. *Standard Edition* 3:287–297.
Freud, S. 1899. Screen Memories. *Standard Edition* 3:299–322.
Freud, S. 1911. The handling of dream-interpretation in psycho-analysis *Standard Edition* 12:91–96.
Freud, S. 1914. Remembering, Repeating and Working-Through. *Standard Edition* 12:147–156.

Freud, S. 1915. The Unconscious. *Standard Edition* 14:159–215.

Freud, S. 1925. Some Additional Notes on Dream-Interpretation as a Whole. *Standard Edition* 19:123–138.

Furlong, A. 1995. Encadrer le cadre: pour une cure moins infernale (Putting a protective frame around the frame: for a less infernal cure). In *La Cure Infernale* edited by François Gauthier, A.p.p.Q., 9–26.

Furlong, A. 1998. The symbolization of Absence under Third Party Payment: Symbolic Markers with Adults. *Canadian Journal of Psychoanalysis* 6:75–98.

Gerald, M. 2011. The Psychoanalytic Office: Past, Present, and Future. *Psychoanalytic Psychology* 28:435–445.

Gill, M. M. 1984a. Psychoanalysis and Psychotherapy: A Revision. *International Review of Psychoanalysis* 11:161–179.

Gill, M. M. 1984b. Transference: A Change in Conception or Only in Emphasis? *Psychoanalytic Inquiry* 4:489–523.

Glick, Y. 2024. Parallel processes, pluri-subjective configurations and the circulation of desire. *Presentation made to the Canadian Psychoanalytic Society, Quebec English Branch, on January 18, 2024.*

Green, A. 1975. The Analyst, Symbolization and Absence in the Analytic Setting (On Changes in Analytic Practice and Analytic Experience)—In Memory of D. W. Winnicott. *International Journal of Psychoanalysis* 56:1–22.

Greenberg, J. 2016. Editor's Introduction: Is Truth Relevant? *Psychoanalytic Quarterly* 85(2):269–274.

Guedeney, D. 1985. Du plomb dans l'or pur de l'analyse? *Les Cahiers du Centre de Psychanalyse et de Psychothérapie* 11:99–108.

Halpert, 1986. The meaning and effects of insurance in psychotherapy and psychoanalysis. In *The Last Taboo: Money as Symbol and Reality in Psychotherapy and Psychoanalysis*, edited by D. Krueger, 169–174. New York: Brunner/Mazel.

Houde, D. 2022. Factures, rapports d'honoraires professionnels, paiements et reçus. *Psychologie Québec, septembre. https://www.ordrepsy.qc.ca/-/factures-rapports-d-honoraires-professionnels-paiements-et-recus*

Kahn, L. 2021. "Confronting the Unknown" Concerning Disquiet in Analytic Listening. *Translation by Sylvie de Lorimier of Conference Presented to the Société psychanalytic de Montréal*: Kahn, L. (2021) « L'EPREUVE DE L'INCONNU » A PROPOS DE L'INTRANQUILLITE DANS L'ECOUTE ANALYTIQUE. Canadian Journal of Psychoanalysis 29:5-19

Kite, J. V. 2016. The Fundamental Ethical Ambiguity of the Analyst as Person. *Journal of the American Psychoanalytic Association* 64:1153–1171.

Krueger, D. ed. 1986. *The Last Taboo: Money as Symbol and Reality in Psychotherapy and Psychoanalysis*. New York: Brunner/Mazel.

Langs, R. 2007a. One Mind or Two: Divergent Views of the Home-Office Setting Commentary on Maroda (2006). *Psychoanalytic Psychology* 24(1):180–186.

Langs, R. 2007b. On Not Being Heard. Response to Gargiulo (2007) and Mills (2007). *Psychoanalytic Psychology* 24(4):726–730.

Laplanche, J. 1997. Aims of the psychoanalytic process. *European Journal of Psychoanalysis* 1:1–8. https://www.journal-psychoanalysis.eu/articles/aims-of-the-psychoanalytic-process/

Laplanche, J. 2006. Psychoanalysis and psychotherapy. In *Freud and the Sexual: Essays 2000-2006*, Translated by N. Ray, 279–284. International Psychoanalytic Books, 2011.

Letarte, P. 2018. *Entendre La Folie*. Paris: Presses Universitaires de France. Kindle Edition.

Lew, R. 2005. Le Paiement En Psychanalyse. *Che Vuoi?* 24(2):37–60. https://doi.org/10.3917/chev.024.0037

Lipton, S. D. 1977. The Advantages of Freud's Technique as Shown in His Analysis of the Rat Man. *International Journal of Psychoanalysis* 58:255–273.

Little, M. 1985. Winnicott Working in Areas Where Psychotic Anxieties Predominate. A Personal Record. *Free Associations* 1(3):9–42.

Manzano, J., Palacio-Espasa, F., & Abella, A. 2016. *Précis de technique psychanalytique avec son application à la psychothérapie*. Collection: Le Fil Rouge. Paris: Presses Universitaires de France.

Milner, M. 1952. Aspects of Symbolism in Comprehension of the Not-Self. *International Journal of Psychoanalysis* 33:181–194.

Office of Science, US Department of Energy. Consulted January 15, 2024. https://www.energy.gov/science/doe-explainsthe-higgs-boson

Ogden, T. 2012. Comments on transference and countertransference in the initial analytic meeting. In *Initiating Psychoanalysis: Perspectives*, edited by B. Reith, S. Lagerlöf, P. Crick, M. Møller & E. Skale, 173–188. London: Routledge: The New Library of Psychoanalysis Teaching Series, 2012.

Ogden, T. 2018. How I talk with my patients. *The Psychoanalytic Quarterly*, LXXXVII: 399–413. http://dx.doi.org/10.1080/00332828.2018.1495513

Parsons, M. 2007. Raiding the Inarticulate: The Internal Analytic Setting and Listening Beyond Countertransference. *International Journal of Psychoanalysis* 88:1441–1456.

Raney, J. 1986. The effect of fees on the course and outcome of psychotherapy and psychoanalysis. In *The Last Taboo: Money as Symbol and Reality in Psychotherapy and Psychoanalysis*, edited by D. Krueger, 88–101. New York: Brunner/Mazel.

Reid, W. 1994. Aux marges de l'analysable. In *Le premier entretien ou une théorie infantile de la psyché. In Le Premier Entretien et L'écoute Psychanalytique*, edited by B. Tanguay, 9–33. Connecticut: Editions Méridien, 1994.

Reid, W. 1998a. Pour une metapsychologie du cadre ou comment peut-on ne pas être un héros? In *La psychothérapie analytique*, edited by P. Doucet & W. Reid.. Montreal: Gaëton Morin.

Reid, W. 1998b. Annette ou les vertus de la métapsychologie: les premiers entretiens aux limites de l'analysable. *Revue française de psychanalyse* 64(1):153–166. https://doi.org/10.3917/rfp.g1998.62n1.0153

Reid, W. 1999. Le cadre analytique revisité. *Filigrane* 8(2):33–44.

Schafer, R. 1983. *The analytic attitude*. London: Hogarth Press.

Sedlak, V. 2003. The patient's Material as an Aid to the Disciplined Working Through of the Countertransference and Supervision. *International Journal of Psychoanalysis* 84:1487–1500.

Sedlak, V. 2025. Countertransference as an unconscious phenomenon. Presentation to the *Toronto Psychoanalytic Society,* April 26, 2025.

Stern, D. B. 2024. Beginning the Treatment on a Personal Note: Creating Emotional Connection. *The Psychoanalytic Quarterly* 93(4):647–674. https://doi.org/10.1080/0033282 8.2024.2398590

Stern, S. 2009. Session Frequency and the Definition of Psychoanalysis. *Psychoanalytic Dialogues* 19:639–655.

Tisseron, S. & Clément, M.-N. 2017. Entretien Avec Raymond Cahn. *Dans Le Carnet PSY* 6/209:34–43.

Weissberg, J. H. 1989. The Fiscal Blind Spot in Psychotherapy. *Journal of the American Academy of Psychoanalysis* 17:475–482.

Winnicott, D. W. 1951. Transitional objects and transitional phenomena. In *Playing and Reality*. London: Routledge, 1989.

Winnicott, D. W. 1969. The Use of an Object. *The International Journal of Psychoanalysis* 50(4):711–716.

Chapter 2

When the frame groans and putting it to work

Putting the frame to work

It is precisely because either or both patient and analyst will inevitably stumble over some aspect of the framework that its existence does us an inestimable service: it forces the therapeutic couple to soberly reconsider hidden aspects of their relationship. If handled delicately, it recasts and deepens the work. There are many ways that the frame can groan, like – to use a tired metaphor – a creaky door, but when it does the couple has the opportunity of putting the framework to work and opening additional psychic space. The framework is there to be used, which means that it first must exist. We are thus entirely in agreement with Antonini Ferro in his book, *In the Analyst's Consulting Room* (2002/2021) when he makes a point of cautioning analysts not to overreact when the setting is not precisely observed. He shares many vignettes demonstrating "how extraordinarily rich in communication breaches in the setting by the patient can be ... [as long as we are] sufficiently available to consider them in this light" (122). Later in this chapter, we will provide vignettes from other sources which illustrate the same point.

Freud (1913) used the analogy of a chess game for psychoanalytic treatment, observing that, while openings and endgames in chess may be codified, the middle game is open to enormous technical variation and creative exploration. And yet we have learnt from the research done by the *IPA Working Party on Initiating Psychoanalysis* that the opening gambit of analysis is far from codified in actual practice, subject to a startling variety of combinatory moves. Nevertheless, sooner or later, the therapeutic dyad must come to an agreement about how they are to work together ... or do they? I have noticed, in my contact with non-psychoanalytically trained psychotherapists, an odd deliquescence of the framework's installation. Due, perhaps, to anxiety about being paid, or to discomfort with uncertainty about commitment beyond the first session, many of these therapists seem to just "slide" into a given treatment, hoping that the patient will come along. They fail to adequately explore the patient's fantasies and expectations about treatment; they do not formulate a definite proposal for a way of working together nor do they introduce a suspension of decision by inviting the patient to consider the offer for a few days before discussing it further. Both the lack of clarity accompanying the "offer" and the absence of programmed decision-making "afterwardness" cannot but vitiate true consent. The root of these avoidances

DOI: 10.4324/9781003527459-3

may lie in a poorly conceptualized notion of therapeutic function and aim, beyond a vague wish to make the patient feel better by some kind of "understanding of himself". Less experienced psychoanalytic psychotherapists may be so preoccupied with wondering what they should "do" that they cannot convey a relaxed, though alert, readiness to hear. Or it may be related to an unrecognized state of internal disarray which has accompanied the activation of untranslatable psychic stowaways in each (see our reference to this Freudian idea in Chapter 1). Fundamentally, these clinicians have little confidence in the power of words to make a real material difference. They also fail to appreciate that resistance needs to be treated with the same respect, courtesy, and curiosity as symptoms. Moreover, they are easily entangled in their patient's manifest discourse without wondering about its underlying conflicts. There is a veritable bashfulness about saying anything beyond rewording what the patient has said.

Before offering some clinical examples of "putting the frame to work", I want to raise an issue that I cannot solve but which theoretical integrity requires putting before the reader. Boesky (2013, 1164) calls it the "epistemological problem of infinite over-determination of meaning" which he had explained in an earlier article (2008, 442) by quoting Waelder:

> … overdetermination encounters a practical difficulty in psychoanalysis: in the psychoanalytic method of interpretation the introduction of the concept of over-determination offers neither a guideline nor a boundary for the required overinterpretations. Overdetermination is, as it were, open to infinity. No principle of psychoanalytic interpretation can give any guidelines as to how far overdetermination extends or when it should be considered exhausted.

The challenge is not to encompass the complexity of any human interaction which would necessitate the participation of many disciplines other than psychoanalysis (biological, linguistic, anthropological, neurocognitive, to name a few). Psychoanalysis has as quite limited (but pervasive) object of study the participation of dynamically unconscious life to our interactions. At least, that is my understanding. Insofar as every frame, if it is at all coherent, is linked to an implicit psychoanalytic epistemological system, then each analyst's "system" will favour "hearing" certain strands of meaning over others, thus generating "data" for interpretive use when appropriate. But how do we know what we claim to know through our listening Boesky asks? Neither he nor I know the answer to "the vexing problem about the evaluation of the clinical evidence generated in all our various competing theoretic models" (2013, 442) which means that readers will have to judge for themselves whether the clinical examples shared in this book assist in conveying my principal positions about the setting.

Consent with a psychotic patient

Implicit in Aulagnier's preoccupation with understanding why the analytic relationship, supposedly source of an enhanced integration and freedom with one's drives can also collude in the patient's alienation, is her anguish about what constitutes properly informed "consent". There is one place where she explicitly brings up the issue in a sequence I will share in some detail both because it is not available in English and because it is an unusually refined description of the intricacies of consent. An entire chapter of one of her books (Chapter 1, 2004) is devoted to the case of Philippe, a man hospitalized after a psychotic breakdown, in a unit where she was regular consultant. She reports that their relation occurred in two time periods, two spaces, and two therapeutic perspectives. During the first three months, Aulagnier saw Philippe on the ward in the presence of other psychiatric staff where she confined herself to supportive listening; in the last seven months before she wrote up the case, Philippe came to her home office where she had hoped to create "the conditions necessary for analytic work and for interpretation to accomplish its goal" (2004, location 708, Kindle Edition). There is no space here to recount the fascinating details of her reconstruction of the infantile origin of Philippe's delusion nor is that clinical material pertinent to the theme of this book. Aulagnier noticed towards the end of the first period that Philippe seemed to lose interest in efforts to give any meaning to his experiences. Though Aulagnier did not express it in these terms, we might say now that Philippe was dead set on destroying links. A depressive downturn occupied the forefront of his interviews: he was sick of everything particularly the constraints of hospital life and, in any case, he claimed he was never going to get better and there was nothing new to say. Then a dramatic event changed the tone of their relationship: just before an anticipated important separation from his parents was to occur, Philippe made a suicide attempt which prolonged his stay in the psychiatric unit.

When Aulagnier visited him on the unit the following evening, they were for the first time alone without other staff present and Aulagnier had the impression that Philippe opened up more freely about his identification with his father as a "brother" figure, even letting himself explicitly criticize his mother as a entrapping and controlling person for both of them. In the warmth and spontaneity of the moment – she admitted after the fact – her desire to be appreciated as an analyst overcame her usual caution.

> It was at the end of this meeting that I surprised myself by inviting Philippe henceforth to come and see me at my home [office], an offer he immediately accepted with obvious pleasure. But when I had come to meet Philippe that evening [on the ward], I had not planned to do anything of the kind. Up to then, the framework as I saw it in the context of the prior three months of interviews, was only justified in my mind by the fact that I had no intention of making it a prologue for psychotherapy, Even if we admit, which is after all quite possible, that my interest in Philippe could have prompted me into making this proposition, *it is certain that I would have made sure that he had the time, and that I had the time, to reflect on the implications of this transformation of our relationship, to discuss with him the advantages, the drawbacks, and especially the specificity of the framework* ["ses particularités" in the French]".
>
> (added emphasis, 1768–1772 Kindle locations)

Aulagnier recounted that for most of the subsequent six months of psychother-apy, paid for by an anonymous source, she doubted her hasty invitation to invite him into the new one-on-one private setting. Philippe would leave the ward once a week to attend sessions in her home office. However, the mental opening she had observed the night after his suicide attempt closed again: he was distant, polite, a little suspicious. From a relationship with him as an inpatient mediated by the presence of hospital staff, medication, ward schedules, etc., they now only had words between them. Philippe's entire defence system had been aimed at not re-membering; now Aulagnier was asking him to reflect on the pertinence of the past to his present worldview. During this period, she often felt helpless as Philippe tediously rebuffed her comments with the retort: "I don't know what I am doing here" or "You want to change my expectations. That is not possible. Time is a false movement. We think it moves, but that's not true. I have already told you, for me time is circular" (location 1947). When she attempted an interpretation relating to Philippe's need to punish himself for wishing to attack the maternal figure, his mind came undone: "In my thoughts it rolls by, it rolls by, but I cannot formulate my ideas, the connection doesn't come, there is no passageway through" (location 1949). She was up against a colossal internal barrier against thinking, a barrier recognized by other students of psychosis, and the equally gargantuan struggle against an internal force seeking to destroy the subject. Not only had Philippe not asked for an analysis – given his psychic structure such a request was in her opinion impossible – but he hardly asked for anything. Moreover, he was missing a critical subjective experience which Aulagnier had come to believe essential for psychoanalytic work: a sense of perplexity about himself, a questioning of the reference points of what she called his "identificatory field" (location 1864). We will have occasion to come back to this specific element in the next chapter as it pertains to the acceptability to any given patient of an "analytic offer".

For the moment, we must leave Aulagnier to examine further instances where the steadiness and/or the legitimacy of the framework has been toppled by a de-liberate or an accidental act by the therapist or by the patient, forcing them to grapple constructively with fallout. Since these critical moments can come up un-expectedly, the psychoanalyst may be caught off balance. Robert Caper (1992) was evidently speaking from experience when he wrote: "the analyst is not someone who maintains a 'neutral' stance above the fray, but someone who is always being drawn into the frway, could not do analysis if he were not in the fray, and who does analysis largely by figuring out what kind of fray he is in" (289).

A time for understanding and a time of conclusion

I have already intimated that the possibility of reaching informed consent to psy-choanalysis or to a psychoanalytically oriented therapy in a single session is highly unlikely. Most contemporary analysts have distanced themselves from Freud's op-tion of a trial analysis when in doubt as to whether to take on a new patient since serious narcissistic injury might occur if the analysand is eventually declined.

All the same, there may be pressure to conclude as soon as possible the decision to work together or not. For instance, Roger Dufresne, who ran a decades long seminar on the first interview, asserted that a "specific trait of the first interview is the necessity of a conclusion, of committing ourselves one way or another, of giving a reply, rather rapidly. For we cannot delay indefinitely until we have better grasped the latent meaning behind the request for treatment" (1994, 87). Yet, we can question Dufresne's position: instituting some delay does not mean putting off indefinitely. Without leaving the patient (and oneself) some "time for comprehending" (Lacan, 2006), how can one properly reach a "moment for concluding/acting" one's consent?

Lacan undertook several ground-breaking investigations into temporal aspects of the psychoanalytic relationship: such as the now well-known study of Freud's concept of *Nachträglichkeit* (translated as après-coup in French, and "afterwardness" in English by Jean Laplanche (see Laplanche et al, 1992), and his notorious practice of short sessions. Less well known are Lacan's meditations with respect to other aspects of unconscious temporality: the grammatical form of "future anterior" as essential in the fixing of meaning, as well as his invention of the concepts of "temporal tension", "the assertion of anticipated certainty", of "quilting points", and of "scansion". Though each one of these temporal considerations could enlighten our theory of the framework, in the present monograph we will only have space to acknowledge the usefulness of Lacan's exploration of "logical time" (2006/1945) which I wish to use as metaphor for the *intersubjective and necessarily time-related nature of informed consent*.[1] Lacan begins with his own metaphor, asking us to imagine an action occurring in a prison where three prisoners have been brought to the director's office. The director explains that for reasons he does not need to make known, he must release one inmate on this date. To decide which one, he has devised a puzzle: the first prisoner to solve it will be the one receiving his freedom that evening. They are shown five discs, three white and two black, one of which, the director explains, will be put on each of their backs. Thus, they will be able to see the disc on the other prisoners' backs but not their own and they are forbidden to communicate with each other in any way. Their challenge is to correctly guess the colour of the disc on their own back. They are then briefly blindfolded while the director places a white disc on the back of all three prisoners. He watches them look at each other and cogitate in silence. After a period of hesitation, not one but all three prisoners step forward at once with the correct answer.

In Lacan's "sophism", the only pathway to a solution is intersubjective reasoning in the following sense: each one has to imagine what the others might be thinking when they perceive the disc on his (the #1 reference subject) back and on that of the other prisoners (reference subjects 2 and 3). Each man must first ask himself: "If I had a black disk on my back, my fellow prisoners (2 and 3) would each be seeing one white and one black disk, whereas I see two white. In that case, since the others also do not know what is on their back but which I (subject #1) can see, each of the others has to be surmising: 'if there were a black disk on my back (that is the back of one of the two prisoners facing me, subjects #2 and #3), one of the others would be seeing two black disks, and would know right away the color of the disk on his back (it has to be white under those circumstances since there are only two black disks in circulation)'. But I (subjects #1, #2, and #3) do not see anyone heading for the door which must mean that my disk is white because they are hesitating like me". And with that conclusion, all three men step forward. Seeing the others move introduces a momentary doubt in each: perhaps they have seen my disc as black after all? Then each realizes that the others have also doubted, and they move again towards the door with confidence. Lacan homes in on the "modulation of time" in the sophism's "movement" which is composed of three "moments": the Instant of the Glance when the prisoners see the discs on the backs of their fellow inmates, the Time for Comprehending when each silently cogitates upon the meaning of the others' uncertainty all the while anxious about losing out if he misjudges their reasoning, and the Moment of Concluding which is a "subjective assertion" based on the "evidential moments" of perceiving his counterparts' either inertia or movement towards the door. It is the hesitancies of the others which act as signifiers for each individual subject, allowing him to conclude what colour is his disc.

The parable illustrates the lot of the human subject who must pass through other human beings (that is what he imagines others to be thinking) to figure out his identity. It is always a question of interpreting – since one cannot know directly – what the other is thinking to venture a conclusion about oneself.[2] Moreover, it takes time. Unless one does the mental work and carefully observes the other, a quick answer may be erroneous. That an answer is possible at all rests on an assumption of sincerity on the part of all actors, as Jean Brini (2023) has pointed out in a recent re-examination of the parable.[3] If the wish to deceive is added to the mix, none of the actors would be sure of his reasoning and would fall prey to the same tormenting doubt as in Freud's (1901) example of one Jew accusing another of trying to lead astray by telling the truth. How can a patient have faith in our words; how can we have faith in our own, knowing that unconscious conflict can lead us astray too? How can one assent to a treatment, we will ask in Chapter 3, destined – if properly conducted – to unseat the certainties of one's narration-of-self, without struggling with initial (and even ongoing) doubt? How can one consent to a treatment if untranslatable leftovers from childhood enigmas (Laplanche, 2002/2011) have unexpectedly stunned the ego in the first interviews? For these many reasons, in my own consulting room (as described at the end of Chapter 1), I create a temporal gap between my description of my analytic "offer" and the patient's acceptance or disagreement with it. It has been my experience that without instituting an explicit "time of conclusion" regarding the how and the wherefore of working together, patients occasionally misconstrue the nature of the work undertaken by the dyad. Introducing a 'temporal gap' during the initial interviews between 'offer' and 'consent' can be viewed as one framework incarnation of the need in our work to respect the necessary time to understand what is going on in the patient, in the analyst, and between them. Sedlak (2025) refers to this as "reverberation time", a term he credits Dana Birkstein Green (2009) with using.

Disruption to the setting introduced by the clinician

The supervisee, Mr A, a psychoanalytically oriented psychotherapist, opened his session with a confession: "I have acted out: I locked the door on Mrs X this morning!" Since this supervisee works out of a home office, he usually takes care to open the door leading to the waiting room before starting the day's schedule.

That morning, his first patient of the day had found herself locked out on a rather chilly morning. Reacting too quickly to confused sentiments of guilt, Mr A apologized to the patient and explained that he had been feeling "farther away" from Mrs X since the latter had decided to consult a sexologist in parallel to her psychotherapy sessions. In fact, as Mr A then explained, Mrs X had recently decreased the frequency of her psychotherapy to see the sexologist more often. I was taken by the note of suffering suggested in the supervisee's apology to the patient, as though he were feeling bereft. At first, he denied feeling anything of the sort. Instead, he admitted that he often found Mrs X's experiences emotionally resonant, though he seemed unaware of perhaps unconsciously treating her as a double. I mentioned Bowlby's observations of children after an overly long separation from their mother: they treat her coldly when she appears again. Mr A remembered that he had given his own mother the cold shoulder after an illness had forced a separation of several months from her at the age of one. Then we could start to think about Mrs X's experience as an adolescent having to take care of a depressed mother and not being able to spread her wings in sexual experimentation. Had Mr A become a clingy mother in the transference? Was he the one who felt locked out by the patient's wish to explore elsewhere? If so, forgetting to unlock the door was an unmetabolized repetition in the form of enacted thing-presentation piercing the therapist's internal frame. Of course, as Mr A's supervisor, I was not in the position to explore these personal issues further. The example has been adduced to illustrate how unexpected breaks in the frame can come from the side of the therapist, whose guilt and shame over the mishap must be dealt with first before it is possible to explore what comes to mind about it.

Another example comes from Bleger (1967) who deduced that patients can deposit the most primitive part of their personality into the framework. He recounted how a colleague had brought a case for supervision which had become mired in "chronicity and therapeutic inefficacy" though the patient seemed to be cooperating well. Bleger discovered that his colleague had acquiesced from the beginning to the patient's request to use the familiar (in Spanish) form of address with each other.

> It took many months to analyse the therapist's countertransference until he 'found the courage' to rectify the familiar form of address by interpreting to the patient what was happening, and what was hidden inside it. The cancelling of the familiar form, through its systematic analysis, made manifest the narcissistic relation and omnipotent control and the annihilation of the person and role of the therapist, which had become immobilised in the familiar form of address.
>
> (239)

Bleger pointed out that it would probably not have been feasible to modify the familiar form of address from the outset, since the colleague "was not technically equipped to handle a patient with a highly narcissistic organization" (239). Bleger is adamant that analysts should not use the familiar form of address to patients "although he may accept it from the patient and analyse it at the appropriate moment .... The analyst needs to accept the setting brought by the patient (which is the patient's 'meta-ego'), because within it will be found in summary form the primitive unresolved symbiosis. However, we need to state at the same time that accepting the patient's meta-ego (his setting) does not mean giving up the therapist's own, as a function of which it is possible to analyse the process and the setting itself when this has been transformed into process" (239–240).

The modern English language does not afford a similar distinction between familiar forms of address and formal ones as Spanish and French do. As an anglophone learning to speak French to patients, I had to go through a significant learning curve to extricate myself from the same mistake made by Bleger's colleague. Not only was there pressure from patients to adopt the more intimate locutions but also the increasingly casual standard of social and professional relations in contemporary North America played a part. It is a frequent challenge for less experienced psychotherapists to practice this symbolization of asymmetry and reserve with their patients. Overall, Bleger's book, *Symbiosis and Ambiguity*, has been an epiphany for me, presenting both a darker side of the setting and a potentially richer one which has illuminated previously mysterious clinical interactions and developments in my practice. But the supervision referred to above did not end that well: "[t]he change in the form of address through analysis led the analyst to see that it was a question not of phobic character but of a simple schizophrenia with a phobic-obsessional 'façade'" (239). The colleague was called upon to make a "very great effort" both in managing his countertransference and to handle an intense change in the analytic process and a "disruption of the patient's ego" occasioned by the rectification to a formal manner of speaking. One wonders – though this ethical and clinical question is beyond the purview of the present book – whether the increased insight into the patient's precarious psychic equilibrium was acceptable compensation (to the patient) for the destruction of his "phantom" meta-ego.

Is the framework co-created?

The so-called "classic" framework of couch, four or five times a week frequency, with an austere interpretating analyst has been under siege for decades in all three original IPA regions. For one thing, tracing it back to Freud proved to be somewhat erroneous as firsthand reports of his analysands and the archival studies of psychoanalytic historians have made clear. At the same time, ample evidence nevertheless exists of the rigidity and conservatism of the psychoanalytic frame instituted in many American Psychoanalytic Association institutes (APsaA) (cf. Casement, 2005; Goretti, 2006; Kernberg, 2016; Levin, 2014) by the third post-Freudian generation's interpretation of "correct" technique and theory as a medical specialty. There have been many debates over what is "essential" to a psychoanalytic approach and who should be permitted to learn to practice it. Given the depth and breadth of this literature not only in the United States but across the globe, we will have to confine ourselves to a handful of authors within the confines of this book to illustrate theoretical and practical rectifications proposed to redress the much maligned and "outdated" "classical" setting. We will see that though numerous analysts have questioned fixation on the setting as a universal, fixed, concrete entity, they do not always arrive at the same conclusions about how to move forward. In the confines of this chapter, I have chosen to address key arguments put forth in a few representative papers. Let us commence with Steven Stern (2009) who set the stage with a cogent résumé of the "state of dissociation" occurring in the field, a "split between psychoanalysis as we are actually practicing it and psychoanalysis as many of our institutions continue to define it" (640). The source of this split is in part, he said, "the trauma of this culture's repudiation of psychoanalysis as it was regarded and practiced in its heyday". Stern drew a parallel with other professions:

> There is an essential, mutually constituting relationship between a profession's name and its clinical practice. Surgeons operate, family lawyers practice law, and teachers teach. A breach in that relationship, as has occurred in psychoanalysis, is damaging to both the name and the practice. Defining the name, psychoanalysis, such that it is no longer the primary form of practice for the majority of its highly trained practitioners chokes this essential relationship, depriving both the name and its practitioners of life-giving energy.
>
> (639)

The majority of IPA analysts today probably share Stern's cross-examination of a definition of analysis based strictly on what he considered "extrinsic" criteria; I also personally agree when he draws attention to the self-defeating approach of excluding from the fold so many trained psychoanalysts for whom the classical framework is no longer their primary form of practice. It undoubtedly "weakens us internally because of the split between psychoanalysis as we are actually practicing it and psychoanalysis as many of our institutions continue to define it" (640). I am persuaded that this is one of the reasons for the penury of new applicants for training analyst status in the older Canadian psychoanalytic institutes, where settings other than the classic framework of incarnating psychoanalytic knowledge are neither valued nor theorized enough to legitimize their psychoanalytic identity. Nevertheless, it is difficult to follow his argument that psychoanalysis needs to be redefined "by the current realities of the marketplace" and by "contemporary theory" regarding the "co-created, nonlinear nature of the analytic relationship". Do the current realities of the marketplace change the surgeon's relationship to injured or diseased bodies? Or the family lawyer's relationship to the family law he or she defends? Changes in the financial model of medical institutions and third-party payment alter the way surgeons are paid for their services but should not, *in principle*, be a driving force in instituting changes in operating room procedures. Evolving case law and new family constellations may change the engagement of family lawyers with their clients but not their relationship to the law as such. If the surgeon decides to give up the scalpel to move to another medical specialty, he will no longer be referred to as a surgeon. No psychoanalytic clinician would argue about the "nonlinearity" of the analytic relationship, when many non-clinical interactions in life are far from "linear", but the notion of its "co-creation" with the patient gives pause. Since any relationship is a co-creation insofar as it is a dialectical exchange in which each response changes the direction of the interlocutor's riposte, Stern must have had in mind something more substantial. Was he thinking that the "analytic work" is co-created? That idea too would seem to be uncontroversial insofar as the engaged participation of both parties is essential to growth. But if he was asserting that the analytic framework itself is co-created over and above minor negotiations such as the exact fee and frequency or the use of the couch or chair, then he has overextended himself.

The surgeon may negotiate the date of surgery with patients or insert a titanium implant over an alternative cheaper material or ask for the authority ahead of surgery to remove a whole cancer-ridden organ if partial ablation is not adequate to prevent a reoccurrence. Yet you will not see a surgeon "co-create" the operation itself, or the organization of the operating theatre within which it occurs. If the offer is "analysis" or a "psychoanalytic psychotherapy", then there are aspects of the setting which are rather "non-negotiable", because without them, analytic intervention would make no sense, just as removing the surgeon's scalpel or the lawyer's casebook, would make their work impossible. Ultimately, however, these parallels fail to convey the gap between these professions and ours. Analysis, as a professional relationship, is in a category by itself because of its "object" of enlarging the ego's inclusion of unconscious aspects of the psyche, an object which necessitates an asymmetrical interpenetration of psychic material unlike any other human exchange, except that of adult and infant. Not only as we have seen with Bleger might the analyst have to entertain in his own mind two frameworks for a while, the analytic project and that brought by the patient (without ever relinquishing the former), but as Levine puts it "the *analytic process often begins and must be sustained for long periods of time inside the mind of the analyst"* (original emphasis, 2024, 240). *There is no parallel situation of internal complexity in other professions.*

As a theory of unconscious life, psychoanalysis has always aspired to contribute usefully to human society beyond the confines of the classical setting, such as with children, families, psychotics, delinquents, or groups. In every one of these situations, nevertheless, "if the practitioner is trying to work psychoanalytically, there will be in his or her mind, *a version of the analytic or therapeutic setting as a something to be established, maintained, and protected, and kept as constant as possible"* (author's emphasis, Churcher, 2024, 3). How much of these settings can be "co-created" if the goal is to remain analytic? If concrete factors such as frequency, use of the couch, interpretation of oedipal repetitions, are not intrinsically determinant of analytic process, is the same true of the psychic constellation of patient and therapist? And given the conviction of so many analysts that the concrete setting cannot be dissociated from the analyst's theoretical cathexis of it, to what extent does a given "co-creation" of the frame alter the dyad's internal frame? The opinion of Paulette Letarte (quoted by Tanguay, 2004, 88), whom we met in a clinical vignette in the Introduction and who wrote extensively about the challenge of an analytic approach with severely ill patients, seems to contrast with that of Stern.

> The frame has to be established, not in terms of a fixed rule, but rather in terms of the possibility each patient has to tolerate its effects, both stimulating and frustrating. The analytic setup ["dispositif" in French] must take into account the relationship of each patient to his internal world, to his intra-psychic space.

Note that Letarte makes no mention of the marketplace, nor despite her lifelong commerce with psychotics, does she bring up the notion of "non-linear" relationship. The analyst's *internal* frame remains quite classically to "hear what the patient does not say, what he does not know, or what he thinks he does not know" (88). Letarte's "adaptation" is not to new cultural expectations but to provide a setting the *patient can tolerate given his or her psychic functioning*. The analytic goal remains resolutely Freudian: the enlargement of the ego's purview of the mind as in Freud's (1933) metaphor of Holland's reclaiming land from the sea (the Zuiderzee Works[4]), while instituting a framework which respects some patients' need to remain underwater until they can tolerate exposure to dry land. Thus, her views appear consonant with Levine's belief that in some cases the analytic process can and must pre-exist in the analyst's mind long before it can be introjected as a comprehensible ideal for the patient. I wonder whether Stern and other relational psychoanalysts would concur? The impression is that to some extent yes and to some extent no. Like Stern, Bass (2007a, 2007c) attributes framework changes over time to the social and cultural environment and not to post-Freudian insights into aspects of psychic functioning though he is well aware of the latter and has written elsewhere insightfully about them (Bass, 2007b). Consequently, he claims in his 2007a article that "we would expect that the rules and frames of analysis would shift to reflect such changing mores" (11). To be underlined: Bass refers to changing *mores* not changing theoretical *conceptualizations*.

In Bass' view, the analytic frame "is meant to create and stand for, both practically and symbolically, a *therapeutic structure with clear and safe boundaries* in which the process of therapy unfolds" (added emphasis, 2007a, 1). In theorizing the functions of the frame, he argued for a "new perspective on the analytic frame as *cocreated and contextual, reflecting the variability of the psychoanalytic situation and the uniqueness of each dyad*" (added emphasis, 1). This relational view is "two-person" but oddly not "triangulated", at least theoretically speaking. Whereas the French think of the framework as a "third", an external necessity to which both patient and analyst owe due regard, the relational framework is promoted as "safe", "cocreated", and "contextual", a situation one snuggles into rather than defers to? Reporting on a panel on the frame with two relational analysts and one of more traditional views, Levine (2009, 1213) found that all panelists agreed that "fluctuations" can lead to "important enhancement of the psychoanalytic process". But whereas Adrienne Harris viewed the frame as "organic, suitable for negotiation, and always bending", Dale Boesky countered that it was wrong to assume "we have control of the decision to bend or not bend the frame. In fact, we often remain unaware of how we are bending the frame" (1213). Boesky emphasized "that learning what important events preceded the frame bending, why it became necessary, and how the patient understood it in retrospect are all essential in understanding what does and does not work" (Levine, 2009, 1213).

When we look at some of the clinical material shared in the Bass (2007a) publication as illustration of "co-creation" of the frame, we may be observing a modification of the framework which justifies Boesky's concern about papering over unconscious features of the patient's relationship to the world. A subtle but important shift may be happening that is pulling the relational two-person system into a closed two partner mirroring, which is the way Lacan defined the register of the "Imaginary", and which he felt was a major theoretical and technical deficiency among American psychoanalysts (which he unfortunately treated as an undifferentiated clump). Lacan's division of psychic experience into three registers, the Real, the Imaginary, and the Symbolic has left a lasting impact on contemporary French psychoanalytic reflection even when authors are critical of the use that some Lacanians have made of this distinction. There is no space or relevance in this monograph for a deep study of these Lacanian notions; a summary definition will be good enough. The Real is what has not or cannot be symbolized in the external world or inside the psyche; the Imaginary is space in which two subjects seek mutual recognition; the Symbolic is outside of individual subjectivity and control, requiring the acquisition and allegiance to language, law, and culture as third-nesses (forgive the neologism) essential for living in any human society.

The concept of "castration" as reworked by Lacan is crucial for appreciating the qualitative leap between imaginary and symbolic since it denotes an acceptance of curtailment of individual omnipotence. For the post-Lacanian generations of French psychoanalysts, symbolic castration is constantly referred to as a relativizing barrier against the totalizing push for mutual recognition within a dyadic structure. Remember that for Lacan, the Imaginary dyadic register is one of ecstasy *and* alienation, constructive *and* destructive passion. Without triangulation, it can undermine the social fabric. Thus, from the French perspective, there are fundamental aspects of psychoanalytic setups, both concrete contractual details and the therapeutic aim of increased symbolization, which have universal significance and that cannot be co-negotiated by each dyad. This difference of opinion is made more succinctly by Manzano et al. (2016, 11) who refer to separate trends of "maternal" versus "paternal" conceptualizations of the framework in the literature. Perhaps in their indignant iconoclasm about perceived restrictive classical frameworks, the relationists and other "contemporary, self-identified two-person theorists" may have eclipsed something important. Lacan himself was an iconoclast railing against the Freudian revisionists of his day. However, as mentioned in the Introduction, reformers can undo themselves (which critics have demonstrated with regard to elements of Lacan's own theory and practice), regressively slipping into repetition of the rigid authority they have justly questioned.

The framework's status as a "third", or as representative of a paternal, separating, function, is not uppermost for Bass as relational psychoanalyst. His emphasis on the dyad's "negotiating" power, its ability to "create" a functional frame "conjointly" might fit his ideal framework into Manzano et al.'s category of a "maternal" conceptualization. Whereas in the present monograph stress is on the usefulness of an analytic approach to failures in the frame, which usually can be righted afterwards, Bass sees usefulness in negotiating the very setup. When he argues that "the negotiation of framing activity may, itself, be a medium carrying potential therapeutic action" (9), he seems to be indicating a conscious, back-and-forth, dialogue. There is a somewhat self-congratulatory note in the second clause of the same sentence: "in the patient's discovery of a *negotiable relational* world, or the *development of competence* in negotiation, both of which carry interpersonal and object relational implications for change" (emphasis added, 9). What Bass views as therapeutic is an increase in the patient's self-confidence, that is, a narcissistic boost, and a strengthening of the positive transference. No reference is made to the "negotiation" undercovering unconscious aspects of the patient's psychic life which could disrupt the ego's satisfaction with itself; Bass' focuses instead on the felicity of the patient's conscious and successful exchange with an authority figure, an achievement in fact seen as equally benefiting the analyst. The tone is slightly condescending, perhaps legitimate with respect to his target adversary, the rigid analytic technique and framework already referred to which characterized some American Psychoanalytic Institutes: "The capacity to negotiate rules in appropriate ways, emphasizing an intersubjective field of experience, was not yet understood or valued as it is today" (12), The thrill of an increased freedom of thought is palpable in "allowing more play to stretch and fit the unforeseen" (15). In fact, Bass approves of the "option to toss out the book from time to time, to respond with spontaneity and creativity" (7) which he likens to "acts of freedom" crucial to the "analyst's repertoire … highly personal, expressive of the analyst's personality … and integral to the analyst's art. Indeed, I believe these rogue interpretive moments lie at the heart of therapeutic action" (7). He cites Symington (1983) as the source of the notion of acts of freedom.

Though one can hardly object to spontaneity and creativity in an analyst's personal integration of analytic theory, I struggle with skepticism each time I read about the analytic dyad being referred to in this fashion. The context usually suggests the analyst's experience of a release of energy in his or her escape from an inner constriction. Indeed, that was exactly the case in Symington's report, where he gave two examples of having colluded unconsciously with patients' views of themselves: with "Poor Miss M" in her inability to be treated on the same footing as others, in one case, and with another patient's right to control Symington's possible view of him as "pathetic" in the other. Symington's release from countertransference entrapment occurred in the first case when "one day a startling thought occurred to me: 'Why can't Miss M pay the same as all my other patients?'" and in the second when he read a passage from Bion which acted as an *interpretation* of his, Symington's, inhibition. An instantaneous lifting of repression altered a piece of his countertransference position, so that he was able to say and think certain things to and about his patients, which had not previously been possible.

Following Symington's liberation from his unconscious collusion with these patients' projective identifications, Miss M was able to make changes in her life "because she had first been freed from the patronizing attitude of her analyst" (283). In the second case, Symington was able to say to the patient "But I am quite free to think that" (that is that his patient could be 'pathetic'). Though the patient "was much taken aback. It was possible then to see how much he operated by controlling my thoughts and the thoughts of others…. We were able to look at his need to wind himself around me like a boa-constrictor and try to substitute my thinking and feeling for his, to make me into his ego, as it were" (284). Symington proceeds to attribute these beneficial changes to "that moment of inner freedom when I had the unexpected thought … I am calling this act of inner freedom the 'x-phenomenon'" (283).

He *felt* freer yes, yet it is doubtful that the act of freedom was completely "spontaneous". Symington acknowledges that the change in his internal disposition in the second example did not emerge, so to speak, out of his own hat. A strand of discourse in the outside world (the quotation from Bion) had acted *upon* him, as Laplanche would have put it. A similar impact from interpretation of countertransference might have occurred if Symington had been in a supervision session with a colleague. In the first case, though the mechanism may be more hidden, one also can suspect that impetus to change came from "outside" Symington insofar as he attributes a causality lodged in a "startling thought", that is, in the passivity of the ego with respect to a new idea *coming at it*, rather than *coming from it*. Symington goes on to brilliant reflections in the rest of the article, but a distortion has occurred in his attribution of the *source* of the "x-phenomenon". Whereas he began in a position of being the "object" of a message (insofar as an internal transformation was brought about by a stimulus outside the ego in the form of an unexpected thought or from a passage read from Bion), Symington quickly moves to seeing himself as the "subject" of the transformation in an act of "freedom" (the ultimate cause of change posited within the ego). It may have been Symington's misrepresentation of the "source" of his metamorphosis with his patients as self-instigated "acts of freedom" which allowed Bass in turn to use Symington to justify his, Bass', declaration that "rogue" interpretations might lie "at the heart of therapeutic action". In Laplanche's terminology, Symington and Bass have closed back their psychic position inwards, viewing themselves as the "source" of change and thus suppressing acknowledgement of an initial passivity of the ego to the impact of something coming from "outside". An alternative formulation in line with José Bleger and the Barangers might have conceptualized Symington's "acts of freedom" as flushing out the way his two patients had been using the framework as depository of primitive parts of themselves. Were Bass and his patient able to shake the primitive parts of themselves out of the frame?

From his account, Bass seems to have taken a different tack, altering the frame rather than analysing it. Bass uses details from his analysis with Nicole to argue the case for "freely negotiated" frame modifications benefiting both parties of the dyad, with respect to the issues "of money, boundaries, exploitation, control, need, and power" (9) motivating Nicole for treatment. "Her frame and mine often seemed distinctly at odds, leading to conflict in early sessions, at times to disturbing effect"

(20). Almost immediately, a major stumbling block arose: Nicole liked travelling on a regular basis and would not hear of paying for missed sessions, It was not that she could not afford it, but "psychologically, to pay for a session that she was already missing would be adding insult to injury, somehow like missing a session twice. It was bad enough to be missing it once" (20–21). Bass interpreted this as a dissociated sense of agency though other analysts might view it as a splitting, that is, recognizing separation and simultaneously denying it. Much ground, he wrote, "was covered in these explorations, while I sensed that other soil remained untilled" (22). Perhaps because his concern in this particular publication is elsewhere, we hear very little about the "ground" explored, tilled or untilled. Nicole came up with a solution to avoid paying for missed sessions: Could she "make up" sessions in advance by coming more often on a regular basis, thus "banking" the sessions she would ultimately have to miss? Bass was frankly impressed with the novelty of Nicole's solution and viewed his acceptance of it as a corrective emotional experience for her.

> She seemed pleased and surprised that I took her *experience* of the matter and her suggestion seriously, and analytic work continued, including, of course, some ongoing exploration of the *experience* of our way of negotiating and working out what had seemed to be a difficult problem. She was moved to feel that I *was taking her needs seriously* and that I could modify my approach in response to her *creative solution, about which she felt considerable pride and gratitude. She was pleased that she was able to provide a solution* that both of us could accept. It brought to mind and into the analysis other successful solutions that she had found in the past.
>
> (added emphasis, 22)

I have underlined the reference to indications of positive transference and ego satisfaction as outcomes of this first negotiation of the framework, as well as the repetition of the words "experience" and "feel/felt" designating the patient's reactions on a *conscious* level. Bass does not mention any insights regarding the unconscious sources of Nicole's dissociative sense of agency (or splitting). Two years later, Nicole was apparently ready to pay for missed sessions though simultaneously questioning another fixed aspect of the frame: once-a-day meetings, which if modified might provide another way around the conflict. It had never "occurred" to Bass to meet with a patient twice on the same day, with the occasional exception of double sessions when "conditions [had] warranted it" (23), so he acquiesced. Nevertheless, the new arrangement did not prove satisfactory. It was, Bass claimed, "becoming increasingly clear that the issue was not really about money at all" (though he had already noted this fact two years earlier).

> She realized that she felt tantalized by my policy that I would make up sessions when able. We discovered this by way of her associations to an older sister (and later to her father as well), who had always promised to be there for her in a variety of ways but who, when push came to shove, would invariably let her down.
>
> (23)

Bass did not seem to realize that in telling the story this way, he appeared to be avoiding the negative transference conveyed in the word "(a recurring event) tantalize". He seemed intent on remaining a good object. When yet another apparently intractable scheduling conflict comes up, he offered (as a good object should?) to alter the frame again so that the patient would *feel better* about it: "OK, how would it *feel* if when it comes to that particular event [the one raising again the impossibility of being in two places at once] I *won't charge* you for those sessions you miss to attend it?" (added emphasis, 24). Despite his efforts to please, "Either way it was spoiled" for the patient. Nicole found his proposed solution once more "to be quite tantalizing and frustrating to her and expressed a preference that I simply stop attempting to make up sessions altogether, the most galling part of my "policy", and that rather than charging for them, I should simply raise my fee to the point that the economics of it would not be burdensome" (24). Hoisted on his own petard, it was at this point that Bass realized that he had not raised Nicole's fee for some time, which led to his patient analysing his inhibition about it, a turn of events he welcomed as part of their "mutual analysis". Earlier in the paper, he had confessed that though he

> had not regarded collecting fees from my patients as a chronic problem, … several situations began to come to mind in which a patient seemingly 'suddenly' owed me several months' worth of fees, enacting a problem in the transference-countertransference field that remained dissociated from my awareness until it became large enough to threaten the analytic work itself'.
>
> (3)

Bass' complacency about laxity in money matters and lack of concern about what others might see as an indication for a piece of self-analysis is at first surprising until one realizes that in viewing it as "enactment" in a transference-countertransference "field", he may have simply viewed himself as playing a requisite part in a scenario created by the patient, for which he was not directly responsible. Bass ends up deducing that there was something about their (Nicole's and his) "arrangement that perhaps we had both outgrown and no longer seemed to fit either of us" (25), a sentiment with which his patient agrees when he shares it with her. Moreover, she was convinced that "changes in me as a result of my work with her were also being reflected, and she spent some time enumerating the ways that she had seen me change and grow and what she had contributed to these changes" (25–26). And yet … Nicole's symptom of feeling "tantalized" when she could not make the missed session disappear seems to have persisted all through the analysis. It would have been interesting to have heard about Nicole's associations to her choice of the word "tantalize" which has the double valence of signifying "torment" and "enticement".

Other than a brief reference to an older sister and to the father, we never learn about what might have been infantile sources for her torment and enticement. It is true that in this article Bass's aim was to justify his notion of co-creating the frame, and so he probably restricted his reporting of the case to the key turning points in the co-creation with Nicole. Yet, his report is tantalizing to the reader. We might wonder whether what tormented Nicole as a child was the parent's reluctance to clearly state limits to the child, and to himself, and to make clear the distinction between following through with being there when he should have (making a promise involves a commitment which castrates one's enjoyment elsewhere) and another position in which the parent allows himself – without prevarication – to be absent when he does not *need* to be there for the child. Is it not tantalizing – both tormenting and enticing – when the two are confused? There are critical moments all during childhood when parents *should if at all possible be there* for their children, but there are also, increasingly, moments when they *do not need to be present*, confident that adequate substitute parental figures are in place. In these other moments, the child has not been forgotten: a plan has been put in place, a testament to the child having been kept in the parental mind. The parent can thus be absent having seen to an adequate mediating replacement. In hindsight, might Nicole's dilemma make us think of Winnicott's comment about one of his patients: "Much of the material in this analysis has to do with coming to the negative side of relationships; that is to say, with the gradual failure that has to be experienced by the child when the parents are not available" (2011, 121)? These speculations may not be etc. These speculations may not be accurate; we do not know since Bass says so little about "analysing" the symptom, and so much more about "negotiating" with it. Another fertile metaphor introduced by Lacan was his idea of "quilting points" ("points de capiton" in French) in discourse which stop the endless sliding of meaning. Every now and then, the signifier stops, "quilted" to punctuation in the sentence, thereby producing a "necessary illusion of a fixed meaning" (Evans, 1996, 149) which allows the interlocutor to respond. Though she consciously craved the constant papering over of absence, perhaps Nicole was unconsciously tormented by Bass' endless accommodating "unstitching", preventing their grappling with the representation of a gap that could not be filled. What she might have reiteratively found "galling" was *a fee structure which represented the missed session, rather than ambiguous alternate structures which made it (apparently) disappear.*

We are led to conclude that while Bass sounds as if he shares the views of the present author and others in asserting that failures in the setting can lead to useful analytic work, "in other words, the frame embodies the paradox of being both structure and process simultaneously" (16), in fact, his conception of "co-creation" of the analytic situation is significantly different from the idea of "putting it to work". The referents are quite separate. In running aground on Nicole's neurosis about missing sessions, about "really" missing them, Bass may have dealing with a version of the "bastion" described by the Barangers (Baranger, Baranger, & Mom, 1983) as an intimate, scarcely discernable, regressive part of the self, concealed from view and ferociously protected, a situation Bleger might also have suspected given his emphasis on analysing the frame from time to time instead of letting it fade from awareness. The perfect hiding place might have been in Nicole's induction into the role of "wise baby" for Bass' position as grateful parent, where they both could bask in mutual recognition and moral support. Sedlak (2025) has expressed reservation about the 'virtue signalling' of confessional responses by relational analysts to patients' perception of moments of inadequacy on their part. Moreover, while it is true etc. that there is a sense of freedom in not being hidebound by tradition, Nicole and Bass's experiments with the frame have been independently tried by others (the double session days of "condensed" analyses of candidates living far away from IPA recognized institutes, increased length of sessions for some patients, the increase in frequency in weeks before or after forced breaks in analytic work, the acceptance of distance analysis in some institutes) but not – I hope – for the same reason. A widely cited article of Merton Gill (1984a, along with an addendum in 1984b) is a counterpart to Bass and Stern. Gill gently, but firmly, questions assumptions, current at the time, about the necessary traditional ingredients of psychoanalysis as a setup, but only to develop more incisively the careful act of transference interpretation as a skill which can transect psychoanalysis and psychotherapy as practiced by analysts.[5] Letarte's work is rife with instances of framework groaning as she struggled to work with disturbed patients and with patients in states of disturbance. Yet she was always at the helm, tactfully bent against resistance, and tolerating negative transferences as welcome expressions of separation and individuation.

Perhaps I am over-reacting to Bass' exuberance in experimenting with new settings? I believe I have already asserted my position that the framework should not be invested as a sacred cow. Yet, with the Barangers we also know that certain formal aspects affect function itself, as they pointed out in the example of fixed or variable length of the sessions producing two very different types of analytic process. In conjunction with them (and other authors as we have seen and will continue to see), when confronted with impasse or sterility in the process, we must take "a 'second look' in which we see the analytic situation as a field *which involves us* in so far as we fail to know ourselves" (Baranger, Baranger, & Mom, 1983, 2). I hope Bass will forgive me for using his generously shared case material as an opportunity to ask three questions as a concerned and invited observer? The first: was Bass really "freely co-creating" the framework with Nicole, where agency is auto-centered, or were they both inexorably pushed to avoid the anguish of living with, and talking about, a "lack" in their relationship, where the *agency of the unconscious as other outside the purview of the self's subjective control*, is determinant? We are brought back to how each analyst construes the function of the setting. Does the "negotiation" facilitate or suppress the chance of hearing what the patient does not say or know as Letarte put it earlier? With a different vocabulary and on a different continent, Cooper offered a similar aim for the framework: "The setting houses the transition from unrepresented to represented experience" (2019, 1439). Cooper credits Winnicott with teaching us about the dual elements of holding and interpretation in the setting (1440). This leads to my second question: it might be useful in discussing each other's approaches with frame alterations to try to tease apart these two elements, and to wonder how, when, and whether the practice of "holding" (as in the narcissistic gratifications of mutual analysis described by Bass) can occasionally obstruct the route to "representation"? As we shall see in Chapter 5, for many analysts *the gesture of payment has the ramification of separation, an experience only attainable beyond holding.* My third question is inspired by Bleger: might a "co-created setting" lose the exquisite but necessary complexity of Bleger's portrait of "two frames", one belonging to the patient, the other to the analyst?

Reformulating the frame in order to restore it

For many authors, such as Bleger (2013/1967, location 5972), the setting is more of a *strategy* than a technique. The use of the word "strategy" evokes a certain state of mind and a certain goal as opposed to a manualized technique applied regardless of the psychic structures of the subjects involved. The prospect of strategy as an approach to the framework, neither kneejerk rigid nor flabby laissez-faire, seems widely shared by those who have studied the matter and crosses over to some extent the concept of "internal analytic setting" or "analytic attitude" discussed in Chapter 1. Ferro (2002/2021) offers a similar view with the term "target to be aimed for" though in contrast to Bass, this target must in his opinion "be an absolutely rigorous setting" (123). Despite my reservations about Bass' enthusiasm for creative settings, inherent in my (and I believe in his) thinking about the setting is that it is a means and not an end. The fact that it is a means which has shown its efficacy over the test of time commands respect but does not make it a holy grail incapable of alteration in certain circumstances. Delourmel (2013, 133) quotes Green on the theme of framework changes:

> The function of representation appeared to me progressively as the referent of analytic work. Whatever factors oblige us to modify the analytic setting, in the final analysis the essence of analytic action concerns the representation of intrasubjective and intersubjective psychic processes. The rest belongs to a process of reorganisation in the patient in which the analyst plays no part. I would even suggest that the *modifications of the setting have no other function than to facilitate the function of representation.*
>
> (Green, 1990, 296) (added emphasis)

There is ample documentation that the classic framework (and the frameworks of other theoretical orientations as well) can make patients feel worse about themselves, in some cases due to the rigidity and lack of sensitivity of the practitioner or because of unexpected negative therapeutic reactions, and that in the worst circumstances with fragile patients, psychoanalysis can be practised abusively in ways deeply alienating. And then there are individuals whose pathology finds comfort and defensive avoidance via the framework itself. In the latter case, authors have reported having to initiate a "reformulation of the setting".

We have already seen a striking example in the Letarte (2018) vignette of Mme X reported in the Introduction of an analyst reformulating the setting during a treatment when the situation has gone awry. *Slavish devotion to an idealized setting can miss the point: if the patient cannot use it, or if its function of enlarging the ego's purview with hitherto inaccessible repressed, split off, or unrepresented content has been perverted, then the analyst must alter the setting to restore its proper function.* Letarte proposed calling these actions "interventions" by the analyst to distinguish them from the task of interpretation. Such interventions are required "preludes", she contended, for certain patients. She claimed that interpretation is rather easy, at least with respect to content, whereas "the biggest difficulty in our field is intervention" (87). The number of interventions an analyst is called upon to make is directly proportional to the intensity of the patient's anguish and inversely proportional to the narcissistic coherence of the Ego. In the classic cure, the analyst's interventions are relatively discrete: supportive "a-hums", interrogative repetitions of certain words or phrases used by the analysand, and the like. But *Letarte noted that the classic cure is not the most frequent form of analytic situation*[6]; she did not believe that the use of the couch was what makes a treatment psychoanalytic. She defined interpretation as the analyst actively assuming or reinforcing certain functions of the patient's psychic apparatus: an Ego function, a Superego function, or even an Id function integrated by the Ego (89–90). In detailing the case of Mme X, Letarte (2018) illustrated how the analyst may have to "reformulate the setting" at times, on that occasion by temporarily incarnating the superego's role of prohibiting violence and of recognizing generational asymmetry. John Churcher (2005) has pointed to the work of the Argentinian analyst, Alcira Mariam Alizade (1992/2002), in reaching a similar conclusion:

> There will be times when it will be necessary to make a break with the external setting, in order to sustain the analytic process. In these situations, the external setting, even if it is the repository of psychotic anxieties (Bleger, 1967), has to be modified in its form in order to maintain a basis without which the analysis will not be able to continue. . . [Quoting Alizade, Churcher goes on] "If an analyst, due to character faults or to an excess of blind spots, deploys a strict external setting and a correspondingly weak internal setting, the analysis (the psychotherapy) will doubtless serve a cathartic or a holding function, but the results in terms of change and elaboration will be poor or non-existent ".
>
> (10, 11)

It is appropriate, therefore, that I call upon another account from the literature published by a compatriot of Alizade, Samuel Arbiser, for another reformulation of the setting by the analyst, all the more so since it is from him that I have taken the phrase: "Words are nonetheless often insufficient and a decisive move may involve *reformulating the setting*" (original emphasis, Arbiser, 2014, 728). A tense situation was described by Arbiser (1994, 736) who was confronted with perverse acting out on the part of a patient, nicknamed by the analyst as the "man with the bus symptom" because he liked to ride buses so as to masturbate near young female riders. Their psychoanalytic work together had made no dent in the symptom which after a time took an even more unsettling turn from the point of view of the treatment. The patient began to miss sessions because he was riding buses in search of new victims *at the time of his meetings with his analyst.* Arbiser was forced to declare an ultimatum: he told his patient that if, from then on, he were to ride buses in which he masturbated near young female riders during time allotted for sessions, he (Arbiser) "would take this to mean that he [the patient] had no interest in continuing his analysis and I would therefore suspend the treatment". Arbiser justified this intervention because "I found myself shut up in what might be described as a pragmatic paradox, and it became clear to me that, in this serious crisis affecting the process, it was necessary to adopt an heroic measure with the objective of *restoring the setting*, which the patient had damaged to the limit of its continued viability" (original emphasis, 736). In this manner, the analyst had acted as the guardian of the framework. It is instructive to compare Arbiser's declaration of boundaries with Letarte's (2018) clarification of "symptom address" with Mme X (described in the Introduction): both analysts were faced with a "misuse" of the psychoanalytic situation, necessitating a return to a "lawful" setting. Moreover, both analysts were inviting their patients to bring aggressivity into the setting and into the transference, instead of colluding with its evacuation elsewhere. However, we saw in Chapter 1 where Letarte tolerated some abuse of the frame from her patient, Nathalie, because Letarte felt she, as the object of transference, was being constructively "used" in the Winnicottian sense to further the possibility of capturing hidden significance. Nathalie was using the framework as a cushion for, and as a consolidation of, her aggressivity in a transferential address.

Ogden (2021) gives an example of having proposed to end a session early with a man when, after 10 years together, their sessions seemed to be sterile and overcome by 'deadness'. After a few sessions from which the patient left early, he shared with Ogden (16) that "I shouldn't tell you this but I like leaving the session early, particularly when it's dark outside. I like it because I have time to myself in the dark – I can think then". Odgen noted that this coming 'alive' occurred within the official timeframe of the session though the patient was no longer in it. An optimal level of absence/presence had been reached, for this particular patient, which could then be gradually repositioned while in the presence of the analyst. *Rather than acting to inhibit it, the alteration tolerated in the frame had allowed the production of new meaning.* I had a similar experience with a long-term psychoanalytic patient who fell into a crisis of despair, having given up on his marriage, and on me, and soothing himself with pornography. He began to use the couch to retreat into an imperturbable shell of silence. Finally, I insisted that he leave the couch for a few sessions in exchange for the chair where, face-to-face, he could no longer stay comfortably silent. The change did put oomph back into our work. It is important to stress that these "reformulations" initiated by the analyst were considered temporary with the aim of restoring a capacity to work within the more traditional setting, not as a way of giving up on that aim in the name of an adaptive eclecticism.

Pertinent to any question of "reformulation of the setting" be it in response to acting out by the patient (as in Arbiser's example) or by the analyst's impression that he or she must "adapt" to the psychic needs of a given patient (as in Bass's case) is the challenge for the analyst or psychoanalytically oriented psychotherapist to "triangulate" their reformulation with some kind of third-party analytic listening for themselves. A recent article by Leopoldo Bleger (2022) lays forth a cautionary note for analysts of all theoretical backgrounds as in these two quotes:

> One may wonder whether the notion of an internal setting is not invoked as a way to justify dispensing with the difficulty of creating a more or less traditional analytical setting.

(34)

I understand (at least I think so) why the concept of "internal" setting has gained favor: it allows for the introduction of modifications of the setting in the name of clinical necessities. However, to put it briefly: the clinical problems are not simply facts, they are also a creation of the analyst who necessarily organizes his perspective and his understanding of the clinical situation through the lens of his own version of psychoanalysis and psychoanalytical treatment.

(36)

If we really take seriously the unconscious nature of countertransference, analysts cannot vouch for the neutrality of their framework modifications. The best hope for the patients' sake is, as we know, peer supervision of some sort as in the following example of a "modification" taking place more and more frequently in the practice of analysts young and old. A supervisee O asked the author for help after four online consultations with a woman working on a farm some distance from the city, the last interview alarming O. After a major depressive collapse cut short the patient's career as medical professional, she had become a rolling stone, recently immigrated and working for room and board here and there. She had been attracted to a website developed by O who advertised an interest in life's "transitions", such as migration, immigration, parenthood and who offered a "nomadic accompaniment" outside the "usual confines" (hors les murs in French). Reference is made on the site to the use of "imagination in meeting arrangements" within a "rigorous internal and theoretical framework". The psychologist added that she now works out of an office where she can see people in person or via audio-visual communication. The patient had introduced herself on the phone as someone who feels everything intensely, a source of great suffering. She thought that O's "approach would be a precious aid". In mentioning the reference to her website as she spoke to me about the case, O became hesitant, as if starting to realize something as she was telling me about it: "I wanted her to come in person, which would be altering the framework of her request. I am having difficulty operating on another register". O was thus making me, the supervisor, realize that O was navigating a confusion or contradiction in her "offer" as a therapist, on the one hand as a "nomadic accompaniment", on the other as an interpretive listener. The patient mentioned having had a sexual relationship with the male member of the couple who had hired her. Then the patient described getting involved with a small religious group in a local church, feeling "exalted" in the presence of the young man, the "leader" or the "priest", leading the prayers. Her experience of herself seemed to be rapidly deliquescing: "Overwhelming! I have met God, he has pierced through me. You are going to think that I am mad. I am in a state of shock, as though I were made of water. God everywhere. I can't say no". And also: "I have a phobia about being seen by others. I am waiting to be recognized. The only reward is love". O was rightly worried about the patient breaking down again, in a dangerous ecstatic fusion with an idealized, and violating being. And she was hearing all of this over the phone while sensing reticence on the part of the patient! *Where was the framework; where was the consent?*

I suggested to O that it might be useful to her patient for O to talk about the confusion between them, about the ambiguity of O's offer as expressed on the website, and the risk to the patient of saying yes to everything, including continued consultation. *It seemed to me that the patient's fragility in the context of a scarcely discernable framework needed to be acknowledged to create a shared anchoring truth between them.* I thought that O needed to revisit her double "offer" as nomadic comrade and psychotherapist; how did she distinguish and how did she coordinate these two registers; how could she remain a psychoanalytic therapist without intervening with transformative speech? Nomadic or not, the patient was clearly asking for help with her inability to set boundaries and her manic sexualized susceptibility to losing them. Something had to be said which went beyond vague sympathetic mumblings, such as submitting to the patient that her excitement about the religious group was related to her transgression with her employers, that she was expelling her guilt rather than grappling with its source and meaning for her. "But the patient doesn't want to hear of talk of the past or interpretation" O protested helplessly. I have already pointed out earlier that it is often hard for psychoanalytically oriented practitioners to interpret patients' defenses, which is an inhibition and avoidance on their part of the healthy function of aggression in creating separateness and clarity, an inhibition and avoidance, it should be added, which can occur in all of us. Perhaps, at these moments, the psychoanalytic practitioner has the fantasy that he or she is destructively "penetrating" the patient rather than viewing the articulation to the patient of an underlying "truth" between them, the truth of a misconception or ambiguous offer between them. The clarification of an intersubjective truth which is sensed by the patient but not yet admitted by the therapist can help deposit new internal representational structure for patients. It is well known that internally disorganized patients have remarkable finesse in generating befuddled frameworks. With such patients, a neutral clarification of the therapist's contribution to the confusion can appropriately bolster their ego strengths.

In a situation like this, Lipton (1977a) would have provided the patient with information which allows her "to form valid opinions of the analyst in current reality…. Without the actuality of the nontechnical personal relationship, irrational elements of the transference remain imaginary or intellectual. With this actuality and its kernel of truth, the patient can gain conviction about the importance of his covert feelings, about their undue intensity and importance, about their timing and about the importance of tracing them to their historical roots" (271). In a sense, O and her patient had enacted together through the portal of O's ill-defined but romanticized "nomadic" offer a state of bewilderment endemic to the patient's being-in-the-world. Betty Joseph (1985) describes coming to a rather similar conclusion in a clinical seminar where the group came to realize that their dissatisfaction with various explanations for the presenting analyst's state of impasse could be understood as a "projection of the patient's inner world, in which she, the patient, could not understand and, more, could not make sense of what was going on" (448). It was this reflection that Joseph felt needed to be shared with the patient. More recent authors might have seen this situation as one of parallel processes (cf. Mendelsohn, 2012).

There is a thoughtful account by Salberg (2009) which intertwines self-analysis accompanying her initiation of the ending of an analysis, felt to be stuck in an inextricable intersubjective knot, with what might count as a "reformulation of the setting". Seeking help in supervision from two different sources, an internal movement occurred: Salberg felt permission to access her own "positive aggression": "This was an aggression that sets limits, protects and preserves in the face of destructiveness, and an assertiveness which, unwittingly, had been stymied for myself and [my patient]" (715). Salberg was persuaded that "Perhaps much of the most important work of an analysis is done after termination occurs, through a deferred action, an après coup, a nachtraglichkeit" (Salberg, 2009, 716). After eight years of sustained work, Salberg set a deadline for terminating the following year, a date which was honoured in the conviction that the only way to preserve her patient's treatment and the gains they had made, was – paradoxically, or perhaps not if we bear in mind that analytic work can continue after termination? – to end it. When the patient requested a post-termination meeting a few years later, Salberg was blessed with an additional insight she was able to share with her patient: "Suddenly I had a new picture of our work together and my unilateral decision to terminate. I now realized in retrospect that the termination had been an enactment. Just as she had closed the door on her brother [a painful episode in which the patient had set a limit to her brother's deeply troubling intrusions], I had closed the door on [her].... In some way I had to close the door on [her] and say, 'you can't come back', but in a way in which no one died, no one was killed. It was a use of aggression that is positive, it was my way of saying you can live and so can I and we need to discover this" (216). The positive signification lent to separateness, and to a necessary constructive use of aggression to affirm it, stands out in Salberg's rendering of the case, but it is perhaps generally speaking an essential ingredient to fruitful "puttings to work of the frame" by one or the other of the analytic dyad. The psychic work Salberg describes as having devoted to separating from her own analyst, in and through her work with her patient, adds another layer of associations to the meaning of the framework for the analyst him or herself. It makes a remark made by Chianteretto particularly à propos: "the primary issue is to make the work in us linked to the unanalysed aspects of our own analysts, organically interwoven with our own unanalysed parts, liveable, capable of elaboration, and a source of creativity" (2016, 14). In Chapter 3, I will have occasion to refer to my avoidance of conflict over missed sessions in my personal analysis which deferred the psychic work of thinking through some separation issues and denied aggressivity until my own patients forced it upon me.

As time passes and I have moved into a retirement from direct clinical work, I have found myself reimaging the "offer" I might make were I seeing new patients or that supervisees could experiment with in the here-and-now: that of proposing a "slice" of analysis, that is a period of intensive work for one to two years, as a counter-offer to the frequent request nowadays by patients for a diluted treatment of uncertain destiny and duration. This resistance to the time-consuming understanding of unconscious factors undermining psychic growth is made all the more difficult to address because of a wider cultural collusion. Would not a shorter but more intensive treatment constitute a richer and far more useful framework response for many people who wish to confront their demons but are equally desperate to get on with their lives? The French term behind my use of the word "slice" is "une tranche d'analyse", usually employed by francophone colleagues to refer to a second or third analysis undertaken to wrestle with personal issues which have emerged as obstacles in pursuing one's life and career in the years after analytic training. The offer of a "slice" has the advantage of appearing less intimidating, as not colluding with grandiose visions of the acquisition of "perfect" health, and as intimating the possibility of more consultation, as needed, in the future. It would also allow the analyst to see more patients when so many suffering people languish on waiting lists. Moreover, perhaps a *stepwise vision of temporality* is more conducive to many patients' preoccupations than the classic *unlimited offer*? Merton Gill (1984a, 1984b), in the articles referred to earlier, experimented with a time-limited framework of nine months which he felt had been a successful experience. Yet we will see in Chapter 4 when we look at the analytic offer accompanying a workable and breathable framework that some authors have found constructive pathways to support the "time for understanding" that some patients need before committing further. But first, the possibility of truly informed consent in psychoanalysis will be examined in the next chapter.

Notes

1 Lacan uses this metaphor to contend that, paradoxically, human identity ends in an alienation in signifiers, a line of reasoning I have not followed here.
2 Ultimately, Lacan's position went even further in postulating the ego as always a place of alienation, the precipitate of the projections of our first caretakers.
3 Brini's critique is not one hundred percent accurate since Lacan does make a brief allusion (2006, 16) to the impact on the prisoners' reasoning of the possibility of deception as a reason to hurry to a conclusion.
4 Zuiderzee Works. Entry in Wikipedia consulted June 11, 2024. https://en.wikipedia.org/wiki/Zuiderzee_Works
5 A rather different reading of Gill occurs in Stolorow, Atward, and Orange (2006) where Gill's invitation to the analyst to notice what he or she may be contributing to what appears to be "transference" is seen by these relational theorists as an affirmation of their "contextual" approach to "intersubjectivity". This is not the place to take exception to their wish to develop a "philosophy" of psychanalysis rather than a psychoanalytic theory.
6 Stern's (2009) investigation of our profession's tendency to deny this state of affairs was discussed earlier in this chapter.

References

Alizade, A. M. 2002. The Internal Setting: New Contributions. Presented to a joint meeting of the Argentinian and the Paris Psychoanalytical Societies. (Alizade's ideas are also available in English in *Psychoanalysis and Positivity*, 2010, New York: Taylor & Francis.

Arbiser, S. 1994. The Man With the Bus Symptom. *International Journal of Psychoanalysis* 75:729–742.

Arbiser, S. 2014. David Liberman's Legacy. *International Journal of Psychoanalysis* 95:719–738.

Aulagnier, P. 2004. Philippe ou une enfance sans histoire. In L'apprenti-historien et le maître-sorcier: Du discours identifiant au discours délirant (Le fil rouge). Paris: Presses Universitaires de France. Kindle Edition, 2016.

Baranger, M., Baranger, W., & Mom, J. 1983. Process and Non-Process in Analytic Work. *International Journal of Psychoanalysis* 64:1–15.

Bass, A. 2007a. When the Frame doesn't Fit the Picture. *Psychoanalytic Dialogues* 17:1–27.

Bass, A. 2007b. The As-If Patient and the As-If Analyst. *Psychoanalytic Quarterly* 76:365–386.

Bass, A. 2007c. Framing Further Considerations. Reply to Commentaries by Philip Bromberg and Glen Gabbard. *Psychoanalytic Dialogues* 17(6):931–943.

Bleger, J. 2013/1967. Symbiosis and ambiguity: A psychoanalytic study. In *New Library of Psychoanalysis*, Translated by S. Rogers and J. Churcher (edited by J. Churcher and L. Bleger). Taylor and Francis. London: Routledge. Kindle Edition.

Bleger, L. 2022. What is the setting after all? *In Psychoanalysis of the Psychoanalytic Frame Revisited: A New Look at José Bleger's Classic Work*, edited by C. Moguillansky & H. B. Levine, 21–37. New York: Taylor & Francis. Kindle Edition. DOI: 10.4324/9781003252252-3

Boesky, D. 2008. The road to unity in psychoanalytic theory by Leo Rangell Jason Aronson/Rowman Littlefield. New York, 2007; 133 pp; $34.95. *International Journal of Psychoanalysis* 89:441–444.

Boesky, D. 2013. Rejoinder: What Does the Presentation of Case Material Tell Us about What Actually Happened in an Analysis and How Does It Do This? *International Journal of Psychoanalysis* 94:1163–1165.

Brini, J. 2023. Acte, décision, événement. Intervention le 2 et 3 décembre 2023 sur « Le temps logique » de Jacques Lacan, *Les Journées d'étude de l'ALI, Le Collège de Psychiatrie et l'AfB*.

Caper, R. 1992. Does Psychoanalysis Heal? A Contribution to the Theory of Psychoanalytic Technique. *International Journal of Psychoanalysis* 73:283–292.

Casement, P. 2005. The Emperor's Clothes: Some Serious Problems in Psychoanalytic Training. *The International Journal of Psychoanalysis* 86(4):1143–1160. https://doi.org/10.1516/58N3-PXKL-PDGE-VLXA

Chiantaretto, J.-F. 2016. Au Commencement était Le Meurtre. *Le Coq-Héron* 224:10–20.

Churcher, J. 2005. Keeping the psychoanalytic setting in mind. Paper given to the *Annual Conference of Lancaster Psychotherapy Clinic,* September 9th.

Churcher, J. 2024. The Psychoanalytic Setting: José Bleger's *Encuadre. International Journal of Psychoanalysis* 105(2):216–233.

Cooper, S. H. 2019. A Theory of the Setting: The Transformation of Unrepresented Experience and Play. *International Journal of Psychoanalysis* 100:1439–1454.

Delourmel, C. 2013. An Introduction to the Work of André Green. *International Journal of Psychoanalysis* 94:133–156. https://doi.org/10.1111/j.1745-8315.2012.00585.x

Dine, R. 2017. A Religion Without Visual Art? The Rav and the Myth of Jewish Art. Online at https://thelehrhaus.com/commentary/a-religion-without-visual-art-the-rav-and-the-myth-of-jewish-art/#. Consulted Jan 17, 2024.

Dufresne, R. 1994. Le premier entretien analytique: Des indications à l'écoute du désir d'analyse. In *Le Premier Entretien et L'écoute Psychanalytique*, edited by B. Tanguay, 86–109. Connecticut: Editions Méridien, 1994.

Evans, D. 1996. *An Introductory Dictionary of Lacanian Psychoanalysis*. London and New: Routledge.

Ferro, A. 2002. *In the Analyst's Consulting Room*. Translated by P. Slotkin. Hove, UK: Routledge, 2021.

Freud, S. 1901. *The psychopathology of everyday life*. Standard Edition 6: 240–241.

Freud, S. 1913. On Beginning the Treatment (Further Recommendations on the Technique of Psycho-Analysis I). *Standard Edition* 12:121–144.

Freud, S. 1933[1932]. New Introductory Lectures in Psycho-Analysis. *Standard Edition* 22:7–182.

Gill, M. M. 1984a. Psychoanalysis and Psychotherapy: A Revision. *International Review of Psychoanalysis* 11:161–179.

Gill, M. M. 1984b. Transference: A Change in Conception or Only in Emphasis? *Psychoanalytic Inquiry* 4:489–523.

Goretti, G. R. 2006. The Crisis of Psychoanalysis and Psychoanalytical Training: The Suffering of the Candidate on the Long Road Towards Qualification. *International Journal of Psychoanalysis* 87 June (Pt 3):827–842. https://doi.org/10.1516/5QQE-90H0-XY3E-GXNY. PMID: 16854740.

Joseph, B. 1985. Transference: The Total Situation. *International Journal of Psychoanalysis* 66:447–454.

Kernberg, O. 2016. *Psychoanalytic Education at the Crossroads. Reformation, Change and the Future of Psychoanalytic Training*. London: Routledge.

Lacan, J. (2006). Logical Time and the Assertion of Anticipated Certainty. In *Écrits* edited by B. Fink, 161–175. New York & London: W.W Norton.

Laplanche, J. 2002. Failures of translation. In *Freud and the Sexual: Essays 2000–2006*, edited by J. Fletcher, 115–113. London: International Psychoanalytic Books, 2011.

Laplanche, J., Fletcher, J., Stanton, M., & Stanton, M. 1992. Notes on afterwardness. In *Jean Laplanche: Seduction, Translation, Drives*, A dossier compiled by John Fletcher and Martin Stanton, Translations by Martin Stanton, 217–223. London: Institute of Contemporary Arts, 1998. ISBN 0-905263-68-5.

Letarte, P. 2018. *Entendre La Folie*. Paris: Presses Universitaires de France. Kindle Edition.

Levin, C. 2014. Trauma as a way of life in a psychoanalytic institute. In *Traumatic Ruptures: Abandonment and Betrayal in the Analytic Relationship*, edited by R. A. Deutsch, 176–196. New York: Routledge/Taylor & Francis Group.

Levine, A. 2009. Bending the Frame and Judgment Calls in Everyday Practice. *Journal of the American Psychoanalytic Association* 57:1209–1215. https://doi.org/10.1177/0003065109344339

Lipton, S. D. 1977a. The Advantages of Freud's Technique as Shown in His Analysis of the Rat Man. *International Journal of Psychoanalysis* 58:255–273.

Manzano, J., P. E., Palacio-Espasa, F., & Abella, A. 2016. *Précis de technique psychanalytique avec son application à la psychothérapie*. Paris: Collection: Le fil rouge. Presses Universitaires de France.

Mendelsohn, R. 2012. Parallel Process and Projective Identification in Psychoanalytic Supervision. *Psychoanalytic Review* 99(3):297–314. https://doi.org/10.1521/prev.2012.99.3.297

Ogden, T. 2021. What Alive Means: On Winnicott's "Transitional Objects and Transitional Phenomena". *International Journal of Psychoanalysis* 102:837–856. https://doi.org/10.1080/00207578.2021.1935265

Sedlak, V. 2025. Countertransference. Presentation made to the 30th Annual Day in Psychoanalysis, Saturday, April 26, 2025. Location 1:06:15 in audio recording.

Salberg, J. 2009. Leaning Into Termination. *Psychoanalytic Dialogues* 19:704–722.

Stern, S. 2009. Session Frequency and the Definition of Psychoanalysis. *Psychoanalytic Dialogues* 19:639–655.

Symington, N. 1983. The Analyst's Act of Freedom as Agent of Therapeutic Change. *International Review of Psychoanalysis* 10:283–291.

Tanguay, B. 2004. Paulette Letarte ou être psychanalyste. *Filigrane* 12:#2:80 à 92.

Tylim, I. & Harris, A. eds. 2017. *Reconsidering the Moveable Frame in Psychoanalysis Its Function and Structure in Contemporary Psychoanalytic Theory*. New York: Routledge.

Winnicott, D. W. 1951;1971. Transitional objects and transitional phenomena. In *Reading Winnicott*, edited by Lesley Caldwell and Angela Joyce. Routledge: London and New York. 2011, Chapter 5 103–125.

Chapter 3

Informed consent in psychoanalysis

Preliminary remarks

Since I wrote the article some years ago which will be reproduced below, the lack of enthusiasm among psychoanalysts for thinking about informed consent from a psychoanalytic perspective remains. It does not seem to be an explicit part of psychoanalytic training nor is the question raised in clinical presentations. There is no doubt that experienced analysts, perhaps because of their long commerce with the unconscious, intuitively grasp the issue and individually come to ways of ensuring that patients are, on the whole, in agreement with the particular setup of psychoanalytic treatment. But the impression remains that for many analysts, the matter appears too prosaic or too obvious to bother explicating. The experience of Margaret Little (1985) in London during the war when psychoanalysis was viewed as an exciting new and mysterious cure was probably typical of the period: Ella Freeman Sharpe took her on with little ado: "She had a vacancy, and started straightaway, and the fear at once became unbearable" (14). Or, more disconcertingly, they may submit with little resistance to the medical model of informed consent that has become the gold standard nowadays – a mainly cognitive transaction, with co-signed written forms consigned to the dossier. There will be occasion to come back to the inadequacy, in our field, of this model of informed consent which is promoted by professional regulatory bodies. For psychotherapists inspired by other theoretical orientations, treatment starts *after* the preliminary interviews, and after the framework has been explained to patients. When the topic of consent comes up in psychoanalytic literature, it is usually with reference to the first meetings.

One can wonder whether the emotional "storm" (Bion et al., 1979), mentioned above, occurring when analyst or psychotherapist and patient meet for the first time is a third and more decisive factor explaining why informed consent has not received more careful treatment in our field. Reith et al. (2018) observed "On the basis of our case studies, we have come to think that this 'storm' is so powerful that it can influence the psychoanalyst's analytic functioning, and perhaps always influences it to some degree in more or less subtle ways" (14). From the case studies shared in Reith et al.'s book, it appeared that under the pressure and confusion of intense feeling triggered in the first interview, there were analysts tumbling into an

DOI: 10.4324/9781003527459-4

offer of treatment that had not been adequately elaborated. The same phenomenon has been repeatedly observed in my own supervision practice.

Years ago, an older colleague, Roger Dufresne, drew attention to an underlying problem about these beginnings: "The first interview is outside of the framework, even without a framework: the fundamental rule of free association and its corollary the floating attention of the analyst have not yet been announced or accepted[1]" (1994, 86). The initial upheaval spurred by the totally new situation for both partners, "neither a normal meeting, nor yet psychoanalysis" (13), occurs without the protection of an agreed upon frame. In the last decade, the publication of two books by the International Psychoanalytic Association's Working Party on Initiating Psychoanalysis (WPIP) (Reith et al., 2012, 2018) has created a stunning trove of clinical examples and theoretical considerations about first interviews, based on eight years of discussions held in forty-five workshops with some five hundred psychoanalysts from all over the world. Though earlier generations of psychoanalysts were schooled in the ample literature regarding indications for analysis, Reith et al. (2018) observed that subsequent research has consistently failed to find any "patient characteristics which could inform the decision whether psychoanalysis should be initiated or not, or could predict whether a psychoanalysis with a given patient will succeed" (2). WPIP's findings were unexpected: it was not the analyst's skill in making a "change of level" from manifest content to a latent or unconscious meaning – the usual description of analytic work – that seemed determinant in the initial interviews they studied. What made the difference was the analyst's "internal frame", their capacity to "weather the storm" and to make use of it meaningfully. I can only refer briefly to the potential further insight into the intensity of the emotional storm experienced by both parties offered by Laplanche's conceptualization of the "invasive" nature of psychic reality as coming from outside in the form of enigmatic messages the child cannot fully translate. It may be ancient unconscious untranslatable remnants from childhood inadvertently reactivated with hallucinatory intensity by unexpected aspects of the physical proximity of analyst and patient in their first meetings which attack both participants from within.

The Working Party's conclusions are consistent with earlier contributions to the issue of consent which came from studies of the analyst's paradoxical and sometimes unconscious resistance to starting psychoanalysis with new patients. First there was Rothstein (1994, 1997, 2002, 2006, 2010) and then a series of articles by Ehrlich (2004, 2010, 2013, 2016, 2020) which had already reversed the *scrutiny on positive or negative indications for analysis from patients to the analysts themselves*. "Analysis", Ehrlich (2013, 1) argued, "begins in the analyst's mind: how analysts think about their function, their patients, and the analytic process determines in great measure whether analysis will begin". Deeply appreciating the analyst's unconscious participation in determining the outcome of patients' consent for psychoanalytic work should not surprise us, and yet it continues to disconcert, as it did for the WPIP. Since we are never rid of our own conflicts and unfinished translations of past relationships, there will always be patients who encroach upon our comfortable and established boundaries. Moreover, as though grappling with the turbulence of the first encounter of what could (and ideally should) become developmental growth for both parties were not enough, nowadays psychoanalysts are subject to the discombobulating expectations of third parties in the form, not just of family members as in Freud's generation, but of contemporary professional deontological codes and third-party payors. Respecting psychoanalytic ethics while meeting these expectations will be a periodic concern in this book. Informed consent in psychoanalysis as we understand it almost always involves putting the frame to work, as needed, at the inception of the engagement, as well as periodically later on, as opposed to the informational model of consent used in research and by regulatory bodies.

Consenting and assenting to psychoanalytic work[2]

This paper hopes to contribute a psychoanalytic view on the question of informed consent, a crucial concept within the professional practice of medicine and psychology. Consent is less about the patient's intellectual awareness of the various aspects of the analytic setting proposed at the beginning of treatment, and much more about *the patient's ongoing learning about his or her unconscious response to the setting and to the analyst who presides over it*. This learning makes possible the patient's active assent to starting and continuing a psychoanalytic process. This unconscious response inevitably entails a remobilization of the patient's particular infantile wish to be loved and regarded. How many times do details in how the analyst manages the frame (for instance, policy regarding missed sessions, how the analyst presents her own absences, how phone calls, texts, and email are responded to, how deaths in the family, illness, or breakdowns in public transport are dealt with) become critical events in the relationship insofar as they are experienced as failures in love or empathy on the part of the analyst. In our view of informed consent, on each of these occasions an effort of psychic work is required by both members of the dyad to discern and work through new unconscious reservations which curtail full engagement in the treatment. Some reflection exists in the literature about what might hold back the analyst from fully "consenting" to accepting a new patient in analysis (Ehrlich, 2004, 2010, 2013; Rothstein, 1994, 2010). The focus here will be on the patient's side of things, since until recently the literature on informed consent has been particularly meagre in this respect. In this paper, no distinction is necessary between a classic analytic framework and psychoanalytically oriented psychotherapies. As long as the aim is to increase the ego's scope over the irrational forces within the "soul" of the individual – without coercion, suggestion, or an invitation to an alienating copying of a non-self generated ideal – the conundrums we are attempting to look at will be essentially similar.[3]

We find it useful to introduce a distinction between *informed consenting and good enough assenting*. Inspiration for separating the two terms comes from the unlikely source of an article on sibling rivalry by Paul-Laurent Assoun (2001). Assoun contends that the birth of a sibling throws the elder and formerly only child before a trial or ordeal of consent (an "épreuve du consentement" in the original French). Without a psychic "treatment" of the initial murderous refusal of fraternity, the child cannot move to an acceptance of narcissistic loss and an "assent" ("assentiment" in French as opposed to "consentement") to a brotherly or sisterly tie (44). There are subtle differences in meaning between the two terms in both English and in French that can help bring out clearly the main contention in this paper: while the patient needs to have access to a certain amount of information about the analytic setting in order to *consent* to beginning treatment, deeper *assent* will come through the insight about himself in the form of the working through of unexpected emotional responses to aspects (usually disruptive) of the frame and of the person of the analyst. Assent and consent are mostly synonymous – they both mean to agree – but assent connotes a greater degree of enthusiasm, and consent often comes with reluctance. To consent is to give permission, which could have been withheld. It implies a power relationship where the consent is granted by the party with more power. To assent is to agree with a statement made by an equal. So, consent is historically associated with the granting of permission while assent has been used to express agreement. For expository reasons, let us carve out a distinction from these nuances. One can consent to a set of conditions proposed by the analyst as part of a project of self-development aimed at learning about mysterious parts of oneself or of one's behaviour. After all, very few would openly admit that self-knowledge is not a worthy goal for anyone. However, the direct experiencing of unpleasant reactions to, or unexpected implications of, the specialized relationship with the analyst can throw this project into disarray. As well, the patient may not comprehend at first, or may periodically lose sight of, the symbolic potential of thought.

   Our investigations into what a consent procedure specific to psychoanalysis would look like have been spurred in part by the realization that for those patients whose internal life is not felt to be interior,[4] or in moments of intimate crisis with other patients, the analyst's offer to listen beyond the manifest content and manifest demand may make no sense. The prospect then becomes a communication operating on different levels: one interactive and cognitive, and the other blind drive and wounded narcissism. Can there be – at least with certain patients – an *illusion of informed consent* insofar as the operating assumptions of the framework consciously or unconsciously assumed by the patient are not necessarily identical to those held by the analyst?[5] In fact, the very discovery of transference implies that at some level, at some moment, in every psychoanalytic treatment – and these moments are, as noted above, frequently precipitated by some kind of "misunderstanding" about the frame – "consent" can be expected to vacillate. *We will argue that true assent to the psychoanalytic process has to be arrived at after a struggle, that is, after experiencing an inner movement of refusal and/or questioning which if sensitively addressed leads to a deeper appreciation and engagement with the process.*[6] We also advocate using the gerund form for these terms as a way of communicating ongoing movement rather than the acquisition of a fixed state of mind.[7]

There is also another source for our interest in this question: our discomfort with the position taken by some analysts who believe that the existence of the unconscious precludes truly informed consent. It is argued that patients cannot consent because they do not yet know enough about their unconscious motivations. For example, Jonathan Lear (2003) evokes an image of colonial bravado in questioning to what extent a person can give informed consent to the use of his clinical material outside the consulting room, another area of ethical preoccupation in current professional practice. Can a person really speak for his own unconscious, wonders Lear? "[I]f I stand up boldly and say, "I hereby give you informed consent to let the unfolding of my unconscious be public property", it is unclear … of whom or for what I am speaking" (7).

A counterpoint to the impossibility of informed consent in analysis will be developed later in this paper. In the meantime, the real-life flag planting of Captain James Cook during his explorations of the Pacific region can provide us with a metaphor for both our first and second concerns. In a review of a new edition of Captain James Cook's *Journals,* Uglow (2019) notes that Cook had taken with him a sealed set of instructions from the Admiralty. Besides charging him to "endeavour by all proper means to cultivate a Friendship and Alliance with [the Natives]", he was told, "You are also with the *Consent of the Natives* to take possession of Convenient Situations in the Country in the name of the King of Great Britain" (added emphasis). In uninhabited lands he was simply to "take Possession for his Majesty". As Uglow comments, the notion of "consent" was meaningless *without any system of shared values or laws*, but Cook cheerfully raised the British flag wherever possible, marking trees as he left with the ship's name and the date. In his journal entry for August 23, 1770, at Possession Island off present-day northern Australia, he wrote that,

> I now once more hoisted English coulers and in the Name of His Majesty King George the Third took possession of the whole eastern coast …, together with all the bays, harbours rivers and islands situate upon the said coast, after which we fired three volleys of small arms which were answered by the like number from the ship.
>
> (quoted by Uglow in his review)

Psychologically naïve patients are not at first in the position of sharing our psychoanalytic assumptions about the value of the framework we propose to them, nor may they have any idea of the unconscious "flags" burning within them until they stumble upon them in the course of treatment. But whereas Lear's solution in 2003 was to "think hard about how we might build up a good analytic character" (17), the thrust of this paper will be elsewhere. We will argue that internal effort is called upon from both analyst and patient in moving from the initial "flag-planting" of the first meeting to informed consent to treatment, and that a meaningful assent can only be achieved over time and repeated psychic labour.[8] We should not forget how often Freud referred to psychic work, *arbeit* in German standing for work, job, test, effort, labour, such as in his terms abarbeit (working-off mechanism), *culturarbeit* (the work of culture), *durcharbeitung* (working through), *trauerarbeit* (work of mourning), and *traumarbeit* (the work of dreaming). Not being aware of certain responses to the analyst and to the setting complexifies the process of consent but does not negate it, particularly if the analyst remains attuned to signs of the patient's unconscious ambivalence.

Some prior analytic contributions to the subject of informed consent

Before developing this idea further, let us look at pre-existing contributions from writers of quite different theoretical orientations who have already given reasons to suppose the risk of misunderstandings about consent. Lacan's warnings about the analyst's imaginary position in the transference as the subject-who-is supposed to know (1977) remains a valuable guide in these matters. To be able to listen carefully to manifestations of the unconscious in the dyad's work, the analyst needs to separate herself in her own mind from the analysand's idealized projections of superior knowledge and mastery which can easily lead to the latter's unconscious submission. Similarly, Kohut (1971) pointed out the clinical virtue of respecting the patient's idealization while gradually reserving the right to interpret it. On yet another continent and in another language, Bleger (1967) argued that "there are actually *two settings*: one which is proposed and maintained by the psychoanalyst, and accepted consciously by the patient, and another, that of the 'phantom world' into which the patient projects" (233, original emphasis).[9] It was "the desire to put thinking to death" that concerned Aulagnier (1979) when both partners in treatment want to put the analyst's theories on a pedestal. In the alienation she observed in certain patients coming for second analyses, she found a total lack of awareness of the violence being done to them in the first analysis by virtue of an uncritical introjection of the former analyst's socially trendy theory. We view this as a possible outcome if informed consent is assumed to be a rather straight-forward process of intellectually informed acquiescence where the analyst is not listening for warning flags of unconscious incomprehension or unease in the patient about beginning treatment. Other French writers such as Laplanche (1999), Green (2005), and Donnet (2001) have all pointed out the trap of the analyst substituting her thinking for that of the patient. If the analyst merely "recommends" an analytic treatment with a list of requirements, and awaits a global agreement, is there not a chance that the analyst is substituting her thinking for that of the patient? In America, the thoughts of A. Goldberg (2001, 2004) on insufficiently elaborated moral and technical tenets of the framework are both pertinent and provocative:

> There should be little doubt that many if not all of the tried and true principles of psychoanalysis may profit from being subjected to periodic re-examination and scrutiny to see if their status remains as telling and relevant today as it did when first developed and observed.
>
> (2004, 301–302)

We can give an example from our own background. Having cheerfully born the cost of missed sessions during the vagaries of life's existence in our own analysis, and proud of our enlightenment, the present author only achieved a less defensive and idealized appreciation of the representational value of some form of "rule of indenture" (Eissler, 1974) for financial responsibility for missed sessions when shaken by transferential explosions in our own practice. Confronted by patient rebellion vis-à-vis ourselves as analyst, a belated reworking of our unrecognized ambivalence about this aspect of the frame was required of us (Furlong, 1992). As we now see it, periodic recasting of one's assent to the analytic setting is a necessary part of the process of self-inquiry and self-knowledge acquired in the relationship with one's analyst.

Other than an initial minimal setup, Freud paid scant attention to other aspects of the frame, such as conflicts of interest, confidentiality, informed consent, third-party payment, record-keeping, and related administrative offshoots of clinical work. As his international reputation increased, most of Freud's patients came having read some of his writings and with an explicit request for "psychoanalysis" from the now famous man, a request which could be – and was – taken at face value. In the spring of 1921, Freud accepted into analysis Anna G. (May, 2009) without having met her nor having evaluated the appropriateness of her request. He based his agreement entirely on the letters of recommendation of two Swiss colleagues and on the patient's written agreement to abide by his conditions of time and fee. We know that this was the way he proceeded at the time with other patients (May, 2009, 267). In the early decades of the psychoanalytic movement, patients seem to have more or less submitted wholesale to the conditions of analysis as it was explained to them. It was only gradually, painfully, and, on occasion tragically, that the first generation of analysts came to appreciate the ethical and clinical implications of details of framework management on their own internal frameworks and those of their patients. A more rigorous procedure seemed called for which became almost sacrosanct in some institutes with candidates regularly instructed on how to assess the analysability of potential patients and warned about the pitfalls of anti-analytic parameters. While there were authors who, as we shall see, questioned the legitimacy of this approach, on the whole a broad cultural agreement may have existed (at least for a time in the mainstream psychoanalysis in North America familiar to us) about what strict framework analysts were expected to impose. Patients "knew" (or at least thought they did) what they were getting into in consulting a psychoanalyst: use of the couch, the analyst's relative "reserve", free association, confidentiality, expectations of interpretation and not advice, payment for missed sessions, avoidance of social interactions outside of the office, etc.

This consensus about the analytic setting has buckled under the scrutiny of the latest generation of psychoanalysts, both from those purporting to extend the Freudian vision and those who have found it wanting in various ways. But the psychoanalytic situation also finds itself increasingly out of sync with ethical, legal, and administrative standards that have derived from other, non-analytic, types of practice. Focussing on informed consent, the present article would like to contribute to discussion among analysts about consideration from a psycho-analytic framework of the latest professional norms in medicine and psychology. In the perspective to be presented here, it is assumed that the frame is not just a helpful container for analytic work but an integral part of the method's associ-ative-digestive-thinking apparatus. The concern about proper technique among second-generation analysts may have inadvertently externalized the issue of con-sent and displaced it onto to evaluations of patient analysibility, thus bypassing the patient's self-reflective participation in the decision. One hears and reads of analysts "recommending" psychoanalysis, as though placing themselves in a po-sition of medical expertise, with the patient seemingly in the passive position of acceding more or less globally to their suggestion. There is merit therefore in the opinion of a recent commentator (Dailey, 2014) that "analyst practice on the initiation of psychoanalytic treatment is in urgent need of review and revision" (1123). We have a responsibility (Wilson, 2016) to try to explain to ourselves (and if need be to our patients, though that may not be necessary if we understand ourselves) why the usual conditions of informed consent in other fields feel so uncomfortable for us.

What does the patient understand?

In any cure, though it is not usually cast in this manner, various dimensions of the framework itself – here gathered under the rubric of their contribution to informed consent – need periodic analysis. We have been slowly appreciating, as mentioned earlier, that the interpretive approach can miss the mark for patients of sub-neurotic structure, whose subjective assumption and mentalization of drive and emotion are insufficient. An example comes to mind from the present author's experience as outside reader of a candidate's fourth-year clinical case study. In the report a patient had been persuaded to move from face-to-face psychotherapy to a classical psycho-analytic position to serve as a training case. There was little description of how this transition had been handled, yet it was clear from the detailed clinical material that though ostensibly agreeing with the transformation, the patient had reacted with a great deal of anxiety. The analyst-in-training's efforts to understand this anxiety in terms of the patient's history seemed to be having little effect. Moreover, though the patient repeatedly referred to the new setting as culprit for her malaise, the analyst did not take up the possibility that she had agreed to something the rigours of which she had not really understood and for which she was not psychologically ready. Perhaps in her wish to please her therapist, she had not fully appreciated the psychological implications of the new setting and the archaic fears which it was mobilizing. One could argue that her consent had not been adequately "informed" and that it might have been more helpful to address her new wave of disquieting transference as it related to the change of setting which had been asked (uncon-sciously required?) of her.[10] In this project of an analytic cure, the analyst may have failed to realise that he had not created "the conditions in which free association proves to be praticable, interpretable and beneficial" (Donnet, op. cit., 129).

Undertaking a rare empirical study, Saks and Golshan (2013) found that there was extremely wide variation among analysts with respect to the proper scope of informed consent and that many did not obtain even a modicum of informed consent. They concluded that informed consent is generally inadequately treated by the psychoanalytic community. Psychoanalysts would thus appear to be out of step with the model which informs most modern biomedical ethical treatment and research codes, and which requires potential subjects to "be adequately informed of the aims, methods, anticipated benefits, and potential hazards" (14) of any medical intervention. Saks and Golshan are well aware of the myriad ways full disclosure of risks and benefits according to the contemporary medical ethical model "may violate the norms of analytic neutrality, abstinence, and anonymity, considered by some to be crucial to the treatment" (40–41). Yet in the name of patient autonomy, Saks and Golshan contend "the reasonable patient would want more information than currently gets disclosed, including the risk of intense transference feelings, malignant regression (particularly to psychosis), and self-destructive acting out" (1124).

It is difficult to gauge the meaningfulness and scope of such a startling recommendation of disclosure. Saks and Golshan do not address in what way an intellectual awareness of such risks is of more than cognitive value to prospective analysands. One reviewer of the book (Tillinghast, 2015, 368) believes that "[e]ngaging a patient in substantive discussions about the risks and benefits of treatment, and possible alternatives, can substantially strengthen the therapeutic alliance, by making the patient feel respected and valued as a collaborator with a healthy side". Yet Tillinghast seems to be sidestepping the psychoanalytic question as to whether ego-to-ego exchanges of this sort should be favoured over a position of carefully listening for the patient's unconscious doubts as they come up over time. Nor does she mention the hidden fantasy of a corrective emotional experience in this proffered "healthy" exchange.

It is true that numerous individual case studies, both historical and current, are available of the categories of negative patient reactions (the risk of intense transference feelings, malignant regression, particularly to psychosis, and self-destructive acting out, (1124) mentioned by Saks and Golshan (for example: Aulagnier 1979, Freud 1923, Gabbard 1977, Pontalis 2014, Rosenblum 2005, Winnicott 1954, 1967). Moreover, we also know that counter-transference complications must also be counted as potential negative side-effects of psychoanalytic treatment. As Freud pointed out since one cannot destroy someone in effigy (1912, 108), we are constrained to working with "highly explosive forces" (1915a, 170). Understanding intense transference and counter-transference reactions is supposed to be an essential aspect of psychoanalytic training but the capacity to predict them is limited. Ultimately, however, the argument against disclosing documented negative reactions to psychoanalysis has to be based on the fact that any analysis is a totally unique experience, emerging from the intersubjective dynamic emerging in the intimate relationship of two personalities each with a partially unknown unconscious component.

For this reason, it is proposed here that the best way to assess "risk" will come from the analysand's capacity to scrutinize what comes to light in the *experience of the psychoanalytic setting* itself. From the psychoanalytic viewpoint, *what the patient needs to be informed about is already a part, an unconscious or split off part, of herself,* perhaps emerging in the initial meeting as a dread of catastrophe. Making a distinction between manifest and latent content not made by Saks and Golshan, Ogden (1992) observes that the sense of danger mobilized in *both* patient and analyst is the "prospect of a fresh encounter with one's inner world and the internal world of another person" (227) (see also Crick 2014). Developing an awareness of the conflict within oneself about beginning a psychoanalytic treatment is also a pathway towards informed consent, and an integral heart of the *intrasubjective and intersubjective exploration which frames the decision to begin analysis.* Being able to perceive and address this conflict is part and parcel of the "analytic process of transformative investigation" as Donnet so nicely puts it (2001, 129).

To make matters more complicated, contemporary psychoanalytic thinking about informed consent would want to take into account the patient's unconscious perception of the analyst herself, and whether or not the dyad can make some sense of this. Perhaps Freud did not stress enough the extent to which unconscious conflict also poses a barrier to the perception of the external reality of others, in this case the analyst, or that resistance can be generated by the unique bi-personal field which develops in a particular practitioner's office. The capacity to perceive and mentalise unconscious conflict and/or deception on the part of significant others is also part of access to relational truth. Beyond the resistance of "discourse itself" Lacan (1982) zeroed in on the resistance which can emanate from the analyst's ego. We know that aspects of the patient's communications can be unconscious commentary on unconscious perceptions of his or her analyst. Van Lysabeth-Ledent (2016) gives an example of what she calls the dream's metabolisation of a real impact on a patient of a session in which the analyst was "psychically absent" due to illness, an external "event" which had been "perceived" but not consciously acknowledged by the patient.[11]

It would seem inherent in a psychoanalytic ethic to help the patient develop her own risk assessment abilities rather than having the analyst enumerate them in a pre-emptive paternalistic list. How could an analyst opine, for instance, that "there is an X% chance that you will regress, or become psychotic" when no specific probability can likely ever be affirmed with respect to this unique dyad? Not only does the "holding" capacity of the "field" vary considerably from couple to couple, but also from session to session, if not from moment to moment, and in ways that cannot always be anticipated. Explaining risks and benefits to patients, which is so helpful in making decisions in other medical and para-medical fields, can easily fall – in the psychoanalytic situation – into the spiral of intersubjective permutations mentioned by Freud (1905) in the joke about one Jew responding to an inquiry by the another as to his destination. When the second replies that he is going to Cracow, his questioner accuses him of trying to deceive by telling the truth. "Is it the truth" inquires Freud, "if we describe things as they are without troubling to consider how our hearer will understand what we say?" (115).

The point is not to minimize, but to complexify the ethical challenge experts like Saks and Golshan put before us. Even before the patient calls an analyst for a consultation, he or she may be misled about a fundamental premise of psychoanalytic treatment if analysts start to follow the pathway a number of mental health orders have taken in inviting their members to indicate "areas of expertise" in their dealings with the public. The list is long: one can indicate on one's website - or be qualified as such on the registrar of the professional order - expertise in the handling of particular diagnoses, such as anxiety and obsessive–compulsive disorders, problems of sexual impotence (male and female), sexual orientation issues, insomnia, attention disorders, capacity for violence, and many other mental and emotional troubles. Despite the fact that the public may seek the security of consulting an acknowledged expert in a specific category of complaint, this kind of professional presentation contravenes long-standing technical and ethical psychoanalytic reservations on three levels: (1) in departing from a position of benevolent neutrality to accede to the patient's wish for the imaginary authority decried by Lacan; (2) by implicitly giving a particular aim to treatment of freeing the patient from a manifest symptom, before knowing what role it plays in his or her unconscious economy, and (3) implying that symptoms share commonalities across individuals which an analyst can know and treat based on *a prior* knowledge. It is quite simply a form of false advertising. Wilson (2016) expresses it clearly: "the psychoanalyst is always interested in the particular, the singular, the first-person point of view. We are *anti-generalists*" (1191, original emphasis).

Interestingly, Freud seems to have drawn attention to the rigours of analytic treatment more often than to its risks. Exemplary is this quote from "On beginning the treatment" (1913): "I consider it altogether more honourable, and also more expedient to draw [the prospective patient's] attention – without trying to frighten him off, but at the very beginning – to the difficulties and sacrifices which analytic treatment involves" (129).

It is enlightening in this context to double back to José Bleger's classic 1967 article, "Psycho-Analysis of the Psycho-Analytic Frame", referred to above, in which he claimed that in every analysis, even one with an ideally kept frame, the frame itself must become an object of analysis. The very steadiness of the frame makes it the perfect depository for the "primitive undifferentiation of the first stages of the organization of personality" (518). Bleger's work is pertinent as a counter-point to well-meaning interventions based upon reassuring the patient about his right to be informed or upon sustaining a therapeutic alliance by engaging in intellectual discussion of his or her fears of treatment, or by providing information about alternative treatments, or explanations about what psychoanalysis entails, or how much expertise one has with this or that particular expression of psychic suffering. All of these interventions can be seen as inducing subtle intersubjective muddles. Yet on all of these fronts, the analyst has the opportunity to enter into co-reflection with the patient about the phantom world, as Bleger terms it, which has been brought to the consultation as an expectation of the analyst and the frame, his or her invisible ego-syntonic expectation that reality conform to certain infantile wishes for protection and non-differentiation. There is no doubt that recognizing the risk of colluding with this archaic part without prematurely disrupting the patient's narcissistic integrity requires adroit technique and subtle double-mindedness in the analyst. In these areas, less experienced analysts perhaps struggle the most for what is required is keeping in mind multiple levels of reality, in particular respect for where the patient is at in his or her personal evolution without sacrificing the fulcrum which will permit addressing later, at a more opportune moment, these fragile zones of mental functioning. Bleger outlines the required considerable skill in technique, timing, and tact:

> The analyst needs to accept the setting brought by the patient …because within it will be found in summary form the primitive unresolved symbiosis. However, we need to state at the same time that accepting the patient's … setting does not mean giving up the therapist's own, as a function of which it is possible to *analyse the process and the setting itself when this has been transformed into process.*
>
> (239, added emphasis)

This is a very tall order, to say the least. How in the world is the analyst supposed to manage this delicate and paradoxical management during the evaluation stage and beginning of treatment? *How to transform into process the question of consent?*

Does the existence of the unconscious prevent informed consent?

We mentioned earlier that many analysts feel that one must be reserved about the possibility of informed consent in our work. It is the notion of the rational, autonomous subject which both patient suffering and the existence of the unconscious turn upside down. In an essay in the Journal of the American Psychoanalytic Association a few years ago, Dailey (2014), a legal and psychoanalytic scholar, contended that "informed consent to psychoanalysis may simply not be possible in any meaningful sense. Consent appears to be the navel of psychoanalytic treatment, the moment from which all psychoanalytic treatment springs, but which itself remains opaque to analytic understanding and insight" (1129).

Not many analysts, however, would follow Dailey to her conclusion that a "founding departure from neutrality" (1130) is called for. Unable to decide for her or himself, the patient should rely on the analyst's guidance in contemplating and assessing the risks and benefits of psychoanalytic treatment. Dailey is aware of the aporia she has reached: "The informed consent process thus becomes a decidedly unanalytic moment that sets the analytic treatment in motion even as it threatens the integrity of the treatment that follows" (1131). And "we confront a … contradiction: that analytic treatment comes into being through a fundamentally unanalytic moment of supportive guidance" (1132).

Nevertheless, Dailey's essay joins the concerns of other analysts in inviting us to take a fresh look at an old controversy: does the existence of an unconscious make informed consent impossible in any walk of life? Posited in this way immediately moves the argument beyond the relatively limited area of patient consent to the much larger issue of free choice for any human being since the Freudian conception of unconscious life is a universal one. Speculation about the contribution of the Freudian *oeuvre* to the conundrum of free choice is not new. Freud (1931), himself, indirectly broached this question in his "Expert opinion in the Halsmann case" where he was asked to comment on an alleged parricide. It is noteworthy that Freud was doubtful about referring to an unconscious complex in assessing responsibility: "Precisely because it is always present, the Oedipus complex is not suited to provide a decision on the question of guilt" (1931, 252).

The whole vista of free will is too enormous to tackle in this paper,[12] though it needs to be addressed however briefly in any serious thinking about the topic of consent. The reader will have already noted threads in another line of reasoning being sketched here in favour of a way out of the apparent contradiction, one that is familiar to many psychoanalytic practitioners as the founding faith in the value of their work. To begin with, there are Freud's contributions to facing this conundrum. The obligation to complete candour on the part of both patient and analyst was a point that Freud made many times, but he (1916) also warned against suggestion, such as "enticing" the patient to speak of a specific content. On more than one occasion, he addressed the puzzling ownership of unconscious thoughts, each time rejecting a split in moral responsibility (1900, 1916, 1925). For example:

> Unless the content of the dream … is inspired by alien spirits, it is a part of my own being… if, in defence, I say that what is unknown, unconscious and repressed in me is not my 'ego', then I shall not be basing my position upon psychoanalysis.
>
> (1925, 133)

Freud seems to distance himself from a conclusion of abject lack of autonomy:

> The physician will leave it to the jurist to construct for social purposes a responsibility that is artificially limited to the metapsychological ego. It is notorious that the greatest difficulties are encountered by the attempts to derive from such a construction practical consequences which are not in contradiction to human feelings.
>
> (1925, 134)

Yet what he had written more than a decade earlier when commenting on the part played by the patient's "unobjectionable" positive transference in treatment, revealed a more complex view of the role of suggestion:

> To this extent we readily admit that the results of psycho-analysis rest upon suggestion; by suggestion, however, we must understand … the influencing of a

person by means of the transference phenomena which are possible in his case. We take care of the patient's final independence by employing suggestion in order to get him to accomplish a piece of psychical work which has as its necessary result a permanent improvement in his psychical situation.

(1912, 106)

Let us recall that possession of an unconscious mind is completely democratic; it infiltrates the psychic experience of every human being and is not confined to conditions of abject suffering. For every person, autonomy in the intra-psychic sense is surely the broadening of the ego's capacity to integrate within its purview the unknown and unrepresented domains already at play within the psyche in the larger sense. It is this goal of inner freedom, however incremental, fragile, or temporary which has traditionally been the focus of psychoanalytic work (e.g., Bibring, 1943; Friedman, 1965; Rangell, 1969; Smith, 1978). *It is this increased modicum of inner freedom emerging from knowledge-of-self acquired in the analytical situation which is most likely to increase the patient's ability to detect and decide at any point in the treatment, the risk and the benefit to self of the psychological strain of the moment.* Does the accomplishment of this "piece of psychical work" have to pass by the analyst's suggestion?

Dailey (2017) no longer answers yes to this question. Having absorbed broad swathes of psychoanalytic literature in the meantime, she has produced a full-length book on the contribution psychoanalysis can make to the law. She now views the apparent conflict between free will in the legal sense and the reality of unconscious life as "simply wrong" (2017, 74). "[P]sychoanalysis recognizes and fosters a capacity for human agency of its own, more constrained but nevertheless central to its portrait of the psyche" (74). Part of Dailey's analysis is marred by her tendency to make rather sweeping statements about the opinion of "psychoanalysis" as though it were a unitary point of view, and this despite the fact that on many occasions she demonstrates her sensitivity to important and separate theoretical strands in contemporary thinking. However, her overall position that it is "through some measure of self-reflection that the individual intervenes in the mind's causal trajectory and becomes an agent of his or her own life" (87) is one that Freud and present-day analysts of many theoretical stripes share as an underlying goal of their analytic activity.

A criticism – though it may not be fatal to her project – is her adoption of what might be considered the pre-1920 Freudian view of the unconscious as a form of meaning which "make[s] perfect sense when subjected to reasoned investigation" (91). Current thinking about the post-1920 Freudian model of the mind, with its unrepresented drives pressing for actualization and the technical challenges this lack of repression and of representation creates with regard to certain patients, is absent from her treatise. With respect to *this unconscious*, reasoned, self-reflective inquiry does not cut it. It appears to be frequently via non-reasoned, counter-transferential sensitivity that images or words can be found to *construct* a meaning for the forces in play. In order to reach a position of fuller assenting, the process of informed consenting must confront not only resistances to self-awareness (the early Freudian model of repression of "incompatible ideas"), but equally the force of unrequited and unintegrated drives (the post-1920 model of the Id).

One might be tempted to resort to the language of "agency", as Dailey has done above, in trying to grapple with these complexities. Yet let us face it, even when the "I" speaks, it is often in the name of another part of the mind (like Freud's rider pretending to go where the horse takes him). "[W]hat is proved is not the existence of a second consciousness in us, but the existence of psychical acts which lack consciousness" (1915b, 170). Lawrence Kahn (2004, 74) is not alone in contending that Freudian determinism confronts us with an irreducible break between agency, actor, and author in the psychoanalytic view of the mind. In the French literature, one is more likely to read about "subjective appropriation" or "subjectivation" (Cahn, 2002; Kirshner, 2012; Wilson, 2014). I prefer the term "subjective appropriation" or "subjective adoption" because they include the notion of a taking into the ego something which comes from outside, which is other and retains otherness, such as unconscious sexual desire or unconscious masochism. Part of the drive remains resolutely non-subjective, experienced but not mastered by the ego, possibly "owned-up to" but never completely owned. The subject of an analysis (and this is true of all humans even if not recognized as such) comes to realize that he or she is not "one". The process of informed consenting and the becoming of good enough assenting should aim at a recognition of this universal paradox. "The unconscious is not that part of being to be reduced at any price, but a perpetual companion with which we must deal and include within ourselves as much as possible" (Cahn, 2002, 190). So perhaps we should speak of "subjective appropriating" (keeping the gerund form, as advocated above, to indicate an ongoing ever being undone process) in informed consenting and assenting.

The first interview

It is evidently inappropriate to suggest that there is one way to handle this ethical challenge. Fortunately, there is no longer a dearth of reflection on these issues. Pertinent to the question of informed consent is the vigorously renewed look the first interview has been receiving in our professional literature over the past decade (see the series published by Ehrlich, 2004, 2010, 2013). There has been a sea change shift from the traditional goal of evaluating the suitability for analysis of patients to using the consultative process to initiate them into a psychoanalytic frame of mind. There has also been increasing realization that the anxieties mobilized in both patient and analyst during assessment can diminish the analyst's capacity to enlist and sustain a psychoanalytic stance. It is now widely recognized that an "emotional storm" (Reith et al., 2018) is inevitable in psychoanalytic consultation, creating a draw towards "unhelpful enactment" (Crick, 2014). All stages of a potential patient's movement from first contact through to entering into an analysis are receiving careful intersubjective scrutiny. In 2012, a collection of papers appeared brought together by the *Working Party on Initiating Psychoanalysis* of the

European Psychoanalytic Federation (Reith et al., 2012). This has been followed by a second collection in 2018 by some of the same researchers under the title of *Beginning Analysis* (Reith et al., 2018).

This concerted thinking on initiating psychoanalysis has not led to Dailey's original 2013 pessimism about informed consent. Contemporary ethical thinking in psychoanalysis casts the issue in terms of asymmetry (Chetrit-Vatine, 2014; Wilson, 2014) rather than in subjection to the unconscious. The analyst's ethical responsibility arises from the presumption – based on his or her personal analysis and training – that he or she is further de-alienated with respect to psychic pain than the patient. The analyst's tutelary duty of care and caring derives from this (sometimes slight) advantage. In 2016, this journal published an entire section on the "Ethical implications of the analyst as person". Although all five articles (Kattlove, 2016; Kite, 2016; Morris, 2016; Moss, 2016; Wilson, 2016) are helpful reading as background to the ethics of informed consent from a psychoanalytic perspective, we find particularly illuminating the approach taken by Kite. Her conclusion is just as paradoxical as Dailey's but does less damage, we would argue, to patient autonomy. Referring to what she describes as "the fundamental ethical ambiguity of the analyst as person", Kite contends that ethics for analysts "is not a 'thing' or a code. It is quite simply taking responsibility for our largely unconscious impacts on patients, and *theirs on us*" (1161). We have to "remain alive to what we don't know in ourselves… *the [analyst's] ethical unknown*" (1168, original emphases).

Ogden's republished observations in the first Reith et al. book can illustrate an approach to informed consent avoiding the pitfalls of paternalism, suggestion, and the position of established expertise. Ogden's (1992) starting point is that there is no difference between the analytic process in the first meeting and the analytic process of any other analytic meeting. Everything the analyst does in the first face-to-face session is intended as an invitation to the patient to consider the meaning of his experience and the possibility of new significance. Ogden eschews referring to the first meeting as an "evaluation period" or "assessment phase" both because this would convey the idea that the patient is to be relatively passive in this enterprise and also because in Ogden's mind the "nature of the interaction is not simply that of one person evaluating another or even of two people evaluating one another". Instead, it is "an interaction in which two people attempt to generate analytic significance, *including an understanding of the meanings of the decision-making process that is involved in the initial meetings*" (italics added, 229).

Odgen insists on the value of sustaining, not reducing, anxiety in the analytic setting: "Since maintaining psychological strain is not only something we demand of ourselves but is also part of what we ask of the patient, it makes no sense to begin the analytic relationship with an effort at dissipating psychological strain" (231). The risks and benefits of treatment which are at stake are the unconscious explanations of the patient as to why she feels that analysis is a dangerous undertaking and why it is bound to fail. "Everything the analysand says (and does not say) in the first hours can be heard in the light of an unconscious warning to the analyst concerning the reasons why neither the analyst nor the patient should enter into this doomed and dangerous relationship" (236). Borrowing and displacing a term used by Ella Freeman Sharpe (1943), Odgen calls these unconscious fantasies "cautionary tales". Rather than guiding the patient through a cognitively informed-consent process of potential advantages and disadvantages, Odgen illustrates the psychoanalytic way of *enlisting the patient's observing ego to address the patient's own unique anxieties in the transference as they are revealed by his speech and behaviour in the initial session*s. In this, the analytic frame of mind of the first interview is no different than at any other moment in the analytic process. Ogden applies the same analytic method of listening and voicing unconscious anxiety and conflict with seriously disturbed patients as he does with persons in the neurotic register who have consulted him about analytic treatment.

Odgen's perspective dovetails with the upshot of the thesis of the present article: It is in articulating what can be gleaned of the particular patient's fears about treatment, rather than referring to "possible" upheavals (to qualify them as "risks" would imply that they should not be part of the process) noted in some other cases, that the analyst facilitates the patient's capacity to make an informed decision *for himself*. We can expect that the "reasonable" patient who consults an analyst wishes to learn more about the *hidden obstacles within himself*. Rather than founding the therapeutic alliance on cognitively apprehended potential risks, it is more consonant with the psychoanalytic setting to use initial interviews to test the patient's ability to utilize tactful observations regarding unconscious contradictions popping up in his pursuit of aid. Ogden's argument is consistent with a position often defended by André Green (2005) to the effect that:

> Let us recall that it is customary, in French psychoanalytic circles, to interpret as close as possible to the ego, sometimes making use of ellipsis or allusion, proceeding by limited touches, stimulating the associative work, counting on the participation of the patient, the main actor of the analysis who has "to do his analysis" rather than being analysed passively by his analyst.
>
> (85)

So far, without minimizing the criticism about laxity in the approach to informed consent among analysts noted earlier by Saks and Golshan, there are cogent objections to the application, *at least literally*, of current medically derived professional models to the psychoanalytic situation. Most analysts, in fact, would agree that consent is not confined to the beginning of treatment, but – in the form of unconscious resistance and new après-coup transference motions – can be an ongoing or sporadic calling the treatment into question, which if tactfully handled revitalizes the treatment project. Resistance itself might be fruitfully reconsidered as a manifestation of the unconscious withdrawal of consent. Patrick O'Neill (1998), a psychodynamic therapist and researcher, made the notion of periodic renewal of consent the central theme of his book, *Negotiating Consent in Psychotherapy* (see review in Furlong, 2003). It is a powerful idea, perhaps obvious in retrospect,

which merits far more attention than it has received in the psychoanalytic literature so far (cf. Etchells et al., 1996). But it is simultaneously very much an old
idea in so far as it is a perfect extension of psychoanalytic readiness to examine
with equal scientific curiosity every twist and turn in the relationship. Nevertheless, timing is everything and the stakes can be high. In his work, Bleger also
underlines analysing the setting "at the right moment" (2013 [1967]), 237). What
is especially interesting about Bleger's classic study is his ironical insight that the
patient's very consent to the frame can serve to avoid a certain reality and that the
analyst's disruption of it (such as the holidays, cancellations, missed or incomplete
sessions referred at the beginning of this essay) can introduce a 'crack' (235) which
is catastrophic for the patient.

There is another inter-subjective kink to this issue which was hinted at earlier.
What do we do about the fact that analysts can be imperfect in their ability to listen to the unconscious concerns of their patients and that it may be the latter who
pay the price? Though Saks and Golshan deliberately exclude the risks entailed
by the unavoidable "personal factor" of the analyst himself, Tillinghast (2015),
in her independent review of their book cited earlier, mentions a number of ways
in which this can be infelicitous. Tillinghast refers to Fairbairn's opinion (370)
that "most people would rather feel like sinners in the hands of god than worry
about being in the hands of a flawed, careless, or potentially harmful caretaker".
To make matters worse, and despite Freud's transmission of an analytic ideal of
benevolent neutrality and his own personal claim that "an abuse of 'suggestion'
has never occurred in my practice" (1937, 262), the phenomenon of unconscious
suggestion is a well-documented and huge factor for better and for worst in many
situations, analysis included (cf. research on the placebo or "meaning effect", on
the role of suggestion in the formulation of survey questionnaires or marketing
strategies, on recovered and implanted memories, on police interrogations, on
guided imagery, etc.).

As a thought experiment, one can imagine a full disclosure mentioning all the
problems potentially arising from the side of the analyst:

> Your analyst is human. Despite her credentials, she may fail you in a number
> of ways: out of incompetence (temporary, partial, episodic); out of a personal
> blind spot that was not treated in her personal analysis; out of unforeseen erotic
> or negative countertransference; out of carelessness, neglectfulness, or even ex-
> ploitative behaviour; or because she has allowed herself to continue practicing
> despite being compromised by illness, personal problems in her private life, or
> old age. It is equally likely that another analyst might disagree with the inter-
> pretations your analyst has been giving you or dispute her overall formulation
> of the main axes of your personal dynamic or yet again introduce a theoretical
> backdrop from another psychoanalytic school which could substantially reframe
> the analyst's way of working with you. It is the opinion of many in the field that
> an objectively "correct" treatment is an illusion. Each analysis is a product of a
> unique inter-personal field formed by you and your analyst which can only aim

at establishing an open-ended, life-long, engagement with and reassessment of one's life rather than at reaching symptom-free happiness.

All of these caveats are potentially true and yet it is hard to conceive how an avowal of this kind would protect the patient against the derailment of unethical, incompetent, or merely run-of-the-mill patchy analysis.

Similar doubts can be asserted about other aspects of modern professional standards which aim to enlighten the patient about the kind of therapy being of-fered, such as advertised areas of expertise referred to earlier, as well as the expec-tation of written contracts and the emission of explicit caveats about the "limits" of confidentiality before beginning treatment. These gestures activate the same clinical-philosophical disquiet about the analyst's open-ended benevolent neutral-ity. The analyst is drawn into "explaining" as the "subject who really knows" risks and alternatives that he or she has presented to the patient for consideration. The analyst is sending enigmatic messages that – like the sorcerer's apprentice – he assumes he can "manage". Tillinghast ends up wondering: "It may be that the law is not an adequate tool for addressing this problem" (373). The position of this article is more affirmative. It is improbable that the risks in analysis can be allevi-ated by the informed consent guidelines so far developed by legal scholars and professional regulatory bodies. Moreover, one could declare that some psycho-analysts have accepted too readily the legal "reasonable patient" way of looking at the matter.

With the proviso that no clinical vignette can independently demonstrate a theo-retical argument, the reader may find the following description evocative. Baffled by symptoms of anxiety after years of feeling fairly content and productive, Mr X requested analysis though he expressed misgivings about me and the set-up. It was the "antipodes of the enveloping environment" he was longing for. However, he agreed with my proposal that what had suddenly brought his life to a standstill was the reawakened terror of a maternal monster from his childhood. It was the first time he would be consulting a woman, a prospect which was frightening but which he thought might be helpful in getting to the bottom of his childhood fear. After some hesitation, he agreed to start twice-weekly sessions on the couch.

He had been coming for about four months when a nasty flu forced the analyst one evening to cancel – by text message – all of the following day's sessions. Still under the weather at the end of the next day, the analyst cancelled everyone for a second time. Mr X, remembering that he had noticed and worried about the analyst coughing in their last session together, texted back to receive reassurance that the diagnosis was not pneumonia which the analyst did in a brief return message. He later left a voice message as well as texting to ask for confirmation about whether the analyst would be working the subsequent day. These entreaties received no reply: on the one hand, the analyst was put off by the extra attention being solic-ited, and on the other hand, she was convinced that all he had to do was rely on the protocol already established, that is, if she were *not* going to be there, she would be letting him know as she had done on the previous two evenings. On the third day, a Friday, he was the only patient not to show up for his regular time. Shortly after this missed session, he wrote to find out if I were returning to work the following week. I return texted that I was already back. A few hours later, he pointed out that I had not returned his messages asking about my plans. Later still, I answered in another text message that my other patients had attended their sessions and that if it had not been for his anxiety, he would have known the answer to his own query.

Needless to say, in the wake of the triple breach in the framework introduced by the analyst's double cancellation and inappropriate counterattack through texting to his anxiety-ridden dependency, Mr X arrived distraught and enraged at his next appointment. He refused to lie down, accusing me of making an interpretation which made him entirely responsible for having missed the last session. He began to wonder whether we were a good "fit". He was hurt, I had not been reassuring; I had chosen rigidity over suppleness. He compared the situation to videos of children disturbed by their mothers' abruptly blank faces. He had not brought his end-of-the-month check because he did not want to pay for the missed Friday session. I acknowledged that my "interpretation" had been out of line, especially in text form, as well as wounding for him. But I also wondered whether rather than a question of fit, what was at stake was being able to talk to my face about his criticism. When he spontaneously associated to elements of repetition in his reaction, I suggested that he consider paying half of the missed session in recognition of his part.

On one level, the analysis was derailed for a full month as Mr X called off sessions to consult another, and male, analyst or asked for phone sessions instead. Nevertheless, at the same time, a lot of psychic work was undertaken by both of us. I accepted only one session by phone during which I expressed my belief that if he quit his work with me, he would be transporting an intact maternal monster with him. He had created-and-found this persecutory object in me. It was the conviction that I was right about this which persuaded him to eventually continue with me, and in the succeeding weeks, to request increasing the frequency of his sessions. He decided against paying anything for the Friday session, nor for the sessions missed in conferring with someone else, though he did assume responsibility during this period for one rendezvous annulled by him at the last minute. I think we both felt that I had been fairly "punished" for my part in the debacle. Since then, I have realized how the acting out of my counter-transferential irritation was itself for him a repetition of the lack of tenderness with which he was often treated by his parents. I have also had many occasions to remark upon the hallucinatory quality of the threat of losing the love of people experienced as parental figures, a fear a rational part of himself decried but which was also nourished by his submissive and conflicted, undercover, attacks on them. Our work has brought to light, moreover, how destructive to his own capacity for thought and play have been his pleas for reassurance (and self-castration) from the flipped-over, sanitized, version of the forbidding other.

A few more remarks may be made about this vignette before concluding. Moments of doubt about the work – if tolerated and worked though – do not always have to be as dramatic as the crisis shared here. However, this example illustrates vividly how for the patient the person of the analyst is part and parcel of the framework and methodology of psychoanalysis. We have not enlarged upon, in this article, this facet of consent though it is probably safe to say that patients do not generally speaking consent to psychoanalysis as a category; *rather they undertake and assent (sometimes sooner, sometimes later) to an analysis with a particular analyst.* The man in the vignette was psychologically sophisticated. He was aware of how features of his relationship to his mother continued to be replayed in his ties to women. He had, nevertheless, to a significant extent hitherto avoided facing the extent of the Medusa phantasy by choosing male analysts and by not realizing, really realizing, the degree to which he carried this figure ready-made within him.

Conclusion

Dialogue between evolving case law and legal theory and psychoanalytic practice and theory is inevitable and mutually enriching, but attempts to bind them together, or – as was more common in the past – to impose the law on top of psychoanalytic ethics, should be avoided. The law cannot prescribe "best practice" though it can integrate – or at least dialogue with – contemporary scientific (psychoanalysis is considered here as a scientific study of the unconscious) consensus. Psychoanalysis has its own tripartite professional response to ethical concerns about patient autonomy in the form of (1) the protection offered by high professional standards of clinical training, (2) the recommended lifelong immersion of analysts in the triangulating experience of inter-analytic space (Donnet, 2001), and (3) continued psychoanalytic research on the matter. Intellectual information does not reach or obviate the real clinical pitfalls. Aspirations to develop general uniform guidelines of informed consent in psychoanalysis are counter-analytic insofar as they lead patients (and analysts) to believe that there are common hurdles and expectable solutions to fundamentally unique and unpredictable intersubjective personal histories and experience. It is the psychic work the analyst guides the patient to undertake (and the analyst will have their own labour to achieve this) which increases his or her ability to a good enough assenting or dissenting. Initial, unconsciously apprehensive, consenting will be inevitably subject to ordeals of doubt and resistance which provide opportunities for growth that can widen and deepen this assenting to the process.

The attempt to reconcile the legal-regulatory and psychoanalytic points of view on informed consent is a worthy one in as much as – and this is the crux of the matter – it encourages analysts to put into words, or to illustrate by their manner of listening and responding, the paradoxical nature of their work. The discussion of risks and benefits can indeed take place, though not in the straightforward, transparent manner envisaged by legal scholars. This discussion takes the form of an exploration where it is assumed that fantasies can be real or imagined or both: where it is possible that the patient might break down or that the therapist might transgress and – at the same time – it might be an unconscious projection on the part of one or the other of the dyad. It is this paradox that we do not want to quickly reduce in order that the patient can continue to freely associate to her uncertainties and eventually make her own judgments. The treasure-hunting ground permitted *within* the psychoanalytic framework allows the suspension of the need to decide so that all unconscious derivatives may see the light of the ego's scrutiny and play. Is there not here a necessary paradox: the patient must have the right to refuse the analytic setup at the same time as she or he accepts it? It is at least partially in this manner that patients can come to making their analyses uniquely and subjectively theirs. Psychoanalysis' answer to the "autonomous subject" is what Donnet has called its "methodic unreason" (2001, 82).[13]

Notes

1 All translations from original French texts are by the present author.
2 With minor editorial corrections, the following appears as it was originally published in 2020 in the *Journal of the American Psychoanalytic Association, 64*:583–613. We thank Sage Publications for permission to reuse it here.
3 Though, for simplicity of presentation, the terms analytic setting, framework, and situation will be here used interchangeably, several authors have offered distinctions (cf. Cooper, 2019; Donnet, 2001; Tabakin, 2017) – indirectly relevant to the concerns of this paper – by seeking to include representation of the non-material, inter-subjective aspects of the relationship emanating from both patient and analyst and the related qualitative changes in their working alliance.
4 For these patients, the drive can be as much external "as can a clap of thunder or a hit" and thus, not a part of the self (Winnicott, 1960, 141).
5 This point came up in a long-term seminar on *Psychoanalytic Culture* bringing together analysts from two linguistic groups. The group's exchanges made us realize the risk of dyads proceeding in an "as if", compliant mode in ignorance of a hidden mutual misunderstanding of what they are doing together. Our thanks to Ron Brown, Sylvie de Lorimier, Martin Gauthier, Gabriela Legorreta, and Jacques Mauger.
6 Some time after writing this, I realized that I had forgotten the attention given by Piera Aulagnier (1979, 2001) *to the test/labour of doubt (l'épreuve du doute)* in the construction of the "I" (as opposed to the ego as a forum of imaginary identifications) in the face of change and disappointment. It is possible that Assoun may have been influenced by her insistence on the capacity for doubt in a healthy, non-alienated, individual. However, it is equally probably that both Aulagnier and Assoun were inspired by Lacan's (2006b) metaphor of the three prisoners who must pass through the imagined subjectivity of each other and *moments of doubt* in order to reason their way to their own respective identities.
7 In a recent article Saketopoulou (2019) also wonders whether the purview of informed consent as understood in the medical profession (what she calls "affirmative consent") is not "insufficiently nuanced" (139) for our field. She too tries to articulate a different quality of consent to the psychoanalytic situation by proposing the concept of "limit consent" which "is predicated not on setting and observing limits, but on initiating and responding to an invitation to transgress them" (140) which echoes somewhat our notion of the necessary "labour" of assent. Her call for the analytic dyad's openness to "excess" and "dysregulation" to allow for the creation of "new translations" of patients' core enigmas is an innovative use of both Laplanche's and Stein's work and a dramatic retake on the notion of risk both parties take in assenting to their work together. There are the arresting overlaps in theoretical references and concerns with our purpose here,

though Saketopoulou's endeavour to make sense of a specific and highly charged interpersonal dynamic leads her elsewhere. To our ears, her invention of a new term "the draw to overwhelm" is more akin to Bion's negative capacity than to a way of thinking about consent to a psychoanalytic treatment.

8 I want to thank Mitchell Wilson for drawing my attention to a noble precursor in Immanual Kant's moral philosophy for our proposition that assent involves a labour which must overcome ambivalence and resistance. This precedent might be discerned in Kant's view of the participation of an act of "will" in moral reasoning. For Kant, "willing an end involves more than desiring: it requires actively choosing or committing to the end rather than merely finding oneself with a passive desire for it" (Kant's Moral Philosophy in the *Standford Encylopedia of Philosophy*, 7). Virtue is, for Kant, "strength of will" (16) and thus would seem to entail *effort*.

9 The *International Journal of Psychoanalysis* 1967 version of Bleger's paper uses the term "ghost world" but I agree with Bleger and Churcher's (see Churcher, 2024) proposed alternate translation of "phantom world" as truer to Bleger's evocation of body schema and a loss inflicted upon it.

10 Even in the context of medical research, a series of studies undertaken by Lidz and his colleagues (Lidz, 2006) demonstrates that the doctrine of informed consent rests on untenable empirical assumptions. They argue that since most individuals are subject to "therapeutic misconceptions" which lead to "context-bound, not context-free, decisions" (545), we cannot and should not "rely simply on the accuracy of information disclosed to protect subjects from risky or inappropriate clinical trials" (545).

11 Since the publication of this article in 2020, I have discovered that an article of Vic Sedlak (2003) proposed that the patient's material, if listened to attentively, may alert the analyst of unconscious countertransference. His article also contains thoughtful conjectures about why theorists of countertransference have avoided "spelling out the importance of the patient's observations on the analyst's state of mind" (1489).

12 The author has pursued this topic in later work, for example, in an article published in the *Canadian Journal of Psychoanalysis 30* (44–60) in 2022: Nous avons toujours été ainsi.

13 My gratitude goes to the editor-in-chief of *JAPA* and anonymous reviewers for the stimulating feedback which improved earlier drafts.

References

Assoun, P. L. 2001/2002. L'épreuve du consentment: À propos du lien fraternal. *La lettre de l'enfance et de l adolescence* 44(2):39–49.

Aulagnier, P. 1979. *Les destins du Plaisir – alienation, amour, passion*. Paris: PUF.

Aulagnier, P. 2001. *The Violence of Interpretation: From Pictogram to Statement*. Philadelphia: Brunner-Routledge.

Bibring, E. 1943. The Conception of the Repetition Compulsion. *Psychoanalytic Quarterly* XII:486–516.

Bion, W. R. 1979. Making the best of a bad job. In *Clinical Seminars and Four Papers*, edited by W.R. Bion & F. Bion, 247–257. Abingdon, UK: Fleetwood Press, 1987. Quoted in Reith et al.

Bleger, J. 1967. Psychoanalysis of the psychoanalytic setting. In *Symbiosis and Ambiguity. A Psychoanalytic Study*, edited by J. Churcher & L. Bleger, 233–242. New York: Routledge, 2013.

Cahn, R. 2002. *La Fin Du Divan?* Paris: Odile Jacob.

Chetrit-Vatine, V. 2014. *The Ethical Seduction of the Analytic Situation*. London: Karnac Books.

Churcher, J. 2024. The Psychoanalytic Setting: José Bleger's *Encuadre*. *International Journal of Psychoanalysis* 105(2):216–233.

Cooper, S. H. 2019. A Theory of the Setting: The Transformation of Unrepresented Experi-ence and Play. *The International Journal of Psychoanalysis* 100: 1439–1454.

Crick, P. 2014. Selecting a Patient or Initiating a Psychoanalytic Process? *International Journal of Psychoanalysis* 95:465–484.

Dailey, A. C. 2014. Abject or Autonomous? Patient Consent to Psychoanalytic Treatment. *Journal of the American Psychoanalytic Association* 62:1119–1132.

Dailey, A. C. 2017. *Law and the Unconscious: A Psychoanalytic Perspective*. New Haven, Connecticut: Yale University Press. Dictionary online: https://www.google.ca/search? q=meaning+abject&ie=utf-8&oe=utf-8&gws_rd=cr&ei=VICqVsDSEMnw-AGP2JLYBg

Donnet, J.-L. 2001. From the Fundamental Rule to the Analysing Situation. *International Journal of Psychoanalysis* 82:129–140.

Dufresne, R. 1994. Le premier entretien analytique: Des indications à l'écoute du désir d'analyse. In *Le Premier Entretien et L'écoute Psychanalytique*, edited by B. Tanguay, 86–109. Laval, Québec: Editions Méridien.

Ehrlich, L. T. 2004. The Analyst's Reluctance to Begin a New Analysis. *Journal of the American Psychoanalytic Association* 52:1075–1093.

Ehrlich, L. T. 2010. The Analyst's Ambivalence about Continuing and Deepening an Analysis. *Journal of the American Psychoanalytic Association* 58:515–532.

Ehrlich, L. T. 2013. Analysis Begins in the Analyst's Mind: Conceptual and Technical Considerations on Recommending Analysis. *Journal of the American Psychoanalytic Association* 61:1077–1107.

Ehrlich, L. T. 2016. Finding Control Cases and Maintaining Immersion. *Journal of the American Psychoanalytic Association* 64(5):983–1012. https://doi.org/10.1177/0003065116671306

Ehrlich, L. T. 2020. *Psychoanalysis from the Inside Out: Developing and Sustaining an Analytic Identity and Practice*. London: Routledge.

Eissler, K. 1974. On Some Theoretical and Technical Problems Regarding the Payment of Fees for Psychoanalytic Treatment. *International Review of Psychoanalysis* 1:73–101.

Etchells, E., Sharpe, G., Burgess, M., & Singer, P. 1996. Bioethics for Clinicians: 2; Disclosure. *Canadian Medical Association Journal* 155:387–391.

Freud, S. 1900. The Moral Sense of Dreams. *The Interpretation of Dreams. Standard Edition* 4:66–74.

Freud, S. 1905. Jokes and Their Relation to the Unconscious. *Standard Edition* 8:9–236.

Freud, S. 1912. The Dynamics of Transference. *Standard Edition* 12:99–106.

Freud, S. 1913. On Beginning the Treatment. *Standard Edition* 12:123–144.

Freud, S. 1915a. Observations on Transference Love. *Standard Edition* 12:157–171.

Freud, S. 1915b. The Unconscious. *Standard Edition* 14:166–204.

Freud, S. 1916. Introductory Lectures on Psycho-Analysis. *Standard Edition* 15:1915–1916: 15–239.

Freud, S. 1923. The Ego and the Id. *Standard Edition* 19:12–66.

Freud, S. 1925. Some Additional Notes on Dream-Interpretation as a Whole. *Standard Edition* 19:127–138.

Freud, S. 1931. The Expert Opinion in the Halsmann Case. *Standard Edition* 21:251–253.

Freud, S. 1937. Constructions in Analysis. *Standard Edition* 23:256–269.

Friedman, L. 1965. The Significance of Determinism and Free Will. *International Journal of Psychoanalysis* 46:515–520.

Furlong, A. 1992. Some Technical and Theoretical Considerations Regarding the Missed Session. *The International Journal of Psycho-Analysis* 73:701–718.

Furlong, A. 2003. Negotiating Consent in Psychotherapy: Patrick O'Neill. *Canadian Journal of Psychoanalysis* 11:567–576.

Gabbard, G. 1977. *Love and Hate in the Analytic Setting*. Lanham, Maryland: Jason Aronson.

Goldberg, A. 2001. Postmodern Psychoanalysis. *International Journal of Psychoanalysis* 82:123–128.

Goldberg, A. 2004. A Risk of Confidentiality. *International Journal of Psychoanalysis* 85:301–310.

Green, A. 2005. Issues of Interpretation; Conjectures on Construction. *Fédération Européenne de Psychanalyse*. Bulletin 59:81–100.

Kahn, L. 2004. Destin du destin. *Libres cahiers pour la psychanalyse* 9:65–86.

Kattlove, S. 2016. Acknowledging the "Analyst as Person": A Developmental Achievement. *Journal of the American Psychoanalytic Association* 64:1207–1261.

Kirshner, L. 2012. Towards an Ethics of Psychoanalysis: A Critical Reading of Lacan's Ethics. *Journal of the American Psychoanalytic Association* 60:1223–1242.

Kite, J. 2016. The Fundamental Ethical Ambiguity of the Analyst as Person. *Journal of the American Psychoanalytic Association* 646:1153–1171.

Kohut, H. 1971. *The Analysis of the Self*. New York: International Universities Press.

Lacan, J. 1982. The Freudian thing, or the meaning of the return to Freud in psychoanalysis. In *Lacan and Language. A Reader's Guide to Écrits*, edited by J. Muller & W. Richardson, 123–141. New York: International Universities Press.

Lacan, J. 2006b. Logical time and the assertion of anticipated certainty. In B. Fink (Ed.), *Écrits*, 161–175. New York & London: W.W Norton. (Original work published 1945).

Laplanche, J. 1999. The unfinished Copernican revolution. In *Essays on Otherness*, 53–85. London and New York: Routledge.

Lear, J. 2003. Confidentiality as a virtue. In *Confidentiality. Ethical Perspectives and Clinical Dilemmas*, edited by C. Levin, A. Furlong & M. K. O'Neil, 4–17. Hillsdale, New Jersey: The Analytic Press.

Lidz, C. W. 2006. The Therapeutic Misconception and Our Models of Competency and Informed Consent. *Behavioral Sciences and the Law* 24:535–546.

Little, M. I. 1985. Winnicott Working in Areas Where Psychotic Anxieties Predominate: A Personal Record. *Free Associations* 1:9–42.

May, U. 2009. Freud travaillait autrement. Remarques sur le journal de l'analyse d'Anna G. In *Mon Analyse avec le Professeur Freud*, edited by A. Koellreuter. Paris: Aubier, 2009.

Morris, H. 2016. The Analyst's Offer. *Journal of the American Psychoanalytic Association* 64:1173–1187.

Moss, D. 2016. Me Here, You There – Now What? Commentary on Kite, Morris, Wilson, and Kattlove. *Journal of the American Psychoanalytic Association* 64:1217–1224.

O'Neill, P. 1998. *Negotiating Consent in Psychotherapy*. New York: New York University Press.

Ogden, T. 1992. Comments on Transference and Countertransference in the Initial Analytic Meeting. *Psychoanalytic Inquiry* 12:225–257.

Pontalis, J.-B. 2014. No, Twice No: An Attempt to Define and Dismantle the 'Negative Therapeutic Reaction'. *International Journal of Psychoanalysis* 95:533–551.

Rangell, L. 1969. Choice-Conflict and the Decision-Making Function of the Ego: A Psychoanalytic Contribution to Decision Theory. *International Journal of Psychoanalysis* 50:599–602.

Reith, B., Lagerlof, S., Crick, P., Moller, M., & Skale, E. 2012. *Initiating Psychoanalysis. Perspectives*. London: New Library of Congress.

Reith, B., Moller, M., Boots, J., Crick, P., Gibeault, A., Jaffè, R., Lagerlöf, S., & Vermote, R. 2018. *Beginninag Analysis. On the Processes of Initiating Psychoanalysis*. London & New York: Routledge.

Rosenblum, R. 2005. Cure ou répétition du trauma? *Revue française de psychosomatique* 28:69–90.

Rothstein, A. 1994. A Perspective on Doing a Consultation and Making the Recommendation of Analysis to a Prospective Analysand. *Psychoanalytic Quarterly* 63:680–695.

Rothstein, A. 1995. Psychoanalytic Technique And The Creation Of Analysands: On Beginning Analysis With Patients Who Are Reluctant To Pay The Analyst's Fee. *Psychoanalytic Quarterly* 64:306–325.

Rothstein, A. 1997. Response to Charles Spezzano's Review of Psychoanalytic Technique and the Creation of Analytic Patients. *Contemporary Psychoanalysis* 33:654–655.

Rothstein, A. 2002. Reflections on Creative Aspects of Psychoanalytic Diagnosing. *Psychoanalytic Quarterly* 71:301–326.

Rothstein, A. 2006. Reflections on the Concept "Analyzability". *Psychoanalytic Review* 93:827833.

Rothstein, A. 2010. Psychoanalytic Technique and the Creation of Analytic Patients: An Addendum. *Psychoanalytic Quarterly* 793:785–794.

Saketopoulou, A. 2019. The Draw to Overwhelm: Consent, Risk, and the Retranslation of Enigma. *Journal of the American Psychoanalytic Association* 67:133–167.

Saks, E. & Golshan, S. 2013. *Informed Consent to Psychoanalysis: The Law, the Theory, and the Data*. New York: Fordham University Press.

Sedlak, V. 2003. The patient's material as an aid to the disciplined working through of the countertransference and supervision. *International Journal of Psychoanalysis* 84: 1487–1500.

Sharpe, E. F. 1943. Cautionary Tales. *International Journal of Psycho-Analysis* 24:41–45.

Smith, J. H. 1978. Psychoanalytic Understanding of Human Freedom: Freedom from and Freedom for. *JAPA* 26:87–107.

Stanford Encyclopedia of Philosophy 2016. Kant's Moral Philosophy. https://plato.stanford.edu/entries/kant-moral/ Consulted January 9, 2020.

Tabakin, J. 2017. The setting and the frame: Subjectivity and objectivity in the psychoanalytic relationship. In *Reconsidering the Moveable Frame in Psychoanalysis*, edited by I. Tylim & A. Harris. London: Routledge, Chapter 4.

Tillinghast, E. 2015. A Review of Informed Consent to Psychoanalysis: The Law, the Theory, and the Data. *Contemporary Psychoanalysis* 512:365–375.

Uglow, J. 2019. Island Hopping. *New York Review of Books*, February 7 issue.

Van Lysabeth-Ledent, M. 2016. Le travail onirique du moi inconscient *Revue française de la psychanalyse* 81:1365–1431.

Wilson, M. 2014. The Ethical Position of the Analyst-as-Mother: Respect and Responsibility for the "other". *International Journal of Psychoanalysis, Open*. pep-web.org

Wilson, M. 2016. The Ethical Foundation of Analytic Action. *Journal of the American Psychoanalytic Association* 64:1189–1205.

Winnicott, D. W. 1954. Withdrawal and Regression. In *Collected Papers: Through Paediatrics to Psycho-Analysis*, 255–261. London: The Hogarth Press and the Institute of Psycho-Analysis, 1978.

Winnicott, D. W. 1960. Ego distortion in terms of true and false self. In *The Maturational Processes and the Facilitating Environment*, 140–152. New York: International Universities Press, 1982.

Winnicott, D. W. 1967. The concept of clinical regression compared with that of defence organisation. In *Chapter 29 in D.W. Winnicott: Psycho-Analytic Explorations*, edited by C. Winnicott, R. Shepherd & M. Davis, 193–199. London and Cambridge: Harvard University Press, 1989.

Chapter 4

The framework offer as an identificatory project

The analytic offer precedes the request

It has already been stressed several times how closely intricated the analytic setup is with the analytically oriented clinician's internal frame. When Bleger referred to the "ideally normal setting" (1967, 22), he did not have in mind a specific concrete organization. It is, he wrote: "similar to what physicists call a thought experiment: a problem that does not occur totally or precisely in the form in which it is defined or presented, but which is of great usefulness (theoretical and practical)" (36). In a rather similar vein, the setting is more of a *strategy* than a technique. Compared to the manualized techniques for psychotherapy proposing pre-digested patterns which can be applied to a wide array of patients by relatively unskilled personnel, and which are an increasingly favoured part of public mental health care in England, Canada, and the United States, the word "strategy", in this instance, implies adding to open-ended listening a requisite psychic preparedness for being surprised.

A distortion has crept into the broader cultural setting regarding the therapist's duty of care. The therapist is expected, or expects from herself, to "adapt" to the patient's self-pronounced "needs". Doctoral students and psychiatric residents are currently taught several different theoretical models so as to possess a technical armamentarium "flexible" enough and eclectic enough to meet patient demand. This training is both reassuring and useful by providing students with a toolbox to offer distressed patients. Students do not meet patients empty handed, nor, it has to be recognized, are they fielding requests for psychoanalysis. But, what about the budding psychoanalytically oriented therapist? Other than introductory (often dry) theory and some post-hoc supervision during their training, what have they metabolized as a future "offer" to patients and do they have a psychoanalytic toolbox to greet them? Why, we might ask, having cycled through other psycho-therapeutic approaches, have they chosen to become a psychoanalytically oriented practitioner? No doubt exposure to psychoanalysis has enriched their own lives and living, motivating a wish to transmit this benefit. Yet without a full psychoanalytic training to deepen and theorize one's individual psychosexual history, which re-mains the best route to deeper competence, how does one refashion internal growth into a receptacle for the psychic growth of others? My impression is that many

DOI: 10.4324/9781003527459-5

psychoanalytically oriented practitioners are unclear about how they can embody this therapeutic model. How will it come across pragmatically speaking? Do they know how to translate what was transformative in their personal therapies into a psychic posture[1] with which to receive the pain of others?

Psychoanalytic listening is a specialized offer. In the psychoanalytic circle of my training years, we were told many times not to be led astray by the manifest wishes of the patient, that we must not become overly preoccupied by the symptoms per se that patients bring to treatment since examining the underlying conflicts and displacements they represent is more important for structural change. That vision nowadays seems to have lost its focus for many, diluted into a rather amorphous offer of an open mind and nonjudgemental listening. But if there is no direction to our listening, are we not back to a therapeutic model of catharsis and corrective emotional experience, where patients unburden themselves into sympathetic ears, feeling not only better, but better about themselves and more hopeful about their lives having met such a kind therapist? Perhaps one secretly imagines that the offer of a place for spontaneous conversation in the form of "free association" is inherently curative?

Yet, patients come to therapists in the hope of relief from their suffering. They may have put off a consultation for a long time, or tried other therapists, and they may not even know that we are of a psychoanalytic bent. Nowadays, they will expect us, usually sooner than later, to "do something"; they are unlikely to be complaisant with our continued silence after the relief of the first, or the first few, sessions. Even a practiced Rogerian tactic, skillfully feeding back reformulations of what has been expressed, is unlikely to be tolerated for long. And they might start asking about our training and our specializations or begin begging for guidance as to what topics to broach. We are going to feel disarmed and in disarray, mumbling something formulaic about what we have learnt in school, unless we have prepared ourselves by thinking about what our listening "is doing" in sessions. Psychotherapy research undertaken in university clinics and community centres has found that most patients are "satisfied" with a small number of sessions with relatively inexperienced therapists. Agreeing with other studies, Nordmo et al. (2021) concluded that patients with mild symptoms achieve "remoralization" (18) relatively easily in a relationship with a sympathetic listener. These patients would seem content with a time-limited and eclectic offer. In contrast, when supervisees wishing to develop a psychoanalytically inspired practice lose patients after a few sessions or, at best, a few months, it is not usually a positive sign. Their patients have often been expressing doubt about the work with the feeling of treading water. As I write these lines, I have received a text from a supervisee who has himself received a text from a patient:

> Hello, I forgot to write to you last week. I have decided to stop therapy. I have not been seeing any difference in my day-to-day life. Thank you for everything. I have much appreciated your engagement and patience. You seem to be very good at what you do, so I am thinking that therapy is maybe just not for me. I apologize for being so disorganized lately. I have made a payment for the last few sessions. Let me know if there are any issues. Again, apologies and thanks for everything.

This kind of departure is quite common, I believe, for psychoanalytic therapists early in their careers. A fizzle rather than a bang. A flummoxed ending for both parties. The patient is trying to be kind to someone he perceives as having endeavoured to be kind to him, but he has not felt helped in whatever inner struggle he had brought to the therapy.

A central premise of this book is that if the therapist does not hold an adequate framework in mind before psychoanalytic psychotherapy begins, and of course without the specialized listening that goes with it, many patients nowadays will not appreciate the qualitative difference between listening together in sessions for conflictual or contradictory patterns beneath manifest content from other kinds of listening offered by non-analytic psychotherapists. Bion's famous dictum to approach each session without memory or desire might work for experienced psychoanalysts but it is frankly confusing for less experienced clinicians. The archival research of Aguayo (2014) sheds light on the context of Bion's (1967) proscriptive "Notes on memory and desire", concluding that "the analyst's true trajectory was toward the unknown. It was important to forget what one knows in the immediacy of the current session, so that some new (and heretofore unknown) pattern might be allowed to evolve" (894). Bion is said to have linked his idea to Freud's advice on "evenly suspended attention" and to his own notion of "negative capability" which makes his views, in this light, completely consonant with other analysts like Laurence Kahn, who in wishing to make room for the psychic stowaway, are expressing a similar idea. Yet Aguayo's research also leaves the reader with doubts about the universal usefulness of the famous dictum since Bion was presenting sessions with severely disturbed patients and the few interpretations reported by him according to Aguayo are in line with known Kleinian "deep" reconstructions. Moreover, Bion depicts himself as unabashedly perplexed by the onslaught of incoherent, hostile, material from some patients. He comes across as courageous and modest – even chastened – with a decidedly reserved view of the therapeutic value of his work.

With respect to the themes of this book, I feel justified in taking the view that a psychoanalyst or psychoanalytically oriented therapist must first refine the conception of "offer" before meeting any "demand". The analytic offer precedes the patient's consultation and is intrinsically part of the frame, conceived of as the material environment, the clinician's provisional theory of listening plus the contract of the analytic relationship. For Piera Aulagnier (1967, 1968, 1984), the psychoanalytic offer precedes and shapes the patient's "demand", just as the mother's offer precedes and interprets the baby's cry as a "demand" addressed to her.

[I]f we agree that the request [la demande], whatever it is, is induced by the field which awaits it … The request [la demande] for analysis does not escape the rule: before anything else, it must be heard as a response to the offer vouched for by the analyst"… [Thus] any request [toute demande] … implies that the petitioner [le demandeur] has imagined what the object of desire is of the person addressed.[2]

Manzano et al. (2016) agree: "The 'psychoanalytic situation' ... is established right from the first interview by the 'mental attitude of the psychoanalyst' (the 'state of mind' of Anglo-Saxon thinkers)" (5) (See Chapter 1 where we discussed the similar notion of 'internal frame'). The unstructured nature of the psychoanalytically oriented interview makes the "mental attitude of the psychoanalyst" particularly crucial as a valuable magnet for the patient's thoughts, both attracting and supporting those thoughts. Behind the relatively silent listening of the therapist, the patient needs to feel his or her alert thoughtfulness for what slides behind what is being said. The therapist's *desire to analyse* presented to the patient as an *offer to analyse* is not necessarily supportive or reassuring to the ego of the patient, but it carries with it a real hope for internal transformation. This offer cannot be "co-created" in the customary sense because it has to *start* with the analytically oriented therapist and it has to *withstand* the patient's necessary (and welcome for observation) attempts to turn it into something else, more narcissistically rewarding or libidinally satisfying. If the necessary dependency of the human subject on a psychic passage through the other is fully appreciated, we are led to concur with Aulagnier that there is an unavoidable violence of interpretation inherent in the psychoanalytic offer. Since the existence of the unconscious makes it impossible for us to completely know ourselves, what the other can sense beyond our perceptual ken will unseat us in some way. That is why the analytic offer must precede the patient's demand for interpretation, gently keeping ajar the ego's wish to close back on itself in a self-sufficient circle.

On another level, the analytic offer contains within it what Chiantaretto (2018, 93) has described as an "internal posture [the word "posture" again] permitting the analyst to bear a double responsibility: on the one hand, for his/her implication in and through the patient's transference, on the other, for undertaking après-coup an auto-observation of this implication". Referring to the work of André Green and Michel Neyraut, Chiantaretto (2018, 93) observes that they agree about the "precession" of countertranference with regard to transference, quoting Neyraut as asserting "not only is countertransference not a response but it constitutes a demand". Though Chiantaretto is echoing the position of French analysts in the wake of Lacan and Laplanche's views, on the American side of the Atlantic, there are analysts who have taken a similar view of the precession of the analytic offer and its implied responsibility for transference phenomenon (see Gill 1984a; Kite 2016; Lipton 1977a). The theoretically "two-person" paradigm of these analysts assumes a not-to-be-bypassed asymmetry in the analytic relationship. Having undertaken a satisfactory personal analysis provides precious protective experience for the clinician willing to assume these ethical and clinical challenges.

In the initial encounters when the two participants know so little about each other, the identificatory dialectic set in motion in both can take unpredictable turns, adding another reason to the ones already marshalled in Chapter 2 for the therapist to try to slow down and cool down the process of integration. It does happen that – having felt rather "good" about the initial exchanges – the analyst or therapist is caught by surprise as the interview draws to a close by the patient's expression of wildly unrealistic expectations for a cure. In an example shared in Dufresne's text (1994) we brought up in a previous chapter, a patient stated that he was ready to begin treatment and that he would accept "all the necessary conditions". He added, however, that he needed a cure for his sexual condition before his upcoming marriage in three months! Dufresne felt "obliged" to explain that analysis usually takes longer and that one cannot predict its outcome. The young man was never heard from again. Dufresne's intervention would have been considered correct at the time, but nowadays, one might wonder if exposing the huge gap between the patient's hopes and the analyst's capacity to help might not have been less traumatic if it had been postponed until after a second or even a third appointment[3]? As noted in Chapter 3, Bleger (1967) argued that "there are actually *two settings*: one which is proposed and maintained by the psychoanalyst, and accepted consciously by the patient, and another, that of the 'phantom world' into which the patient projects" (233, original emphasis). Dufresne's explanation of "his" framework must have had the effect of stomping on the phantom world the patient had been silently projecting in the earlier part of their meeting.

By way of contrast, consider that Ogden (2018) ended a first meeting with an exceptionally skittish patient by simply asking her if she would like to meet again. He went on to permit her control of the frequency of their framework by accepting appointments on a "one time only" basis. This lasted two months before Ms Y asked to meet regularly. Odgen had reported a similar attunement to a patient's reservations in an earlier article (2004) where he did not dispute the wish "not to have analysis" already asserted in the phone call to set up a first appointment. In the course of the first several months, a schedule of daily meetings became established, presumably after the patient had become convinced of the value of Ogden's listening. In the second or third session, Ogden told the patient that he thought he would be able to work best with him if the patient used the couch, a recasting of the frame readily accepted. It is noteworthy that Odgen proposed the couch as *an arrangement useful to him, the analyst*, thus a petition, not an imposition. Though younger psychotherapists are often faced with requests for two-week intervals between sessions, a frequency much harder for a working therapist to tolerate, and Ogden had the requisite patience and flexibility not all therapists can afford, his example does show that a willingness to let patients take their time before committing can pay off. More examples of this approach will be shared in the next section.

The identificatory dialectic precipitated by the analytic offer

Some of Aulagnier's earliest work (1967, 1968) looked at what she called "the identificatory dialectic" between "offer and demand", her integration and elaboration of ideas she was being exposed to at the time in Jacques Lacan's seminar. He was introducing a new categorization of inter-human expectations, defining three levels of inter-subjective exchange: need, demand, and desire and the helpful clarification of analytic listening these levels provide. Though this distinction has informed French psychoanalysts so deeply after forty years that it has become a permanent backdrop to their thinking, it seems to have scarcely touched English-speaking psychoanalytic clinicians, outside of Lacanian societies. Yet, its application is potentially universally useful, regardless of psychoanalytic school, insofar as it alters our conception of the framework's function, which is why a short detour will be taken to introduce these terms.

In the original French, Lacan spoke of the registers of "besoin, demande, et désir". "Besoin" or "need" is the expression of vital bodily requirements, such as air, food, and water, but amongst human beings, especially at the beginning of life, it cannot be satisfied without the assistance of another. In contrast, for example, the mediation of a plant's own hormones causes cells on the shady side to grow larger thereby bending its stem towards the light. The plant can take care of itself without the intervention of another, more mature, plant. At the beginning of our lives, as well as ever after, "besoin", as a lack addressed in various disorganized non-verbal gestures to the adult taking care of us, has to pass nevertheless through language and speech, specifically via the interpretation of the adult called upon to intervene. This adult puts words onto and into the infant's appeal and on the objects brought to quench it. It is this passage through the narrow "corridor" (the French is "defilé") of language and speech which permanently displaces and colours "besoin" with a host of interpersonal and cultural meanings. In the process, "besoin" gradually transforms into "demande", which Lacan pointed out is always in the end – because of its circuit through the intersubjective conscious and unconscious projections of primary caretakers – an "appeal/demand" for love. When the patient says he "needs" something from the analyst (a special favour, a particular gesture), the realization that a biological need is not in question clarifies the ethical tenure of the analyst's refusal to respond in kind. In the Bass case presented in some detail in chapter Two, was Nicole's problem in paying for missed sessions a "need" or a "demand"?

The level of "désir" is even trickier, affirmed Lacan, since it harkens back to an impossible wish for a *fantasied lack of lack*, when one felt gloriously whole, fantasized as a state having existed or of having been frustrated in the past, in the form of a psychic union with another. Through the various stages of life, we move from one "demande" to another, never satisfied because "le désir" for completeness can never be fully or permanently satisfied. "Need" is a good translation for the French "besoin" and the French "désir" can be adequately translated into English by "desire". However, the translation of Lacan's notion of "la demande" as "demand" which is the current official translation into English is more problematic (cf. Evans, 1996, 34). "Demande" in French has the flavour of "request", or "supplication", or "application" by which a subject *asks for* something whereas the English "demand" is closer to an "exigency" or "insistence" or "requirement", where the subject's expectation of a response is felt to be more *imperious*. As long as we keep this caveat in mind, accepting "demand" as the English translation of the French original is probably nevertheless the best choice so as to keep the unity of Lacan's concept. At the same time, as we will see, the nuance between request/ supplication and exigency/insistence is a significant one in my conception of the setting as an offer rather than an imposition.

Aulagnier (1967) observed that patients' requests for psychoanalysis variously aligned with what was perceived to be the analytic *zeitgeist*. When Lacan claimed to be following Freud in pronouncing the "cure" to be an inconsequential side-line of the enlightenment of proper psychoanalytic work, patients downplayed their wish for therapeutic relief in their initial interviews with her. In their wish to be taken into treatment, patients were ready to sacrifice themselves on the altar of the idealized knowledge attributed to the analyst. At the time, psychoanalysis was enjoying a heyday of prestige; psychoanalytic knowledge carried an aura of mystery and excitement with patients flocking to Paris and New York to consult well-known analysts. In my wider circle in Montreal, there were young people in the sixties and seventies leaving for Paris in the hope of consulting Lacan or one of his disciples. I even dreamed of going there myself but did not have the funds. Deeply perturbed by the unhappy fallout around her of this public seduction and naiveté, Aulagnier began a lifelong reflection on what she viewed as the risk of *mutual* alienation, particularly important in psychoanalysis. The case of *Odette*, a "second analysis" shared in her 1984 book, *The Apprentice Historian and the Master Sorcerer* (author's translation), and which has unfortunately not yet been translated into English, contains a fine investigation of this risk in a vulnerable, pre-psychotic, patient.[4"] Yet, Aulagnier's theoretical reflections on this unfortunate outcome were already being voiced several years earlier in a seminar held in 1977 and 1978 at Sainte-Anne Hospital in Paris, subsequently published much later in 2009 as *Destinies of Pleasure*, and which carries the subtitle of *Alienation, love, and passion.*

Aulagnier offers an intriguing illustration of the dialectic of offer and demand from Freud's case of the Rat Man. She points out that before the Rat Man ac-cidently came upon one of Freud's writings, scarcely read in fact, his original in-tention was to seek a medical certificate claiming that his obsessional vow to pay a favour back to the wrong person was necessary for his return to health (Freud 1909, 173). The passage he had seen in Freud had "reminded him of some of his own 'efforts of thought' in connection with his ideas" (1909, 159). Thus, a nar-rative and a ritual which had until then seemed senseless were transformed into a "phantasied après-coup sense" (Aulagnier 1967, 5). "[I]t is at this precise mo-ment that the subject accepts what I refer to as the hypothesis (and the mortgage) (in French "l'hypothèse" and "l'hypothèque") of the unconscious that the object of his appeal (la demande) permutates and that transference begins" (Aulagnier 1967, 4). The transference began by virtue of an awakened quest in the Rat Man to understand his symptom rather than rely on it simply to ease his anguish. He is thereby moved to make a psychic pivot, to seek out Freud as psychoanalyst rather than as physician, imagining Freud as possessor of vital knowledge rather than as a medical professional vouchsafing the symptom. Consequently, when the Rat Man meets Freud, he puts forward details of his sexual life because that is what he has heard about psychoanalytic doctrine.

There is a wordplay in French in this text between the terms "hypothèse" and "hypothèque" which are back-to-back entries in my old paper versions of the *Petit Robert de la langue française* and the *Larousse Dictionnaire Encyclopédique*. The "hypothèse" corresponds to the English term of "hypothesis" and "hypothèque" to the English "mortgage" as a future financial pledge to another for the use of a property now. But in both languages, "hypothèque" and "mortgage" can be used metaphorically to mean "burden" or "obstacle" undermining development, as when someone is seen as "mortgaging his future because of a gambling addiction". The concept has a bidirectional temporality in so far as a pledge to pay later can become a burden in the present, and an unfortunate condition in the present can compromise the future. Intriguingly, the word "mortgage" in English comes from the old French for "mort-gage", literally a "dead pledge". Was Aulagnier intimating that the hypothesis/inkling of misunderstood forces within oneself might include sensing an unconscious "pledge" with the past? In any case, until this prior psychic pivot of puzzlement about the self occurs, she did not believe that the psychoanalyst's "offer" has a chance of being meaningful to the patient. The case of Philippe described in Chapter 2 evinces the resulting impotence in the analyst.

> I think that any wish for analysis takes root in that precise point of speech when a 'lack of sense' [that is, when the symptom appears senseless] appears to the patient in his own spoken history; as long as the subject does not bump into/trip over [buter sur] the unknown or the nonsensical [in himself], we cannot accept the request [because in this state of mind, interpretation of the symptom would be incomprehensible to the patient].
>
> (1967, 8)

Consequently, in Aulagnier's view the inaugural experience of the analytic meeting cannot be reduced to pure repetition. It requires the expectation by the patient of learning something new about himself before the meeting can become meaningful. There must be an inkling of the elusive existence of a highly personal and enigmatic message to oneself in one's apparently meaningless behaviour. If this intimation has not already occurred to the patient, some preliminary experience of the setting may be necessary for it to emerge.

I have taken the time to share Aulagnier's views on the first interview because these writings are not yet available to English-speakers. Yet her reflections and the historical context of psychoanalytic excitement and institutional warfare in which she developed them (see Roudinesco, 1990) remain relevant today as much in their rupture as in their continuity with what I am trying to articulate as a preliminary psychoanalytic "offer" in contemporary English-speaking analysis. This is not the place to review the extensive literature beginning in the seventies of inquiry into a widespread decline in psychoanalytic practice (cf. Green's watershed article of 1975). Yet the risk today may be less mutual alienation than a fading of passionate hope in both clinicians and patients for help from psychoanalysis as anything more than a benign encounter between two well-meaning individuals? In order to be ready to undertake psychoanalytically oriented work, the clinician can gain from preparing his/her own mind, which brings us back to the question of an *analytic offer* and how to go about thinking about it as part of the frame.

A recent article in a local newspaper caught my attention. A reporter (Fine, 2024) wanted to improve his hockey skating skills by taking lessons from a world-class skating coach. Other than running though drills, and critiquing videos of his stride with the coach, Fine was introduced into the technique of visualization, now part of any elite athletic training. He consulted a clinical neuroscientist specializing in muscle memory and brain plasticity, Dr Gallucci, who is quoted as saying using visualization is a way of "hacking the system". "You can actually build the fibres [in neural networks] because large portions of the brain don't know the difference between whether you're doing it or not doing it". I doubt that Dr Gallucci or Mr Fine are aware that this description corresponds practically word for word with Freud's discovery of the unconscious mind's incapacity to distinguish hallucinated images from perceptual ones. It was one of the reasons he gave in a letter to Fliess on September 21, 1897 (see Masson 1985, 275–265) for giving up his *"neurotica"*, that is, his belief that all hysterical symptoms can be traced back to childhood sexual abuse. It may not be entirely tongue in cheek to wonder whether students of psychoanalysis might try visualizing their offers before they actually make them. It is certainly true that in our discipline, professional learning is handicapped by the paucity of opportunities to "see" analysts at work. Almost all psychoanalytic training and continuing education is either purely theoretical or supervisory "word of mouth" and after the fact. We study what we say to each other about what has happened between ourselves and our patients. We are always once removed, spatially and temporally. Yet, of course, as students of the unconscious, we are forced to admit that even if we could "be" there with each other, enlightenment might still elude us. Neither direct "watching" or "hearing" a session can replace the "hearing *about* it" since resistance, linguistic ambiguity, and unconscious derivatives are transmitted via the other's mind and must be divined rather than shown in the sharing.

All the same, the metaphor of visualization may not be as outlandish as it first appears as a way to "prepare" a psychoanalytic offer as an offer to analyse. For example, "visualizing" ahead of time that one will be aiming to "understand" the patient may be less effective than "visualizing" ahead of time that one expects "not to understand". *Less experienced therapists assume they understand what their patients are saying.* They accept the manifest content of their culture's common bromides, not tarrying to decorticate them: a phrase such as "I am attracted to father figures" might be left as though self-explanatory. Or "I know I have to please everyone", "I'm a control freak", "I have anger issues", "I haven't mourned the loss of X, Y, or Z", or other hackneyed phrases that have lost their mystery and mislead the therapist into believing that they come from a place of insight. It may not occur to the therapist to express Colombo-like curiosity about what the patient means in using such phrases. Some of us will recall the homicide detective, Colombo, from the long-lived TV series of that name whose character was deceptively naïve. Viewers already knew who the perpetrator was since every episode started by showing the murder. The delicious twist in premise was to watch Colombo, with hair askew and always in the same crumpled raincoat, bumble around the crime scene looking for clues while the murderer looked on with contempt. Just when the murderer was sure that he had gotten away with his crime, Colombo would turn back from the door he was about to exit, and with an apologetic smile state: "One more thing …" after which he would proceed to pose an embarrassing, unexpected question putting the murderer on the spot. Eventually, of course, after several similar unexpected inquiries, Colombo would unspool an exact reconstruction of the dastardly deed, to the dismay of the murderer. *There is an acquirable art in conveying non-confronting curiosity* which is the equivalent in our field of the somewhat feigned perplexity of Detective Colombo: "Oh! Does an example come to mind?", "I'm not sure what you mean? Can you say more?", "Wait a moment, I am not sure I have understood".

The neophyte clinician's illusion of understanding patients puts them repeatedly in the position of prematurely attempting to "say something therapeutic". It is not surprising, therefore, that their comments do not particularly further the process. I often have recourse to another metaphor complimenting that of Detective Colombo, that of the "*microdot*" which was an espionage technique used in the world wars. A microdot is text or image substantially reduced in size to prevent detection by unintended recipients. Microdots are normally circular and around one millimetre in diameter, about the size and shape of a typographical dot. At the 1925 International Congress of Photography in Paris, Emanuel Goldberg introduced an apparatus capable of producing extreme reduction of normal sized document pages as well as a way of restoring them back again to original size. The reduction was such that a page of text would be legibly reproduced at the size of a dot. Wikipedia (see Microdot. Wikipedia) tells us that this density is comparable to the entire text of the Bible fifty times over in one square inch! I use this metaphor to convey the stupendous material of overlooked associations hidden in the banal crevasses of the ordinary speech patients bring to the consulting room. This material is invisible unless the therapist shows curiosity to open up the condensation and elision present in the spontaneous discourse of their patients, where like the individual elements of dreams a variety of memories, ideas, perceptions, and other psychic material can lie compacted together. For example, a recently psychoanalytically oriented supervisee had not realized the extent to which he had accepted at face value the patient's recounting of a tender attachment to the father during latency and had not inquired more about the patient's explanation that the father's later depression was triggered when his children grew mature enough to leave home. The therapist somehow felt that he "understood" this explanation without being surprised by it, without being curious about the hitherto concealed ambiguity and fragility of this paternal figure, and without among other things wondering about the impact on the patient as emerging adult of such a massive loss-of-presence and de-idealization of her parent. Lipton may have been expressing a similar idea when he wrote about the "ambiance of conversation" he developed with patients, by which he meant that he was "convinced that if the analyst does not take up and pursue the suggestive material, it will not come to light" (1977b 470–471).

The offer of psychoanalytic framework as an identificatory project

We have seen how the analytic offer, as a psychic posture and anticipatory listening by the analyst, gives soul and substance to the framework which will be proposed to the patient. We have also seen how this "offer" must precede the patient's request, contextualizing it, transforming it, giving it berth and allotted space within which to exist. Insofar as this offer is to put into words what may be evading the patient's speech, this offer directly engages with the phenomenon of resistance. It is thus accurate in most cases to affirm that making the offer (which in my mind cannot be made in an explicit statement on the part of the analyst, that is, by *saying it*, but rather by explicit speech acts by the analyst in which voice is given to sensed unconscious conflict, that is, *by showing it*) puts the analyst squarely before some resistance. Though Lipton wrote this a long time ago, it is still true especially of less experienced psychoanalytic practitioners, that "certain resistances are not interpreted as frequently as they can be advantageously, and I think that it is quite possible that they are not recognized" (1977b, 463). Sometimes younger clinicians might be disinclined to say anything which goes against the grain of the patient's ego. It may seem obvious, but the analyst must dare to think thoughts that the patient is unwilling to think and to propose them as possibilities with the risk that the patient will disagree. All the evidence suggests that for a psychoanalytic process to engage, the analytic offer and the framework accompanying it have to go out on a limb; they have to be already there to hear the patient in an out-of-the-ordinary way. As Lipton goes on to say in the same article "in regard to the material [these particular resistances] I have described, nothing will appear in the analysis if the analyst waits for the material to unfold" (469). In another article published in the same year, Lipton (1977a) writes: the "analyst will be forced to define the limits of the analytic situation, both for himself and the patient; will have to try to induce the patient to include in the analysis what the patient wants to exclude" (269).

I would like to make a further proposition to qualify the offer of a framework made at the beginning of treatment. This proposition may only be new by being made explicit. It is inspired by Aulagnier's work on what she calls the *identificatory project* (1989), a developmental acquisition made after the (relative) resolution of the oedipal complex, in which the subject gives up his or her wish to be his early caretaker's prized possession, in the here-and-now, for an ego-ideal in the future in the form of a project to be realized. In so doing, the subject both renounces early caretakers as continuous libidinal object choices and introduces a new deferred temporality wherein he/she becomes an agent, a creator of a personal story which will not and should not be an exact copy of the past. The project – I want to become this or that, when I grow up, I want to do this or that – by preventing the individual from coinciding with himself, introduces a certain tension into identity. It also offers the individual a way out of the determinations which have weighed upon him as a child. For Aulagnier, the development of an identificatory project is a crucial task for the adolescent; its absence weighs upon the future adult who often brings it to the analysis as a symptom (I don't know what to do with my life; I don't know what career or partner to choose; I feel like I am going nowhere).

Referencing Aulagnier, Ridel (2004) associates the lack of a project to a being "stuck to or in what the subject imagines to be the desire of the other" (92), a "regressive project" as it were. The word Ridel uses in French is "engluement", which comes from the ancient practice of catching birds by smearing glue on a stick, and which Lacan used to describe the dilemma of the subject rivetted to the original object, both pathetic and grandiose. Moving forward entails « castration », giving up the grandiose project of the infantile past for the uncertainty of a personalized future with persons other than the primary caretakers. The adhesive power of glue in Ridel and Lacan's metaphor points to the *regredient* pull behind the analysand's wish for change which is why conceptualizing the offer of a psychoanalytic framework as support for the *progredient* elements of patients' identificatory projects can be a good counterpoint. The analytic setting is an *offer not an imposition; it is an invitation for the future, or more accurately, an offer to join the patient's quest to look forward to a better psychic future.* It is not a *push* towards the future. It should be communicated in alliance with patients' identificatory ideals: their wishes to become parents, to become better educated, to quarrel less with their co-workers or their spouses, their wish to overcome inhibitions in the development of certain talents, etc., if the therapist listens for the expression of these wishes in the material brought to the first sessions. There is a qualitative and temporal distinction between viewing one's personal therapy project as a "treatment" to expunge bothersome symptoms, presumably leaving the rest of the personality intact, and as a project in alliance with the therapist to move forward towards transformative ego-ideals.

Aulagnier reconstructed *the necessary relational undergirding to the development of an identificatory project, which she sees as a function, not a particular content.* It allows the child to envisage taking over the place (perhaps in a different manner) now occupied by caretakers and other adults without feeling that he or she is committing an act of "murder". "In order for this potentiality to be invested, it would have been necessary for the mother and the father to have already recognized and valued its existence and indeed they should have, from the beginning, presented it to this child as an active possibility and a realizable promise in the future" (1989, 736). Fortunately for most of the patients consulting us, the identificatory project has been under construction, though parts of it have been repressed or otherwise thwarted. It still needs our help as repository of that potential. This means, as Aulagnier carefully laid out, reconstructing the past in order to uncover the pieces of the identificatory puzzle confounding the patient's attempts to move on with life. The wonder of Aulagnier's theorizing is her constant reminder that psychic maturity is not a "renunciation" of past as forbidden fruit, so much as a remodelling of it as an acceptable pleasure for the future. Accordingly, she finishes her article by stating that the framework has to be a "wish and not an injunction for we are well placed to measure the difficulty of such a task, never terminated, which we all have to reprise for ourselves and through ourselves" (740).

In adopting this perspective Aulagnier was implicitly agreeing with Freud who had argued in 1908 that "we can never give anything up; we only exchange one thing for another. What appears to be a renunciation is really the formation of a substitute or surrogate" (145). It was in the same article that Freud argued that phantasy participates in "three periods of time" (151): the present, the past, and the future in that order. In decorticating the time-related sequence of phantasy, Freud was looking at a psychic temporality quite different from the decision-making one we outlined in Chapter 2 as inherent to informed consent. Freud was not here describing either a temporal circularity or an intersubjective dialectic but rather a rebound towards the past from the present with an anticipatory impact on the future. An incident in the present precipitates a wish that unconsciously triggers an associative link to the past, which is then constructed into a phantasy as "picture of the future" (148). The identificatory project of psychoanalysis mobilizes a similar temporality, where present anguish and breakdown are found to have displaced connections with antecedents in the patient's personal history, and which if adequately worked through allow investment in transformed projections for the future.

Less experienced clinicians are regularly stymied by an all too frequent defensive declaration made by patients nowadays: "I don't want to talk about the past!" The appropriate response to this position might simply be: "Fine, as you wish. All that I ask if you wish to continue working with me is that you say what comes to your mind here. If the past happens to come to mind, then I encourage you to share that". I have often advised supervisees to be alert for signs of resistance in their new clients, in the form of passing references to limited financial resources, to the presence of insurance companies as third parties whose financial support is constricted to a certain number of sessions, or to confusion or discouragement with their "progress". Since these may be signs of doubts about the therapy, the clinician should consider whether their listening has been missing something. In fact, it may be particularly useful to hear the obstacles to continuing as expressions *of the patient's loss of faith in his or her identificatory project of feeling better*. This state of affairs is more prevalent when the analytic offer and informed consent have been inadequately elaborated at the beginning. It might helpfully orient the therapist at this juncture to cast back to the preliminary interviews and to implicit identificatory project (or projects) shared then. The patient's doubts may stem from a sense that the dyad has missed addressing the inner barriers to achieving those projects. Some colleagues have referred to similar comments as the "patient's unconscious supervision" of the analyst,[5] potentially valuable to the work if heeded by the clinician. It is equally easy to miss the hope expressed in material brought by patients which expresses an identificatory project, not necessarily explicit, in their coming for help and that too needs to be somehow acknowledged in the "contract". When the inevitable "twisting of the frame" (Manzano et al. 2016, 7) occurs, we should bear in mind that the patient may be unconsciously expressing both progressive and regressive aspects of the identificatory project.

In a remarkable series of articles over a twenty-year period, Arnold Rothstein (1994, 1995, 2002, 2006, 2010) explained how he kept a full analytic practice while his peers complained of having few analysands in their practices. Rothstein argued that most of his analytic patients had been "made" not "found". In all but his use of Aulagnier's term – unavailable in English at the time – Rothstein's personal "solution" was a conception of psychoanalysis as the ideal identificatory project for most of the patients consulting him as a psychoanalyst. He began with the "premise that the analyst's optimistic attitude toward the efficacy of analysis significantly enhances the possibility of success in helping prospective analysands accept the recommendation of analysis" (1994, 680), that is, he began with a welcoming analytic offer. He argued strongly against the "evaluative model of deciding analyzability", which as mentioned in the preceding chapter Reith et al. (2018), has not turned out to be particularly helpful in predicting the outcome of analytic treatment. Rothstein also warned against a "pathological" bent in diagnosing patients. "If you want to have a successful analytic practice, welcome disturbing patients. Privilege self-analytic inquiry into your experience of them as disturbing" (792). He encouraged analysts to create new psychodynamic formulations "that are intended to facilitate the analyst's ability to interpret" (2002, 321) by which I take him to mean formulations that help the analyst understand the internal difficulties being faced by the patient. Rather than culling unsuitable persons from eligibility, Rothstein insisted that "all human beings have the capacity to symbolize; however, that capacity may not immediately be obvious or manifest" (2006, 827). He calls his solution a "trusting" model for doing a consultation and beginning an analysis: "I trust that people who come seeking help really do want our help. Regardless of their presenting complaints and/or deficiencies, which I conceive of as analogous to the manifest content of dreams, *I trust that they want to improve their lives*" (added emphasis, 2006, 829). He greets prospective analysands armed with the conviction that analysis is the optimal treatment for them, that is, Aulagnier's identificatory project, from the analyst's viewpoint. "To communicate such a belief, an analyst must have conviction concerning the therapeutic efficacy of psychoanalysis. I optimistically trust that *we* will be successful in our collaborative enterprise. I assume that patients are analyzable until they prove they are unanalyzable in a trial analysis" (2006, 829).

When in his "trusting" model", Rothstein would make an offer of analysis, the patient's reticence was not only received as an expression of resistance but also as genuine challenge to him as the analyst: "How can I help this person begin a trial of analysis with me at this time in our lives?" Instead of digging his heels in with regard to an optimal framework, when a patient objects to one or more of the parameters that define the analytic situation, such as frequency and/or the use of the couch, Rothstein agreed to begin analytic work with the patient at any frequency the patient desired "*with the understanding that an aspect of the work will be our effort to understand why he or she objects*" (added emphasis, 2006, 830). His approach "frames the patient's reluctance as a self-defeating masochistic enactment and, in collaboration with the patient, focuses an aspect of the early work on understanding" (2006, 831). Rothstein developed a style of dealing with reluctant patients that put the frame to work right at the beginning of treatment by paradoxically acquiescing to an aspect of the patient's resistance "in order to bring their transference potential, expressed as enactment resistances, under more focused analytic scrutiny" (1995, 323).

His idea of "making" analysands rather than "finding" them did not mean, Rothstein argued, that he was "creating" them; it meant that he was hoping to "develop" a potential some analysands did not realize already existed within. Rothstein was opening a "site" for the analysand to inhabit (Donnet (2001) would have approved). Mariela Aisenstein (1998), writing about the challenge of working with psychosomatic patients whose operational thinking severely curtails their emotional integration, confessed that "I do not hesitate to evoke here 'a *measured seduction*' in the message 'come then to dream and think with me'" (added emphasis, 38–39). Laplanche also wrote about the baby's vital need for an "optimal" seduction which can be seen as the counterpoint of Aulagnier's vision of an "optimal" violence of "interpretation". The analytic offer can convey an optimal seduction via its belief in the patient's potential psychic expansion, in what Aisenstein refered to as "something of the order of an anticipatory illusion of shared pleasure in mental functioning" (31).

In his version of allowing the patient to keep "his own frame" for a time (Bleger (1967) would have approved) in a defensive but potentially transformative use-of-the-object (Winnicott (1969) would have approved), Rothstein advised: "A good deal of tolerance for this kind of abuse, played out in the consultation, is required to help such patients experience themselves as participants in an analytic collaboration…. Begin the trial in any way the patient is able to begin" (2006, 831). In a perspective now familiar to us, Rothstein sums up "that, particularly in a consultation and at the beginnings of an analysis, it is not primarily the parameters of the analytic situation that define a treatment as an analysis. It is the analyst's attitude toward the patient and the patient's behavior and verbal associations that fundamentally define a treatment as a psychoanalysis" (2006, 831). That "attitude" holds an identificatory project open for patients where they can meet and eventually share it.

In fact, holding this project open for a future date seemed to have contributed to Rothstein's equanimity in letting certain patients go who declined his offer of analysis. "*I maintained an attitude that communicated that analysis was the optimal treatment to initiate at some future time in order to help protect the patient from a recurrence of her acute state* (original emphasis, 1994, 691). In the meantime, rather than attempting to offer significant help to individuals with serious personality issues and chaotic lives on a once-a-week basis, as I see so many younger psychotherapists do nowadays, Rothstein used to explain to these patients that "they will be better off working with someone less intensively who believes that such a psychotherapy is the optimal treatment for them" (1995, 315). I find that beginning or even mid-career psychoanalytically oriented clinicians resist recognizing, and resist communicating, that they will not be able to help some patients who are not prepared to invest more time in their analytic work. At the same time, these same clinicians may not allow themselves the initial uncertainty of gradually developing a shared analytic project with their patients as Rothstein reported having done. Another author reporting the same flexibility is Thomas Ogden (2018, 411) in a case mentioned earlier in this chapter. Ogden described permitting a patient to keep her own frame for a while by acquiescing to "Ms. Y's wish" to meet on a "one time only" basis for about two months before she asked to meet regularly. They went on to slowly increase the frequency of the analysis to four-sessions per week.

An unusual acting out on the part of a former patient of mine might have led to an angry rejection from some analysts. In the building in which my office is situated, the patient leased space almost directly across the hallway to mine. Then a few weeks later, she requested a consultation. Though she had undertaken a "slice" of analysis several years earlier, she wanted to return to work on unfinished business, a central part of which was the persistance of some transference feelings which had not been apparent in our earlier work. At the beginning of my career, I might have felt suffocated by the physical proximity of our offices during the ensuring period of highly emotional exploration of how much I resembled her mother. On the contrary, it seemed to me to be a wonderful opportunity to elaborate with me abandoned aspects of her identificatory project as a young woman, caught between a passionate, overbearing, mother figure who seemed to discourage access to a retiring father figure, a dilemma which had found symptomatic expression in the straddling of two careers of equal symbolic significance all her adult life. Aulagnier's conviction that an identificatory position is always part of sexual desire made it important that I not deprive the patient of the opportunity to treat the divide within her. In any case, as many authors previously cited (such as Chiantaretto, Gill, Kite, Lipton, Laplanche) have pointed out, not only are patients inescapably influenced by the personality of the analyst, it is our responsibility to become aware of unintended effects of our personality, behaviour, and appearance on patients which leak "enigmatic messages" into the frame. By inadvertently reminding this woman of her mother, I was conveying enigmatic messages which needed to be taken into account, though only when she was on my couch where the identificatory offer held sway. And so we continued: as carefully circumspect same floor neighbours if we passed in the hallway, and as analyst–patient once she passed the door of my office.

Notes

1 I borrow the phrase "psychic posture" from Marie Desrosiers (2019). The term "psychic posture" conveys some muscular tension to hold the body in a certain way, a more felicitous comparison for the internal effort inherent in the analytic offer than the more passive sounding and static image of "psychic position".

2 All translations from the original French are by the author.
3 The "framework" of Dufresne's hospital-based seminar did not allow for proper postponement.
4 I recently heard Sophie de Mijolla-Mellor, who knew Aulagnier and has studied her work, share similar stories of the alienating impact of some Lacanian practices revealed in second analyses with her (Conference at the annual colloquium of the *Société psychanalytique de Montréal*, April 27, 2024).
5 Oral communication from Lise Monette. This idea echos the thoughts of other authors referred to in Chapter 3.

References

Aguayo, J. 2014. Bion's Notes on Memory and Desire – Its Initial Clinical Reception in the United States: A Note on Archival Material. *International Journal of Psychoanalysis* 95:889–910.

Aisenstein, M. 1998. La deuxième rencontre. *Revue française de psychanalyse* 62:31–40.

Aulagnier, P. 1967. La spécificité d'une demande ou la première séance. *Interprétation* 1:3–21.

Aulagnier, P. 1968. Demande et identification. In *Un interprète en quête de sens*, 161–198. Paris: Ramsay.

Aulagnier, P. 1984. *L'Apprenti historien et le maître-sorcier. Du discours identifiant au discours délirant.* Paris: PUF.

Aulagnier, P. 1989. Se construire un passé (Building a past for oneself). *Adolescence* 33(4):713–740. 2015. https://doi.org/10.3917/ado.094.0713

Aulagnier, P. 2009. *Les destins du plaisir: aliénation-amour-passion (The destinies of pleasure: alienation, love, and passion).* Paris: PUF. 1979. Third edition.

Birksted - Breen, D. 2009.'Reverberation Time', Dreaming and the Capacity to Dream. *International Journal of Psychoanalysis*, 90(1):35–51.

Bion, W. R. 1967. Notes on Memory & Desire. *Psychoanalytic Forum* 2(3):272–273, 279–280.

Bleger, J. 1967. Psychoanalysis of the psychoanalytic setting. In *Symbiosis and Ambiguity. A Psychoanalytic Study*, edited by J. Churcher & L. Bleger, New York: Routledge, 2013, pp. 233–242.

Chiantaretto, J.-F. 2018. Cadre interne, transfert et contre-transfert. *Filigrane* 27:91–100.

Desrosiers, M. 2019. La théorie. Conference delivered at a scientific meeting of the Société psychanalytique de Montréal, January 17, 2019.

Donnet, J.-L. 2001. From the Fundamental Rule to the Analysing Situation, Trans A. Weller. *International Journal of Psychoanalysis* 82:129–140.

Dufresne, R. 1994. Le premier entretien analytique: Des indications à l'écoute du désir d'analyse. In *Le Premier Entretien et L'écoute Psychanalytique*, edited by B. Tanguay, 86–109. Westport, Connecticut: Editions Méridien.

Evans, D. 1996. *An Introductory Dictionary of Lacanian Psychoanalysis.* London and New York: Routledge.

Fine, S. 2024. Lightning fast: Testing the limits of muscle memory with lessons from a word-class skating coach. *The Globe and Mail*, April 16, 2024 p A1 and A8-A9.

Freud, S. 1908. Creative Writers and Day-Dreaming. *Standard Edition* 9:141–153.

Freud, S. 1909. Notes upon a Case of Obsessional Neurosis. *Standard Edition* 10:155–257.

Gill, M. M. 1984a. Psychoanalysis and Psychotherapy: A Revision. *International Review of Psychoanalysis* 11:161–179.

Green, A. 1975. The Analyst, Symbolization and Absence in the Analytic Setting (On Changes in Analytic Practice and Analytic Experience)—In Memory of D. W. Winnicott. *International Journal of Psychoanalysis* 56:1–22.

Kite, J. V. 2016. The Fundamental Ethical Ambiguity of the Analyst as Person. *Journal of the American Psychoanalytic Association* 64:1153–1171.

Lipton, S. D. 1977a. The Advantages of Freud's Technique as Shown in his Analysis of the Rat Man. *International Journal of Psychoanalysis* 58:255–273.

Lipton, S. D. 1977b. Clinical Observations on Resistance to the Transference. *International Journal of Psychoanalysis* 58:463–472.

Manzano, J., Palacio-Espasa, F., & Abella, A. 2016. *Précis de technique psychanalytique avec son application à la psychothérapie*. Collection: Le fil rouge. Paris: Presses Universitaires de France.

Masson, J. M. 1985. *The Complete Letters of Sigmund Freud to Wilhelm Fliess 1887–1904*. Cambridge: Massachusetts: Belknap Press.

Microdot. Wikipedia, consulted December 19, 2024. https://en.wikipedia.org/wiki/Microdot

Nordmo, M., Monsen, J. T., Høglend, P. A., & Solbakken, O. A. 2021. Investigating the Dose-Response Effect in Open-Ended Psychotherapy. *Psychotherapy Research* 31(7):859–869. https://doi.org/10.1080/10503307.2020.1861359

Ogden, T. H. 2004. An Introduction to the Reading of Bion. *International Journal of Psychoanalysis* 85:285–300.

Ogden, T. 2018. How I Talk With My Patients. *The Psychoanalytic Quarterly* LXXXVII:399–413. http://dx.doi.org/10.1080/00332828.2018.1495513

Reith, B. Møller, M. Boots, J. Crick, P. Gibeault, A. Jaffè, R. Lagerlöf, S. & Vermote, R. 2018. *Beginning Analysis: On the Process of Initiating Psychoanalysis*. London & New York: Routledge.

Ridel, L. 2004. Les temps du projet (The Time of a Project). *Topique* 86:87–95.

Rothstein, A. 1994. A Perspective on Doing a Consultation and Making the Recommendation of Analysis to a Prospective Analysand. *Psychoanalytic Quarterly* 63:680–695.

Rothstein, A. 1995. Psychoanalytic Technique and the Creation of Analysands: On Beginning Analysis with Patients Who Are Reluctant to Pay the Analyst's Fee. *Psychoanalytic Quarterly* 64:306–325.

Rothstein, A. 2002. Reflections on Creative Aspects of Psychoanalytic Diagnosing. *Psychoanalytic Quarterly* 71:301–326.

Rothstein, A. 2006. Reflections on the Concept "Analyzability". *Psychoanalytic Review* 93:827–833.

Rothstein, A. 2010. Psychoanalytic Technique and the Creation of Analytic Patients: An Addendum. *Psychoanalytic Quarterly* 79:785–794.

Roudinesco, E. 1990. *Jacques Lacan & Co: A History of Psychoanalysis in France, 1925-1985*, trans. J. Mehlman. Chicago: University of Chicago Press.

The Internal Setting: New Contributions" to a joint meeting of the Argentinian and the Paris Psychoanalytical Societies in 2002.

Winnicott, D. W. 1969. The use of an object. *International Journal of Psychoanalysis* 50:711–716.

Chapter 5

The shared suffering of the missed session

Why the missed session needs to exist

Strachey made a remark in his 1934 article on the nature of therapeutic action in psychoanalysis (1969/1934) which remains so incisive and challenging that it could have been included in every chapter of this monograph. Despite its length, it is worth quoting in full since it is often relevant to the difficulties psychoanalysts at all stages in their careers have in making full interpretive use of challenges to the framework[1]:

> Mrs Klein has suggested to me that there must be some quite special internal difficulty to be overcome by the analyst in giving interpretations. And this, I am sure, applies particularly to the giving of mutative interpretations. This is shown in their avoidance by psychotherapists of non-analytic schools; but many psychoanalysts will be aware of traces of the same tendency in themselves. It may be rationalized into the difficulty of deciding whether or not the particular moment has come for making an interpretation. But behind this there is sometimes a lurking difficulty in the actual giving of the interpretation, for there seems to be a constant temptation for the analyst to do something else instead. He may ask questions, or he may give reassurances or advice or discourses upon theory, or he may give interpretations—but interpretations that are not mutative, extra-transference interpretations, interpretations that are non-immediate, or ambiguous, or inexact—or he may give two or more alternative interpretations simultaneously, or he may give interpretations and at the same time show his own skepticism about them. All of this strongly suggests that the giving of a mutative interpretation is a crucial act for the analyst as well as for the patient, and that he is exposing himself to some great danger in doing so. And this in turn will become intelligible when we reflect that at the moment of interpretation the analyst is in fact deliberately evoking a quantity of the patient's id-energy while it is alive and actual and unambiguous and aimed directly at himself. Such a moment must above all others put to the test his relations with his own unconscious impulses.

(289–290)

DOI: 10.4324/9781003527459-6

How could a surgeon plunge a scalpel into the abdomen of a patient if he or she were not persuaded that it will ultimately improve that person's quality of life? A clearly integrated conceptualization of the role of the missed session in psychoanalytic work bolsters the analyst's capacity to titrate the patient's discomfort without betraying either the need to make a living or the framework's resilience in tracking unconscious meaning. The suffering experienced by the dyad concerning missed sessions is so widespread it would seem that Mrs Klein's intuition that "there must be some quite special internal difficulty to be overcome by the analyst" is applicable to this aspect of practice. The theoretical and clinical interest of protocols for dealing with missed sessions is intimately related to what French authors have designated as the "gesture of payment". By this term, they mean a gesture, a symbol, or a transaction which signifies the mutual dependence of patient and analyst, one needing help with an unconscious sabotage of self and the other needing remuneration to maintain a specialized, non-biased, listening. I started my career in the heady days of community psychiatry when multi-disciplinary teams operated out of a building "embedded" – as they say nowadays – in the community served. It was in this context that I began my psychoanalytic training. I was intrigued by the comparison between my rather classic personal psychoanalytic experience on the couch and the institutional framework of psychotherapy I was offering to patients. Though I was learning to think as an analyst, my status as salaried government employee eliminated the need for patients to pay me. According to Hilda Doolittle's journal of her analysis in 1934 with Freud (Lohser & Newton, 1996), he inferred reference to third-party payment in a dream in which Doolittle found herself riding a two-headed horse. Freud gathered that a friend's paying for the analysis had contributed to her resistance.

The need to distinguish theoretically between the "material act of payment" and the "fantacized payment" has been stressed by some analysts. Regardless of the patient's actual paying or not, they believe that it is essential to analyse the patient's personal fantasies, conscious and unconscious, about the "circulation of money" in the treatment. Zimeray (1985, 121) puts it this way:

> What counts in fact is not money as such, paid or not paid: it is the fantasized money with the possibility of placing these fantasies in the workable analytic field that counts. Because as long as money is not fantasized, whether actually paid or not, we are essentially in the same boat.

It is patently not a question of doubting that people who do not pay for their psychoanalysis or psychoanalytic therapy miss out on the benefits of noticing the impact of the unconscious on their lives, but rather as Zimeray points out, it can be easy to overlook the conflictual aspects of money exchanges if an effort is not made to discern the fantasies which might accrue to them, a point also made by several older generation analysts (Eissler, 1974; Halpert, 1986; Lorand & Console, 1958). I began wondering as a hospital employee offering psychoanalytic psychotherapy to patients who were randomly assigned to me what the non-representation of money circulation and the absence of a gesture of payment might mean in this context?

Encouraged by the effort of theorization referred to above by French analysts working in state-sponsored psychoanalytic clinics in Paris (cf. Aisenstein, 1986; Cahn, 1985), I embarked on an experiment which as far as I know, has remained unique. It was inspired by Françoise Dolto's introduction of symbolic payments in her work with young children who were not paying for their treatment. She felt that it ethically necessary for children to be able to express their agreement with seeing her. In an interview published in 2008, she explained: "It was on account of the negative transference that I understood the role of the child's symbolic pay-ment... [She would tell children] 'you are quite free not to want to come and talk to me, if your parents bring you to me... but I will never receive you if you don't ask to come to me ... bring me a sign that you want to talk to me'. [T]his is very important, because if a child brings a symbolic payment, whether it is a stone, a small piece of paper, or a fake stamp (...) I have a system that is symbolic" (quoted in Guedes, 2024, 11).

Over an approximate two-year period, I introduced the idea of "symbolic mark-ers" to every new psychotherapy patient referred to me as salaried psychologist in an out-patient hospital setting. Technical specifics can be found in a subsequent publication (Furlong, 1998). The critical feedback of colleagues disabused me of thinking of the tokens my patients used as legitimate equivalents for money. However, if one lets go of the pretension of substituting for money in the sense of a fixed exchange value, a symbolic marker can nevertheless serve a valuable representational function. For a symbolic marker to be effective, it must be both symbolic and real, i.e., real in the sense that it can be lacking (such as forgotten at home) and hence can confront the psyche with an otherness. Rereading my paper twenty-five years later, I still find the experiment enhanced my psychoanalytically oriented listening at the time in several ways: by introducing a gesture of exchange, the symbolic token became a conduit for payment-related associations; it acted to encourage mental representation of the hidden third party; and it provided a *ready-made transference instrument* in a setting where low frequency, the anonymity of the institutional service offering, and lack of psychological mindedness usually preclude transference associations. It also stood as a marker for the patient's un-conscious place in the therapy, whether present or absent. "In particular", I wrote, "by its restituting presence, the symbolic marker [could] fundamentally alter in the après-coup the psychological meaning of the patient's *missed sessions*" (emphasis added, op. cit., 94).

With the more intrapsychically compromised patients who can be part of psy-chiatric outpatient populations, "we are often under the impression of a *mental disappearance* on their part that brings our work to a standstill" (op. cit., 92). The technique of symbolic markers, along with an interpretative analysis of their manipulation, allowed for a kind of playfulness with these patients, encouraging them to recognize and undo their psychic evacuations. In one session, the pa-tient described in the paper brought three buttons, one for the current session, one for a session missed the week before, and one to make up for having forgotten to bring one the session before that. It was probably not a coincidence that it was also the first time he reported at dream, a dramatic one, which allowed open discussion of his fusional, death-tinged, impulses toward the women in his life. The dream had occurred *during his absence from his therapy.* Is it not possible that the tokens, by symbolically holding the framework stable despite several interruptions and death anxieties, allowed more psychic elaboration to occur *in absentia?* The framework held steady in the structural sense, because the *gaps* were not filled by supportive elements, and thus afforded the patient an opportunity to generate his own fantasy production, a dream, forcefully bringing home the psychological link between his wife and his mother. For this patient, an observation by Saucier and Bossé was particularly apt: "We have been struck throughout our reflection upon the analytic situation by the very tight link that exists between the payment gesture and the incest interdiction" (1990, 27). It was extremely difficult for this man to consent to any physical or mental separation from his wife.

There is an example in Leopoldo Bleger (2022) of a hidden "bastion" in the lack of payment associated with outpatient psychiatric settings. The bastion, as we referenced it in Chapter 2, is the term used by the Barangers (Baranger, Baranger, & Mom 1983) to describe an intimate and regressive part of the self, concealed from view in the clinical arrangement. When Bleger stopped working in the hospital, one of his patients requested pursuing in private practice but then revealed for the first time that this change of setting was blocked by a strong conviction the patient was embarrassed to reveal. Though he knew how strange it sounded, "to his mind, it was society's responsibility to provide him with free psychotherapy" (Bleger 2022, 22). In a flood of new associations, the whole theme of gratuity and money was linked to the figure of his father, such that the psychotherapy itself up until then had been experienced as a hidden act of stealing, identified with the father's admonition to make money "no matter how". As L. Bleger concluded, referring to his own father's (José Bleger) work, this vignette "points to aspects which can easily remain hidden to the analyst, silently embedded in the 'reality' of the setting" (22).

Many analysts would concur with viewing payment for psychoanalytic services as a symbolically separating act. For Aulagnier, the analyst's request to be paid "allows the patient to recognize that analysis is not something that has been given to him, nor something he has to put up with, but actually the object of an acknowledged wish on his part" (quoted by de Mijolla-Mellor, 1998, 200). In Chapter 3, we found Assoun's (2001) distinction between "consent" and "assent" felicitous with respect to acceptance of a framework. Whereas "consent" can mean expressing agreement with something or simply accepting that something occurs, "assent", he argued, is the outcome of a struggle with loss. A distressing component of payment for missed sessions is precisely the implicit confrontation with loss. All the same, paradoxically, payment *restores the missed session, militating against forgetfulness by either member of the analytic dyad.* I (Furlong, 1992) have compared the "rule of indenture" (Eissler, 1974) whereby the patient pays regardless of his reason for not coming to a dressmaker's dummy which imaginatively gives substance to the time and related psychic space of the absent patient. I went on to write:

> Just as the traditional benevolent neutrality of the analyst restrains him or her from 'plugging holes' in the patient's anguish, just as he or she eschews being supportive in order not to bring about premature closure of the ambiguity of the patient's transferential appeal to him, just as Lacan viewed the ego as an 'orthopedic' and defensive function, so too can the missed session be 'repaired' by a well-meaning 'rational' therapist, carefully peeling off the conflicts into neat layers of reality and resistance, leaving nothing left over, nothing 'lacking'. Patching the 'blank' left by the missed session prevents unconscious derivatives from emerging. The analysand is present most when he is 'absent', i.e. when he is missing from his unconscious train of thought in the form of a lapse or '*acte manqué*'. The verbal slip is something 'missing'. Even the symptom is a 'blank', a mystery to the subject, when it is not rationalized by the ego.
>
> (1992, 708)

The same article of Leopoldo Bleger mentioned above contains an eloquent instance of the *patient* trying to restore a session cancelled *by him* by overpaying. Bleger interpreted the error as demonstrating that the "missed session existed despite the cancellation. Or rather, [the patient] was trying to bring it into existence to help dissipate the turmoil caused by the disruption" (32).

I also feel that therapists put themselves in an awkward position when – racked with guilt about receiving remuneration without services rendered – they try to legislate what is an "adequate" reason for missing a session from a "neurotic" one. While most analysts will concede some flexibility in special circumstances, they do not necessarily suppress the indenture rule as reference point, knowing that even "realistic" motives for absence (illness, career, parenthood, etc.) nevertheless can invite an examination of the possible "contamination" of the real event by the patients' conscious or unconscious fantasies about the wishes of the analyst towards them. At these moments, the missed session homes in on a particularly excruciating aspect of transference – that of the unconsciously intuited and/or projected desire of the Other, as well as upon an explicit intrusion of the therapist's needs into the therapeutic arena. The latter aspect often engenders a complementary anguish on the part of the analyst or psychotherapist: they cannot bear to ask for payment of missed sessions because of their need to protect themselves from any trace of there being anything *missing* in their relationship with the patient.

Here is an example of a missed session kerfuffle. The clinician was speaking of her irritation with a patient who recently challenged her about an imminent summer vacation, intimating that the therapist was allowing herself absenteeism privileges denied to the patient under their "contract". It turned out that it was true that the patient had not been informed of these plans at the beginning of their work together, an oversight which the clinician blamed in part on the patient's stop-and-go strategy, attending psychotherapy in intermittent blocks allowed for by an insurance plan. Besides, fumed the therapist, everyone takes a summer vacation and the patient should have expected as much! The previous day the patient had cancelled because of a flight delay and here we were in the last few days before the therapist's own departure. The psychotherapist was exasperated and anxious: why had the patient not asked for a replacement time? "She always wants a place but then she does not take it!" The patient had texted to inform her of the inability to attend the session and to inquire what their next appointment would be after the therapist's holidays. In a return text message, the therapist reminded her of their missed session protocol and that they had already scheduled an appointment upon the therapist's return. Recounting the sequence to me, the therapist shared an additional annoyance that the patient had not properly paid her the previous month. In going over elements of the patient's history, we realized together how painful the thematic of "place" was, since the patient had been left with her maternal grandmother for the first decade of her life before returning to live with an overwhelmed and unstable parental couple. No one in the family liked to hear any complaints.

In this instance of missed session, as proposed earlier, it is clarifying to think in terms of a double causality: there is the causality of the airplane snafu and there is the causality of a transference wish. Since the two are intertwined, it can be a very delicate maneuver to tease them apart for separate appreciation. This work cannot be done at a distance, such as in a text or an email. Even a phone conversation might be inadequate. *The "operation of elaboration" needs to be inhabited and handled with kid gloves.* Detective stories have taught us the crucial prohibition against disturbing the scene of a crime before the investigation has been completed. The missed session is similar; it is important not to disturb the "scene of the symptom" until the dyad can pore over it together. Hence the importance of learning to wait before reacting, especially when there is no objective emergency, since the reaction can so easily muddle the "scene" by introducing new elements of anxiety, reproach, or a call to order. The therapist could have simply replied "So sorry to hear you had to miss your appointment. Given that I will be leaving soon on vacation, shall we try to find another time to see each other this week?" Under the circumstances, the clinician might even have wanted to give the patient a "pass" and only charge once. This slight deviation from protocol could be justified as an optimal investment in a treatment with a patient who has reason to replay abandonment, who needs a therapist to be there to be complained about, and who may need to flush out the therapist's commitment to staying engaged.

The literature contains many instances of similar ambiguous scenarios activated at moments of imminent separation, requiring the therapist to find a way to keep the analytic offer alive, and to extend a symbolic hand over the gap created by the missed session. In another text to her therapist (again it was unfortunate that the communication was occurring over a distance instead of in the consulting room together), the patient cast light on a "misunderstanding" which she felt had happened on two levels. For her the "force majeure" which prevented her from attending the session was not part of their agreement since it was in no way "similar to a forgetfulness". The patient had spontaneously distinguished between two causalities. In her mind, she had consented to assuming payment when *she was responsible* for her absence, but not when *she was the victim* of the "irresistible force" of a technology breakdown in an airport. The mixup on the other level, according to the patient, was that she had assumed that there was no time available before the holiday break because the therapist had not immediately offered a makeup session when she had learnt of the patient's inability to attend the session. Remember the psychotherapist had been exasperated with the patient for not having asked about a replacement time. The breakdown in communication needed to be explored, as both partners seemed to be waiting for the other to take the initiative.

Though my 1998 reflections on the missed session were written long ago, a section devoted to "Destiny and Contingency in the Missed Session" still seems relevant today. When patients are prevented from attending because of external circumstances, an occasion may be created for associations to the role of "fate" in their lives. I was marked, at the time, by Lacan's (1954–1955) assertion that identity is fundamentally an "intersection of signifiers" since none of us has a choice in our place of birth, our body, our sex, our maternal language, our parents, our culture, our alienation in the desire of others, or in our inevitable death. On one level, this assessment is deeply disturbing, making us wish to rebel against the "hard necessity" Freud (1913) wrote about in his astonishing analysis of the theme of three caskets where the "choice" of a beautiful woman denies the grip of the third of the three mythical "Fates", Atropos, the inexorable. Yet, at the same time, Lacan's position offers an unexpected possibility of evolution. This is how I expressed it:

> Lacan's work allows an ontological distinction to be derived between a diagnosis, which makes a declaration about *who* and an interpretation, which makes a declaration about *where*. For instance, a diagnosis of depression attributes a certain substance of being to the patient, whereas an interpretation such as 'Your depression is your way of ensuring that you do not humiliate your father by surpassing him' is a statement about that person's locus in the oedipal triangle. An interpretation which can make sense of a given psychological state of being *as a locus*, as a place, in terms of the early significant others, has the liberating effect of transforming a static state, a specific content, into a form, a symbolic function. The latter is not necessarily wedded to any particular content and permits certain permutations and combinations, by virtue of its formal characteristics. A therapeutic goal for the patient thereby can become to disentangle himself from the arbitrary *who* he is alienated in, to assume a more flexible *where* in terms of symbolic function.

When a session is missed because of circumstances beyond the patient's control (and therefore impossible to interpret as a resistance to the treatment), an excellent opportunity presents itself for reflection upon the role of contingency in that individual's history. This contingency can be explored at three levels. First, there is the recognition and acceptance of one's limits, the limit to what gratification to expect from others as well as the limit to what gratification one can offer another. Secondly, there is the anguish of facing the contingency, the arbitrariness of one's life and identity (e.g. ordinal position in the family, ethnic or linguistic community, accidents of biology and environment). Lastly, there is the question of the recognition and acceptance in principle of the separation of contingency between two interconnected lives, such that the success, failure, disease, handicap, or talent of the one does not ricochet unfavourably upon the other.

(1998, 712)

My supervisee's patient did not seem aware that she was assuming (in an inchoate fashion) that her retention at the airport required a parallel "lack" without compensation in the therapist's schedule. Granted these are not elaborations easily grasped in a once-a-week setting, and moreover, it might call upon a good deal of experience to be able to handle the multiple narcissistic precipices involved in talking about it. Yet no individual experiences them as "abstract" whenever "fate" seems to deal a bad hand (notice how the very notion of fate "personifies" a causality beyond our reach or ken). Whatever the protocol for missed sessions offered by the analyst or psychotherapist, Dufresne's advice (1994) should act as essential beacon: "The analytic frame cannot be imposed. It has no inherent efficacy. It must be registered in a complementarity of desires which has previously been agreed upon and fundamentally wished for by the analysand... [As such the] framework is inconceivable unless reciprocally acceptable" (88). The example just shared shows how intersubjectively complex these moments in a psychoanalytically oriented treatment can be, prompting the therapist to act out in rapid tit for tat, instead of offering noncommittal containment until the dyad has the time to examine the situation together. There is a world of difference between technical rigidity and thoughtful resolve. It is better to suspend judgement until the dyad has the time to reflect; this negative capability (the capacity to tolerate not knowing for a time) is easier to preserve if one is persuaded of the rewards of an unhurried attention to particulars.

In the last chapter, I played with the images of the TV character of Detective Colombo and the WWII spy tool of the microdot as analogies to thinking about psychoanalytic work as always gaining when it is able to reach *thicker descriptions* of patients' lives. The notion of "thick description" was developed by the American cultural anthropologist, Clifford Geertz, whose conception of the aim of anthropology was "the enlargement of the universe of human discourse" (1973, 316). There is an overlap, I believe, with the goal of psychoanalysis, though in our case, we are specifically hoping to return and expand meanings to patients' lives *which have been lost* through repression or because unable to find other shareable representation. Geertz' account of the anthropologist's work is very Colombo-like in its vision of the intertwining of studied obtuseness and method:

> Although one starts any effort at thick description, beyond the obvious and superficial, from a state of general bewilderment as to what the devil is going on-trying to find one's feet-one does not start (or ought not) intellectually emptyhanded. Theoretical ideas are not created wholly anew in each study.
>
> (321)

Consistent with my thinking about the missed session is Erna Furman's classic 1982 article in which she wrote movingly about the need for mothers "to be there to be left". The same is frequently true of the psychoanalytically oriented psychotherapist. Very often, inexperienced psychotherapists are under the impression that they must "do something" in situations of ambiguity, not having acquired the crucial capacity to wait. Negative capability is part of the analytic frame of mind and internal reserve, since it encourages the therapist to tolerate uncertainty. Beginning therapists often call patients who have not turned up to their sessions, sometimes even before the session time is over. One therapist practically chastised a patient for missing an hour scheduled at the end of the therapist's workday. In an anxious call to the patient, halfway through his scheduled time, the therapist intimated that he had made her wait fruitlessly at the end of a long working day when she might have been free to go home early. Yet, if one is not open to tolerating some anxiety, some wasted hours and uncertain income, one may not have chosen the right profession. In order for a private psychoanalytically oriented practice to flourish over time, the therapist's long term plan is crucial, and should consider that our offer of listening will always encounter ambivalence. The steadiness of the framework is obviously easier to maintain if the therapist is not juggling more than one work site. *The beauty of Winnicott's concept of the "use of the object" is in helping the therapist twig to the usefulness of tolerating an optimal abuse, disuse, discarding, and retrieval of sessions by patients. Thus, the importance of creating a setting which will not inflict too much pain on the therapist* in the form of overly low fees, neglected payment, scheduling too many hours, frequently switching hours in response to patients' requests, feeling squeezed between office and home duties, etc. Otherwise, patients risk being resented for their neuroses.

Before moving to the next section, let me briefly return to the general protocol for initial interviews shared in Chapter 1 where I related my handling of bills and receipts because I see it as derivative of my understanding of the developmental role of optimal absence and negative capability. *I do not present patients with a written invoice and I do not immediately issue a receipt.* Among my English-speaking colleagues, the tradition of presenting a monthly bill to patients, either by hand or in the mail, is so ensconced that they do not seem to realize how much it deprives them of fertile transferential and counter-transferential information. In my experience, deprived of a tangible piece of paper with a clearly written sum on it to rein in their unconscious dynamics, patients are as liable to overpay as to underpay. And of course, the analyst can also make mistakes which can be equally revelatory. The absence of a tangible bill increases the malleability of the payment gesture; the tangible bill forcloses this expressivity. Even experienced clinicians fudge these matters as another anecdote illustrates. In the course of a supervisory hour, the supervisee casually noted that the mother of a patient had paid twice in the past month. This fact was quickly passed over until the supervisor expressed curiosity about what had been the original financial arrangement of the frame-work. Discussion revealed that the supervisee's own analyst confessed to billing for missed appointments but not bringing them up if patients did not include them in their payments. Another supervisor, equally senior, had the routine (and I have seen this occur in other cases) of offering a receipt before receiving payment as an unspoken reminder that the money was due! The inhibition about acknowledg-ing money matters as potentially potent clinical material was being handed down from one generation of psychoanalysts to another. This inhibition risks preventing aspects of the life of patients from existing as Ogden (1996) has put it "as 'analytic objects', i.e., as events that carried meaning that could be experienced, noticed, considered, and thought about in the context of the network of meanings that were being elaborated" (1134).

Who is responsible for the frame?

The comparison made by Freud between an ideally dispassionate posture on the part of the analyst towards his or her patients and the clinical distance cultivated by the surgeon in the operating room is well known, though it has sometimes been interpreted critically as advocating for an overly "distant" attitude. On the contrary, I believe the metaphor remains useful, particularly if it is further elabo-rated to bring out both the similarities and the differences of the two "fields of operation". Both the surgeon and the psychoanalyst are ultimately responsible for the patient's welfare in the operating and consulting rooms, a responsibil-ity which requires the assumption of authority over the conditions of work. But whereas we have the caricature of the surgeon yelling at para-medical staff when their support is substandard, the psychoanalyst is alone in managing the optimal conditions for psychoanalytic treatment. Another difference is that the patient is anesthetized during an operation, either locally or under a general anesthetic, such that patients do not feel the pain being inflicted upon them until afterwards. After the completion of my husband's complete knee replacement, his surgeon called to say that the operation had gone well, that my husband's bones were strong, and that "he will hate me in a couple of days when the anesthetic I in-stalled in the wound peters out". And this was indeed the case: the catheter deliv-ering a strong analgesic directly into the incision was removed forty-eight hours later and the patient began a prescription of a two-week supply of Dilaudid to be administered orally every four hours. By the tenth day of counting the minutes to his next dose and finding it hard to imagine how he was going to continue without the precious drug, my husband put in a desperate call to the surgeon: Would the latter extend the length of the prescription? The answer was no. Fortunately for my husband, the surgeon's clinical distance was based on years of his own direct experience and the research of others. Soon afterwards, the patient's medical situation turned a corner: he no longer clamoured for relief and was able to accomplish in manageable discomfort the necessary physical rehabilitation of the new knee.

This anecdote brings out a significant divide between the surgeon and the psychoanalyst since the latter is directly exposed to the patient's pain, in real time, during their meetings together whenever the psychoanalyst "administers" beneficial interpretations (however tactful and well-timed) which always contain a minimal "violence" to the integrity of the patient's current defensive equilibrium. The surgeon's framework allows for a safe removal from the direct scene of the pain induced by his or her curing intervention, greatly reducing the training in countertransference tolerance and self-analysis required in surgical specialties. Another substantial divergence, mentioned earlier in this monograph, between our discipline and theirs is that medical students accompany senior physicians in their rounds and gown up to stand at the back of the operating theatre to watch operations unfold. The senior surgeon stands beside the surgical resident as the latter practices various procedures. None of this is possible in our field. Our "operating procedure" which relies on the unfettered speech of patients in confidential one-on-one relationships calls for an unusual indirect learning process. The therapist learns through the speech of others in clinical presentations, through the voices to be found in psychoanalytic literature, and through the reflected echoes in supervision of the transmission of unconscious effects in his or her speech.

Co-signed written contracts?

We have space here to address the conflicts which can occur between psychoanalysts and their local cultural/professional environment by relating in some detail a telling divergence in ethical viewpoints about the therapeutic setting which happened in my professional community of the province of Quebec, Canada. Most psychoanalysts begin their careers in a core discipline, medical or paramedical.[2] Psychoanalysis is not considered a separate mental health discipline, and since generally speaking practicing analysts do not wish to change that extra-territorial status, it means that the majority remain subject to the deontological codes of their original disciplines, even if they no longer identify with these disciplines. Though deontological obligations vary across the jurisdictions of International Psychoanalytical Association (IPA) members, most analysts live under the tension of juggling a psychoanalytic ethical sensibility with the expectations of their core regulatory bodies.

So, even if the details are not the same for all regions of the IPA, readers are likely to find instructive the examination of one instance of this kind of strain. The example will illustrate the importance for analysts of preparing themselves for conflicts of this kind, of deepening their conceptualization of the function of the frame, and of finding appropriate "translations" of their point of view into contemporary regulatory language for use in professional inspections and in other third-party dealings. We will return to these ideas in Chapter 6 when the topic of confidentiality will be treated separately.

The reference point in the present author's case was the Quebec Order of Psychologists (the Ordre des psychologues du Québec, OPQ), mandated to ensure the quality of psychological services offered across the province. Psychologists are licensed to practice by this body and are subject to professional inspections by it on a regular basis. The subsection of the Order handling complaints about members is called the "Syndic" which issues bulletins three times a year in the Order's official magazine to explain guidelines on various aspects of professional practice. These bulletins are considered official policy; no ordinary member is allowed to criticize them within the pages of the magazine. As of 2008, all psychologists, regardless of theoretical orientation, were required to establish a written co-signed contract for any "particular financial agreements" with patients. The main concern from the Order's point of view was the potential for abuse in requiring patients to pay for missed sessions to receive psychological services. In 2011, the Syndic (Poulin, 2011) reminded members of this requirement and added that "it is generally agreed that best practice is to have each service paid for as soon as it is over, notably at the end of a psychotherapy session" (14). Poulin specifically counselled against monthly payments because "one must be conscious of the fact that a failure to pay can have consequences since the client risks not being able to complete his course of treatment if his financial situation deteriorates" (14). Occasionally, it was suggested, psychologists might like to bill ahead of time to protect themselves from a "debt" if a session is cancelled. In 2022, the Syndic (Houde, 2022) issued a further reminder to members of this obligation and set out the Order's justification for it. The main argument for a written, co-signed, contract was to avoid any "ambiguity" since usually professionals are not allowed to bill for services which have not been received. If the psychologist does indeed charge, the payment can only be considered as an administration fee which third party payors will not reimburse. Houde gave five advantages to written contracts:

- They protect against the "distraction" of the patient and the "forgetfulness" of the psychologist [presumably at the moment when the contract is explained, or when it is supposed to be explained].
- They obviate any "risk of misunderstanding".
- They permit the psychologist and her client "to concentrate on the principal objectives of the consultation rather than dealing with the resolution of a misunderstanding".

- They diminish the likelihood that the client "will wonder what was the policy agreed upon [in the initial sessions] when the first instance of cancellation occurs".

Houde concludes "In summary, when the initial agreement is limpid and the client has a written copy of it, there is less chance that he will experience as abusive having to pay administrative fees and [thus] the relationship of confidence can continue" (25). Members were encouraged to personalize written co-signed informed consent templates for their practices.

Yet, – despite the claims of the Houde and Poulin – there are the multiple disadvantages to written agreements in psychotherapeutic work. A conscious, intellectual, contract cannot disentangle the analytic setup from the evolution of treatment. More to the point, rather than to be avoided at all costs, the analysis of "misunderstandings" can be a privileged terrain of the therapy. It is an illusion to expect written, co-signed, contracts to ensure free and informed consent. Not only is spelling out the patient's obligations rather condescending but the unconscious can wreak havoc with any agreement, verbal or written. Why would a psychoanalyst want to create a framework which is aimed at eliminating transference manifestations? In my experience collaborating with younger psychologists, I have noticed that the written contract often becomes an excuse for avoiding full discussion with the patient of all aspects of the frame, particularly the expectation that missed sessions be remunerated. The discussion of money matters is invariably a source of anxiety for younger clinicians, and they are often glad to hurry over this detail by passing the "contract" to the patient at the end of a session with the request to bring it back signed to the next session. Frequently, the document never becomes a topic of direct exchange by the therapeutic couple. The written contract thus can collude with a wish to "forget" these mundane details until, of course, some reality factor will bring them to the fore at a later moment in the treatment. Article 13 of the OPQ's deontological code recognizes that consent is not a one-time act: "The psychologist makes sure that consent remains free and informed *during the entire* professional relationship" (added emphasis). Written contracts, in contrast, give another message: "You have committed to this agreement; there it is written, and there is your signature. Let us no longer talk about it because it is not what is important about our work".

Mr Poulin's assertion that paying at the end of each session is the "state of the art" in our field is also questionable. In fact, it is more likely that most psychotherapists, certainly psychoanalyst psychologists, ask for monthly payments as more consonant with the long-term nature of our treatment vision. On the one hand, *if the patient is not billed and encouraged to add up what is owing at the end of each month*, errors (which can be too little or too much) or defaults in payment are regular topics of exploration in a psychoanalytic approach and are not necessarily "negative consequences". On the other hand, psychoanalysts would never consider their professional service to be "over" at the end of any appointment;

what happens in between sessions is also of interest as are the circumstances and/ or thoughts occurring to the patient when he or she misses an appointment. The service "rendered" transcends any one individual session. In fact, a *psychoanalytically oriented psychotherapy that has not had to treat the question of an "absence" in the clinical relationship would not be "complete"; it would be "missing" an essential dimension.*

Thankfully, after lobbying from psychoanalysts such as myself, the Order finally modified its position which now allows for simple verbal agreements if they are noted in the dossier. The Director of Practice Quality and Development (Marleau, 2020a, 2020b) published two articles on informed consent which overturned Houde and Poulin's positions. "The process of obtaining informed consent should be more significant and complex than the simple deposition of a consent form in the dossier" (2020a). Now the contribution of different theoretical models has been recognized as certainly entailing "variations in the way interviews are conducted, in the taking of notes, of appreciating what is important for the client, in the way of explaining proposed services, and in treatment arrangements (for example, the policy of payment and of cancellation)". *However*, if the psychologist wishes to "*insist* on receiving administrative fees for a missed rendezvous, a written agreement to that effect, signed by the patient, must exist" (added emphasis). The Order was not "prescribing any specific form" because the goal of the Order is to have members "reach a proper comprehension of the scope (la portée) and purpose (la finalité) of the ethical and regulatory challenges (enjeux) inherent to consent". Nevertheless, since some members were asking for more detailed guidance, the Director enclosed one template for informed consent, with the promise that the Order was going to provide more models of consent forms, "adapted to different kinds of practices" among the membership (see 2020b). The 2008a consent model for "psychotherapy" is reproduced in an appendix to this chapter. Note that of the ten suggested aspects of informed consent covered in this template, seven are not obligatory and are to be weighed in context.

This revised interpretation of informed consent by a significant regulatory body in Quebec is more compatible with a psychoanalytic approach. The remaining sticking point is the requirement of a co-signed written agreement to pay for missed sessions. This remains problematic for the reasons mentioned above. Fortunately, paying attention to the Order's use of the word "insist" in the formulation "if the psychologist wishes to "*insist* on receiving administrative fees for a missed rendezvous" gives the psychoanalytic practitioner an honest solution. The French term in the Deontological Code is "exiger". In English, we have the word "*Exigence*" to refer to desperate or urgent situations. To understand the pressing importance of *exigence*, offers Vocabulary.com, look to its Latin source, *exigentia*, "urgency", and its root, *exigere*, "to drive or demand". Exigence demands immediate action or urgent attention, on a small or large scale.

My Order's use of a verb signifying significant constraint has allowed me to recognize the ethical risk of forcing patients to bow to conditions unacceptable to them without the indignity of co-signing a document which pretends to evacuate unconscious infiltration on the part of either party. I have never "insisted" or "compelled" that a patient pay for a missed session when they disagree with the application of the "rule" I had introduced when we started. In my mind, this "rule", like the other "rule of free association" is part of the package of an *ideal way of working* together which I sincerely believe is to the benefit of both parties' engagement. As long as the patient's objections are not an attack on the whole project of an analysis or analytically minded psychotherapy, I am willing to put a particular payment in suspense mode, where it can be reviewed at a later date, if pertinent. See Chapter 3 for an example from my own practice. Consequently, I do not feel "ethically" obliged to ask for a written agreement, since I am not "insisting" on that arrangement. *The insistence is not on paying but rather on the thinking about it.* Once I refused a check sent by the partner of a troubled patient who missed several sessions before dropping out completely. I did not feel that it was the partner's duty to compensate me. I viewed the limited financial loss incurred as the reasonably expectable outcome of the gamble of trying to treat that individual. The recent modifications to our local regulatory environment has made it easier for psychoanalyst-psychologists to co-habit with psychologists of other theoretical orientations, but it would not have evolved without input from them. Even now, despite the Order's increased flexibility, I continue to witness students making use of these contracts to fudge proper discussions of "consent". They continue to be deeply marked by the *fear of being found guilty of improperly documenting consent, ending up paradoxically avoiding a measured consideration of it.*

A student started a Zoom session by announcing she had made mistakes and was ashamed. The context was a difficult one. She had seen a young parent for a single session when the private institution where she had been working for years had suddenly closed. In one week, a whole roster of psychotherapists had to find alternate quarters for their offices. In the melee, the therapist had forgotten the patient's second session, forcing her to quickly set up an alternate meeting online. She felt "discombobulated" and swore during the meeting when her cat jumped on the table and into camera view. The following week the patient cancelled. Rather than wait for him to make contact again, she sent him a bill attached to email. It was only then that she realized that she had never negotiated a proper contract with this person, prompting her to send a written consent form attached to another email. When they had met again the day before our supervision, the patient wanted to talk about "the elephant in the room: the punitive consent form". He continued: "Not only do I miss a session, but I have to pay". Bearing in mind that this man has a handicapped child, one might have had the initial impression that he felt he was losing out twice, first having to reschedule his life when plans for the daughter's care had gone awry, and then having to miss – and pay for – his psychotherapy time. And yet his complaint was made on another level: "Suddenly I felt that there is a difference between us and that you are in control... Is that even legal? What do the insurance companies think?" The therapist, ill prepared to be put on the spot, as well as uncomfortable about talking about money, babbled something about professional distance, the symbolism of money, and the need to make a living. Despite this obviously inadequate bluster, the patient shared that he felt understood by her (!) and went on to share a pertinent association regarding his relationship with a frequently absent father, how he had missed him so much, but that, at least on his birthday, the father had *sent money*. Instead of turning into a disaster, the psychotherapist's ability to stay with the affective reactions of the patient allowed her breach of the setting to open an important historical theme. Her "failure" as a "distracted" or "busy" parental substitute had brought to mind dolorous memories of unrequited desire for closeness with the patient's father.

Let us not be too critical and learn from the initially crumpled setting. Using signed "contracts" with patients gives the wrong message in psychoanalytically oriented treatment on several levels. To begin with, it is as though the patients' verbal assent were not enough; secondly, it as though patients can grasp the psychological impact of the contract for the rest of the treatment by reading about it "noir sur blanc" (black on white) as the French say, whereas we know very well that they cannot. Consent as I maintained in Chapter 3 cannot be treated cognitively; some therapeutic "experience" with us will be required before felt "assent" can be given. Trying to explain what "insight therapy" is rather like trying to teach someone how to skate by describing particular leg motions. Unbeknownst to themselves, the therapists are occupying the position of the subject-who-is-supposed to know, that is as an authority figure, even as their explanations attempt to deny that position. Rather than "explaining", the therapist can strive for a psychic space which will allow meaning to accrue to the project of psychotherapy, by showing in their listening and reflections a different level of working, which hopes to be not just *therapeutic* but *psycho-therapeutic*.

It is more useful to conceptualize the analytic position as an *offer* of an ongoing way of working together which the patient can only embrace partially at any given moment. Moreover, we know that we will "fail" to respect our part of the bargain sooner or later, just as the patient will. The hardest thing on the side of the psychotherapist is to eschew reacting tit for tat, losing the promised as-if listening of the "contract". An often repeated theme of this book is that we have learnt as psychoanalysts that framework breaches can be enormously helpful to both members of the therapeutic dyad if they can weather through the storm of their respective shame and shock to listen to each other more fully and to understand the narcissistic injuries that have arisen (spoken aloud by patients, usually, elaborated in silence within the therapists). Another lesson: email contacts with patients should – usually – be kept to a minimum, only confirming dates for appointment changes. Sending a written contract to a patient before it has even been discussed will obviously have negative consequences, and therapists should ask themselves whether they are not avoiding discussing the frame during sessions.

Moreover, expecting an unsophisticated patient to appreciate a psychoanalytically oriented way of working with symptoms in one (or even many) meetings is unrealistic.

In a recent update of informed consent in research, Bazzano, Durant, and Brantley (2021) declare that "comprehension" has become one of the significant issues in contemporary thought on the matter. They quote major reports that have found that "The manner and context in which information is conveyed is as important as the information itself" (83). Flexibility in the presentation of key information is appropriate if it "facilitates comprehension" and enhances meaningfulness (84). I encourage psychoanalysts of all stripes to bear these references in mind when they have to justify a less cognitive method of seeking informed consent in their consulting rooms than the academic ideal that tends to be promoted by their professional regulatory bodies. Bringing up the extensive literature on the gap between informed consent and what the researchers call "health literacy" not only gives psychoanalysts a common language to explain themselves to outsiders, but it also demonstrates that their concerns are not outliers.

Notes

1 There is a necessary "violence of interpretation" according to Aulagnier (2001), insofar as the meaning ascribed by a parent to a child's movements or utterances, or that ascribed by an analyst to his patient's discourse supercedes the meanings already intuited by the child or patient about themselves.
2 Psychoanalysis has been enormously enriched by the contribution of so-called "lay" analysts who have come from disciplines outside of the medial and paramedical fields. Lamentably, contemporary professionalization of therapeutic practice is gradually closing the door to these people in the name of standardization of training and quality control. Freud would not have approved of this new *Weltanschauung* nor of the market monopoly it creates.

References

Code de déontologie des psychologues, RLRQ c C-26, r 212, <https://canlii.ca/t/pmwv> consulted July 14, 2024.
Vocabulary.com. https://www.vocabulary.com/dictionary/exigence. Consulted July 15, 2024.
Aisenstein, M. 1986. D'un singulier usage du don. *Les Cahiers du Centre de Psychanalyse et de* Psychothérapie 12:21–35.
Aisenstein, M. 1998. La deuxième rencontre. *Revue française de psychanalyse* 62:31–40.
Assoun, P.-L. 2001. L'épreuve du consentement: À propos du lien fraternel. *Revue de l'enfance et de l'adolescence* 44:39–49.
Aulagnier, P. 2001. *The Violence of Interpretation: From Pictogram to Statement*. Philadelphia: Brunner-Routledge.
Baranger, M., Baranger, W., & Mom, J. 1983. Process and Non-Process in Analytic Work. *International Journal of Psychoanalysis* 64:1–15.
Bazzano, L. A., Durant, J., & Brantley, P. R. 2021. A Modern History of Informed Consent and the Role of Key Information. *Ochsner Journal* 21(1):81–85. https://doi.org/10.31486/toj.19.0105

Bleger, L. 2022. What is the setting after all? *In Psychoanalysis of the Psychoanalytic Frame Revisited: A New Look at José Bleger's Classic Work*, edited by C. Moguillansky & H.B. Levine, 21–37. New York: Taylor & Francis. Kindle Edition. https://doi.org/10.4324/9781003252252-3

Cahn, D. 1985. Les infortunes d'un destin et la gratuité dans la cure. *Les Cahiers du Centre de Psychanalyse et de Psychothérapie* 11:11–65.

Dufresne, R. 1994. Le premier entretien analytique: Des indications à l'écoute du désir d'analyse. In *Le Premier Entretien et L'écoute Psychanalytique*, edited by B. Tanguay, 86–109. Westport, Connecticut: Éditions Méridien.

Eissler, K. 1974. On Some Theoretical and Technical Problems Regarding the Payment of Fees for Psychoanalytic Treatment. *International Journal of Psychoanalysis* 1:73–101.

Freud, S. 1913. The Theme of the Three Caskets. *Standard Edition* 12:289–302.

Freud, S. 1933 [1932]. *New Introductory Lectures in Psycho-Analysis. Standard Edition* 22:7–182.

Furlong, A. 1992. Some Technical and Theoretical Considerations Regarding the Missed Session. *International Journal of Psychoanalysis* 73:701–718.

Furlong, A. 1998. The Symbolization of Absence Under Third Party Payment: Symbolic Markers with Adults. *Canadian Journal of Psychoanalysis* 6:75–98.

Furman, E. 1982. Mothers Have to Be There to Be Left. *Psychoanalytic Study of the Child* 37:15–28.

Geertz, C. 1973. Thick description: Toward an interpretative theory of culture. In *The Interpretation of Cultures: Selected Essays*. New York: Basic Books, 311–323.

Guedes, D. D. 2024. The Psychoanalytical Practice of Françoise Dolto and the Use of children's Drawings. *Revista Científica Arbitrada de la Fundación MenteClara* 9(370). https://doi.org/10.32351/rca.v9.370

Halpert, E. 1986. The meaning and effects of insurance in psychotherapy and psychoanalysis. In *The Last Taboo: Money as Symbol and Reality in Psychotherapy and Psychoanalysis*, edited by D Krueger, 169–174. New York Brunner/Mazel.

Houde, D. 2016. Les ententes financières particulières: par écrit, s'il vous plaît. *Psychologie Québec* 33, septembre.

Houde, D. 2022. Factures, Rapports d'honoraires Professionnels, Paiements et Reçus. *Psychologie Québec* 39, septembre.

Lohser, B. & Newton, P. M. 1996. *Unorthodox Freud: The View from the Couch*. New York: Guilford Press. ISBN 9781572301283.

Lorand, S., & Console, W. 1958. Therapeutic results in psycho-analytic treatment without fee. *International Journal of Psychoanalysis*.39: 59–65.

Marleau, I. 2020a. Le consentement libre et éclairé: réflexions et modèles pour les cliniciens. *Psychologie Québec* 37, mars.

Marleau, I. 2020b. Modèles de formulaires pour un consentement libre et éclairé. *Psychologie Québec* 37, septembre.

Mijolla-Mellor, D. 1998. *Penser la psychose. Une lecture de l'œuvre de Piera Aulagnier*. Dunod: Paris.

Ogden, T. 1996. The Perverse Subject of Analysis. *Journal of the American Psychoanalytic Association* 44:1121–1146.

Poulin, B. 2011. À propos des honoraires. *Psychologie Québec* 28(2):14–15.

Saucier, J. & Bossé, J. 1990. De la règle d'or à la règle d'argent (From the Golden Rule to the silver/money Rule). *Bulletin de la Société psychanalytique de Montréal* 2:19–29.

Strachey, J. 1969. The Nature of the Therapeutic Action of Psychoanalysis. *International Journal of Psychoanalysis* 50:275–292. 1934.

Zimeray, C. 1985. L'argent dans la cure: maître ou serviteur. *Les Cahiers du Centre de Psychanalyse et de Psychothérapie* 11:109–126.

Appendix:

Template of an informed consent form (Taken from page 4 of Marleau, 2020a)

PSYCHOTHERAPY SERVICES

Nature of professional service:

_____

_____

Goals of treatment (the patient's request):

_____

_____

Benefits, drawbacks, and alternatives to the treatment proposed:

_____

_____

Theoretical orientation, tools and techniques to be used (if relevant):

_____

_____

How services will be provided (if relevant):

_____

_____

Mutual responsibilities of the parties (including, if it is the case, an agreement concerning payment and modalities of payment):

_____

_____

Information (relevant in the context) regarding the possibility – at any point – of either refusing the offer of professional services or of ceasing to receive them:

_____

_____

The parameters of confidentiality, as well as the limits thereof (according to the context):

_____

_____

The parameters covering any agreement to share confidential information about the professional intervention (according to the context):

_____

_____

I acknowledge the content of this document and that I have obtained satisfactory answers to my questions about it.

Signature of the client:

Signature of the psychologist:

Chapter 6

Lessons learnt about confidentiality in psychoanalytic work

An analyst's theoretical research is often driven by the clinical situations he or she has felt ill prepared to face. My first brush with confidentiality in psychoanalytic work goes back more than forty years when a psychiatric out-patient asked to see her dossier in my first real professional occupation as a psychologist in an outpatient community psychiatry clinic. This experience opened questions for me about the dossier as "third", about the "ownership" of the "story" therein, and the need, as an aspiring psychoanalytic practitioner, to reflect beyond the manifest content of patients' right to information stored about them. Then, two events in 1996 swept me away. In February, Bollas and Sundelson published their trenchant critique (using examples from the United States) of the flabby respect paid to confidentiality by the psychoanalytic profession: *The New Informants: The Betrayal of Confidentiality in Psychoanalysis and Psychotherapy*. In June of the same year, the Supreme Court of the United States published its decision in *Jaffee versus Redmond* to accord psychotherapist-patient privilege in the Federal Rules of Evidence after a consortium of American psychoanalytic associations had deposed an *amicus curiae* (friend to the court) brief. In this brief, the consortium argued that the psychoanalytic therapy of the defendant be protected from disclosure to the suing party in a civil suit alleging wrongful death. These events spurred a group of Canadian psychoanalysts, including myself, to organize an inter-regional and multi-disciplinary conference of the International Psychoanalytic Association in 2000 on the topic "Confidentiality and Society". Some of this material was co-edited and collated for publication in two subsequent books in 2003. The debate with analysts from other theoretical backgrounds and from other jurisdictions as well as with ethical and legal experts invited for the occasion proved transformative for my appreciation of what is at stake, theoretically and clinically, when confidentiality is considered an essential aspect of the psychoanalytic framework. I have continued since then to study and publish on various aspects (and there are many) of confidentiality in psychoanalysis including service on the International Psychoanalytical Association's (IPA) Committee on Confidentiality, and participation in its first Report in 2018.

Far from feeling obsessed with a single topic, I found that each time I took up confidentiality from a different angle I was propelled to deepen my understanding of other aspects of the setting. As Churcher (2005) has written "to give a full account of

DOI: 10.4324/9781003527459-7

any single aspect of the setting ... soon involves one in all the complexity of the setting as a whole" (3). In what follows, I have condensed and synthesized the lessons I have learnt. These elements relate to founding principles of the psychoanalytic frame, and to a lesser extent, other forms of psychotherapy and counselling. On every point, I have reviewed a sizable swath of the literature and discussed the various controversies with other analysts. This leads me to believe that many – though certainly not all – analysts will agree with my opinions, as lessons to be shared. For ease of reading, each lesson has been streamlined and presented without intext references. Since the number of thoughtful studies examining in more detail the various controversies around each point greatly exceeds the space available in this monograph, only a partial list of sources has been provided at the end of each lesson as starting points for interested readers.

Lesson #1: The importance of collective representation of a psychoanalytic point of view

The "lamentable passivity and even collusion" exposed by Bollas and Sundelson of psychoanalytic practitioners and institutions in the undermining of confidentiality in our practice remains, unfortunately, an ever-present possibility. Psychoanalysts do not have the power or the natural inclination – which is baked into the bones of lawyers – to question potential abuse of authority. Nor do they have deep pockets and in-house counsel, which practice as members of large firms affords most lawyers. The concerted intervention in defense of confidentiality of several American psychoanalytic associations in the *Redmond versus Jaffee* case was groundbreaking. American psychoanalytic institutions have continued to lobby for confidentiality protection at both the state and federal levels. In Canada, by contrast, this kind of political activity in defense of professional ethics is far less common. Not one mental health association seemed concerned about the ethical issues at stake, and none intervened in several prominent Canadian court cases which involved the question of access to the private psychotherapy files of victims of alleged rape. We have feminist organizations to thank for the gradual change of legal mindset which led to the enactment in 1997 by the Canadian Parliament of changes in the criminal code strengthening the protection of private psychotherapy files as potential sources of "evidence" before the courts. To my knowledge, the Canadian Psychiatric Association's *amicus curiae* brief in R. *vs* Mills (1999) marked the first time a Canadian mental health professional organization had intervened to make its views public on this matter. I underline this observation in comparison with the alacrity of lawyers in defending any threats to "lawyer-client privilege" (referred to again in Lesson #2). When the Canadian government introduced new rules in 2000 to combat money-laundering, lawyers immediately sought an injunction forcing the government to hold back the application of the requirement for their profession to report private information which was being required from other businesses and professionals. Finally, in 2011, a provincial court judge found the federal legislation intruded unduly into the solicitor-client relationship, failing to adequately protect solicitor-client privilege. Whereas as psychoanalysts, in my jurisdiction of Quebec, we remain subject in our deontological codes to the paradoxical injunction of announcing the "limits of confidentiality" as part of an informed consent procedure before beginning psychotherapy, supposedly a confidential relationship.

Canadian psychoanalysts seem to feel that the pressure other psychotherapists or counsellors are under is not of our concern. And when it does concern an analyst, Canadian colleagues recoil from adopting a formal, institutional, position on "social and cultural" matters, expecting the individuals whose files are being requisitioned to fend for themselves. This portrait is admittedly a little simplistic, but I have learnt over time that there are fifty ways to rationalize a collective lack of action. The work of Richard J. Bonnie and his collaborators on the work of reform of Russian psychiatry after the collapse of the Soviet Union is a cautionary tale for psychoanalysis as an institution in the West. Russian psychiatrists were formerly unable (and may again under the authoritarian rule of Vladimir Putin be unable) to contradict the aims or directives of state officials. The ability and the willingness to say "no" is an essential attribute of professional independence under any kind of government.

The professional community as a containing and supportive environment

The International Psychoanalytic Association decided in 2000 to remove reference in their ethical code to caveats about confidentiality which would make them "subject to local laws and regulations". These caveats were leaving psychoanalysts across the world without any institutional protection when they felt ethically and clinically bound to confidentiality in opposition to third-party interest in their files. The Canadian Psychoanalytic Society (CPS) made a similar change to its ethics code in 2001. Yet when the CPS Ethical Code was revised in 2023, a generation later, subjugation to local laws was re-introduced leading to a spirited debate over accepting them at the annual general meeting of that year. A substantial difference of ethical perspective emerged with some analysts insisting that we cannot hold ourselves "above the law as symbolic third", whereas others felt that the professional autonomy lost under totalitarian regimes necessitates an "optimal reserve" with respect to any given legislation. A compromise was reached: none of the new ethics articles was required to adjust to local laws and regulations if the assembly agreed to the general principle of abiding by a "rule of law". I accepted this compromise under the circumstances, yet given the struggle it took to return to ground achieved twenty-two years earlier I am not confident that an optimal intrapsychic distance from the law has been widely internalized by peers.

Far too much evidence exists that the laws of any nation are neither fixed nor infallible, constantly subject to political, institutional, economic, and community pressures as well as changing social and ethical norms. Laws can be, and have been in certain IPA jurisdictions, directed to ends that are incompatible with psychoanalytic ethics. Since our ethics have derived independently through our century-old experience with psychoanalytic settings, individual analysts and their patients will generally be better protected if ethical guidelines avoid asserting the precedence of the law. *Institutional backing creates a space for conscientious objection.* It allows individual members who have doubts about breaching confidentiality to feel safe in explaining their ethical stance to the relevant authorities. The alternative is to feel alone and somewhat ashamed of "holding back" to "deserving" outside interests. I personally hold that a position of potential conscientious objection, defined as disobedience in the context of respect for and fidelity to the legal system, is a healthy fibre in the analyst's internal framework (referred to in Chapter 1) as demonstrated by the English analyst Anne Hayman in 1965. It is not necessarily unlawful to respectfully contest a specific rule, mandate, or legal direction on the grounds of professional opposition to it. *Should we not bear in mind that the unconscious is neither legally nor politically correct?*

Some references for lesson one

B.C. Supreme Court Exempts Lawyers from Federal Anti-Money Laundering Laws. Blog-Posted on the Lawson Lundell law firm website October 4, 2011. https://www.lawsonlundell.com/Commercial-Litigation-and-Dispute-Resolution-Blog/bc-supremecourt-exempts-lawyers-from-federal-anti-money-laundering-laws

Balsam, R. 2024. Thoughts on the Beginnings of Psychoanalyses. *The Psychoanalytic Quarterly* 93(4):675–699. https://doi.org/10.1080/00332828.2024.2403420

Bollas, C. 2003. Confidentiality and Professionalism in Psychoanalysis. *British Journal of Psychotherapy* 20(2):157–176.

Bonnie, R. 2000. Confidentiality in the formerly communist world: A case study in mental-health reform. *Paper presented at the International Psychoanalytic Association's Inter-Regional Conference on Confidentiality and Society*, Montreal, October 14, 2000.

Bonnie, R. J. & Polubinskaya, S. V. 1995. The meaning of professional independence. *Paper Presented at the Third Meeting of the Network of Reformers in Psychiatry*, Prague, September, 1995.

Churcher, J. 2005. *Keeping the Psychoanalytic Setting in Mind. Paper Given to the Annual Conference of Lancaster Psychotherapy Clinic in Collaboration with the Tavistock Clinic.* Lancaster: St. Martin's College. September 9th.

Code de déontologie de l'Ordre des psychologues du Québec. Disponible à https://www.legisquebec.gouv.qc.ca/fr/document/rc/C-26,%20r.%20212. See article 10. Consulted May 30, 2025.

Hayman, A. 1965. Psychoanalyst Subpoenaed. *Lancet* 286(7416):785–786.

Jaffee v. Redmond, 518 U.S. 1 (1996).

Levin, C. 2003. Civic confidentiality and psychoanalytic confidentiality. In *Confidentiality: Ethical Perspectives and Clinical Dilemmas*, edited by C. Levin, A. Furlong & M. K. Neil, 55–80. Hillsdale, New Jersey: Analytic Press.

Levin, C., Furlong, A., & Koggel, C. 2003. *Confidential Relationships. Psychoanalytic, Ethical, and Legal Contexts.* Amsterdam/New York: Editions Rodopi.

Minow, M. 1991. *Breaking the Law: Lawyers and Clients in Struggles for Social Change 52 Harvard Law Review* 723:741.

Polubinskaya, S. & Bonnie, R. 1996. New Code of Ethics for Russian Psychiatrists. *Bulletin of Medical Ethics* April:13–19.

R v Mills, [1999] 3 S.C.R. 668.

Lesson #2: The questionable contribution to the truth-seeking process of psychoanalytic and other psychotherapeutic records before the courts

The law's double standard

The "as-if" status of our consulting rooms can only survive if the social and political structures of the local community favour the existence of a temporary "retreat" from moral and aesthetic normative pressures. Widespread misunderstandings about the specificity of confidentiality in psychoanalytic work leave practitioners open to the vagaries of cultural fads and projections. Psychological and legal concepts and principles are often conflated. There is also a tendency in contemporary mores to think of psychotherapy as a form of redress or rehabilitation, an inclination some psychoanalysts may share. Pretending to exist in an "extra-territorial" space beyond the reach of "reality" is a precarious option if other social institutions do not agree to maintain the illusion. In a review I undertook of several Canadian court decisions regarding judicial treatment of confidential information, written more than ten years ago as a chapter to a book which was never published because the legal scholar's plan to finish it was interrupted by his death, the "evidence" – at least to my reading – is clear: lawyers consider confidentiality to be more important for their work and of greater societal value than the confidentiality of professional psychotherapists. With due respect to the legal profession, a bias must be recognized in the differential adjudication of matters of access to confidential records by the courts and by legal theorists. Whereas the solicitor–client relationship is accorded the quasi-absolute status of a class privilege, access to the psychotherapeutic relationship must be decided on a case-by-case basis "balanced against other interests". Relevance and balancing are specifically rejected in the very notion of solicitor-client privilege.

But how could this double standard be otherwise unless the dissonant and foreign voice of the "other" profession of psychoanalyst also takes the "stand" to explain the unique function of confidentiality in its field, quite different from that of the solicitor but just as rigorously in need of protection? To undo this historical discrimination, there is a need for a coherent defense of confidentiality which takes into account the specificity of this professional relationship. As Bollas and Sundelson contended, the entire profession's "failure to educate" third-parties has left the latter "so uncertain about one of the competing interests and so familiar with the other, [that] the outcome is a foregone conclusion". The initiative of the American consortium in the *Redmond versus Jaffee* case was exciting because it meant that psychoanalysts were explaining to the courts the actual function of confidentiality in their work as something more than a question of privacy, or intimacy, or of cordoning off information of value to court decisions. *It is also a question of mental integrity for the two partners in a psychoanalytic project.*

Psychoanalysis as deliberative process

I have argued for the pertinence of using a legal concept other than the right to privacy to defend the confidentiality of psychoanalytic work: the *privilege of the deliberative process* which is usually evoked to protect the discussions of cabinet meetings of elected representatives, to foster open-ended exchanges in certain phases of labour arbitration or mediation proceedings, or to shield the personal notes judges make when they are sitting on the bench. According to the Legal Information Institute website:

> The purpose underlying the privilege is to protect the "'quality of agency decisions' by allowing government officials freedom to debate alternative approaches in private." But the deliberative-process privilege applies only to those documents and communications that are *predecisional*, meaning they are created prior to the agency reaching its final decision, and *deliberative*, meaning they relate to the thought process of executive officials and are not purely factual.
>
> (Consulted December 22, 2024)

The notion of deliberate process provides a legitimate comparison to the as-if space the analyst attempts to create in the consulting room,[1] and it has the advantage of not being under the control of the patient's decision to disclose or not his private sharing with his analyst. Would the surgeon give patients the right to control the sanitation of the operating room? The notion of deliberate process might better shield the therapeutic dyad over and above "privacy" as a strictly individual "right". Though the virtual arena evoked in the original legal concept is that of legal or political deliberations, might the privilege of deliberate process just as legitimately apply to psychoanalytic treatment when third-parties in disputes with patients seek information about the therapy? This might happen in contested managed care coverage, life insurance policy claims, child custody battles, allegations of child abuse or of sexual perversion, wrongful dismissal suits, and complaints of professional negligence. Could the fact that this privilege has never been called upon to protect psychotherapists be just another example of legal bias?

Questionable contribution to the truth-seeking process

Psychoanalytic understanding of the multiple forces and representations at work in human minds and its recognition of unconscious psychic life mean that information cannot be lifted from the consulting room to be scrutinized by non-psychoanalytic experts who claim to be able to sift through it for "probative" evidence of one kind or another. This claim is pretentious, misguided, and seriously underestimates the distortion introduced into the therapeutic relationship. It is more likely that "evidence" taken from psychoanalytic/psychotherapeutic treatment will lead astray the pursuit of justice. The bread-and-butter as it were of psychoanalytic work depends on the ambiguity of human speech where it is not immediately evident in whose voice the patient is speaking nor to whom, past or present. Parallel psychological processes are at work which shadow the professional encounter with conscious and unconscious personal meanings. Mutual suggestion, conscious and unconscious, is an unavoidable and completely necessary part of the work patient and analyst do together. The encouragement to suspend conventional, learnt, and expected ways of speaking and to verbalize thoughts without censorship, not only permits patients to unburden themselves of socially unacceptable ideas, but it can allow unexpected, new, thoughts to break through, revealing parts of themselves they were unaware of. Anne Hayman, the British analyst mentioned earlier who successfully refused to testify before a judge despite the patient's permission, wrote at the time "Justice as well as our ethic is likely to be served best by silence". It is for these reasons and others mentioned earlier that the privilege of the deliberative process seems an appropriate, if as yet unused, legal shield. In fact, the former president of the Law Commission of Canada, Roderick Macdonald (1999, see Des Rosiers, 2003), suggested that left undisturbed psychotherapy might belong to those institutions of civil society "better attuned to preventative law and to transformative justice than are courts".

Some references for lesson two

Bollas, C. & Sundelson, D. 1996. *The New Informants: The Betrayal of Confidentiality in Psychoanalysis and Psychotherapy*. Lanham, Maryland: Jason Aronson.

Des Rosiers, N. 2003. Confidentiality, human relationships, and law reform. In *ConfidentialRelationships. Psychoanalytic, Ethical, and Legal Contexts*, edited by C. Levin, A. Furlong, & C. Koggel, 229–248. Amsterdam: Rodopi.

Frank, C. 2019. Breach of trust or the analyst's independent thinking as facilitating third? *Presentation at panel Confidentiality as a Container - Clinical and Theoretical Issues of the International Psychoanalytic Association, Congress of London*, July 2019.

Furlong, A. 1996. The Conflict of Interest between Treatment and Expertise. *The Review of Psychoanalysis and Psychotherapy* 7:45–47.

Furlong, A. 2003. The questionable contribution of psychotherapeutic and psychoanalytic records to the truth-seeking process. In *Confidential Relationships*, edited by C. Koggel, A. Furlong & C. Levin, 13–29. Amsterdam: Editions Rodopi B.V.

Furlong, A. & Lefebvre, M. 1997. La confidentialité des dossiers et la Cour suprême (The Confidentiality of Files and the Supreme Court). *Psychologie Québec, novembre*: 30–31.

Furlong, A. & Lefebvre, M. 1998. Psychotherapy and Disclosure: Recent Court Decisions. *Canadian Journal of Psychiatry* 43:731–736.

Furlong, A. 2012. Introduction to Ron Sklar's Book Section on Confidentiality. Unpublished Manuscript.

Legal Information Institute. Deliberative process privilege and law enforcement privileges. https://www.law.cornell.edu/constitution-conan/article-2/section-3/the-deliberative-process-and-law-enforcement-privileges Consulted December 22, 2024.

Lesson #3: Saying no to requests for information from third-parties

Defensive practice is not good practice

This section refers only to the treatment of time-limited third-party requests for information from psychoanalytic treatment and not the impact of third-party participation in support of treatment. The latter topic deserves an entire book which would research the advantages and disadvantages of state or private business funding of psychoanalysis in Germany, the United States, and some provinces in Canada, studies from psychoanalytic clinics, and other sources. Lesson #3 carries on Bollas and Sundelson's original concern about the license to poach the psychotherapeutic scene for information useful in third-party disputes, which has only increased since the publication of their book with additional social, legal, and economic justifications. Bollas and Sundelson's observations about the passivity and evasion of many psychoanalysts and psychoanalytic organizations in confronting these intrusions head on remain pertinent. The quasi-ubiquitous contemporary position of regulatory bodies that informed consent involves instructing patients of the "limits" of confidentiality kneecaps the pledge to a confidential relationship before patients even begin treatment. Experts have advised psychotherapists to practice defensively or to share only "factual information" in response to requests for information, dodges which nevertheless contaminate the psychic space of the dyad. A plethora of manuals for therapists exists promising "toolboxes" for "risk management" with respect to insurers and court proceedings. Yet, if one truly believes in the importance of confidentiality in our work, in the importance of honest neutrality with respect to the different aspects of the patient's mind, then these compromises are unacceptable.

Analyze patient consent to third-party involvement

Often enough, third-party intrusions are linked to a fifth column inside the dyad, when patients are eager accomplices in attempting to engage their analysts as white knights against the dragons of their imaginary and real universes. The patient's permission to disclose is a major impediment in the capacity for resistance of psychoanalysts who are often confounded when protection of confidentiality is understood solely as an issue of patient privacy, a legal argument flawed by its emphasis on an individual right. This legal grounding means that confidentiality can be broken if the patient consents, a state of affairs which can only be resolved if the analyst undertakes a review of the framework with the patient. This can occur explicitly or implicitly. Analysts can remind patients that using their psychoanalytic work to persuade third-parties to decide in their favour in disputes outside the consulting room sabotages the dyad's ability to freely associate. Or, better still, the analyst can maintain the framework by seeking to understand the unconscious repetition behind the patient's inadvertent masochism. The same British psychoanalyst, Anne Hayman, wrote that respecting the patient's consent for disclosure would have missed "the essential point that he may not be aware of unconscious motives impelling him to give permission".

Cooperation with third-parties is likely to contaminate the "benevolently neutral listening" of the analyst

The psychoanalytic position of "benevolent neutrality" is a professional stance intended to help the dyad from inadvertently repressing issues which may be indirectly and secretly relevant to our patients' problems. Requests from third-parties for information about the treatment or the patient put pressure on the psychoanalyst's neutrality. John Forrester makes a compelling argument that the analyst's rule of *abstinence* is undermined if he or she consents to "acting out" in the real world based on material from analytic sessions.

The why of sharing, not the what

I have argued for an additional distinction. Key to contamination and inhibition of analytic work is whether disclosure serves an analytic end. There is a risk that confidentiality be reified into a thing onto itself instead of a qualification of the analytic relationship. If we go back to fundamentals, we might be hard pressed to see anything inherently sacred about confidentiality aside from the purpose it serves. One might even consider it a technical matter, not a moral goal. *Confidentiality contributes to the healthy functioning of our method of free association and benevolently neutral listening. It is in permitting the suspension of immediate reality claims that confidentiality takes on unique importance in psychoanalytic relationships and not as a transcendent moral claim.* The definition of confidentiality found in some contemporary professional codes relies heavily on the models of privacy and professional secrecy, which though useful and relevant, fail to encompass the transitional, intersubjective space engendered by the analytic process. Defining confidentiality as a promise to "never tell anything" outside the relationship omits evaluation of the impact of the third's listening on the combined freedom of thought and freedom of speech in analyst and analysand. Circulation of information outside the therapeutic couple, such as in a supervisory or collegial intervision context, need not be toxic, need not disrupt the analytic couple's openness to new meaning. I have referred to this way of thinking as an invitation to consider the "why of sharing and not the what".

It is proposed that we regard confidentiality as a "skin" rather than as a "lock". It must breathe, be flexible to context, and, if need be, stretch to contain (not undermine) therapeutic work in extreme situations. Both skins and locks act as containers, but whereas the former is a porous dynamic membrane enveloping the entire analytic unit, the latter is a mechanical device, impervious to ambiance or relationship, designed exclusively for the protection of the patient in whose hand the "key" allegedly lies. Though it moves us outside of the classic individual psychoanalytic framework, the Novicks' model of "dynamic concurrent parent work" throughout the treatment of adolescents is a good example of a similar reworking of the concept of confidentiality. Other analysts might fault the Novicks for engaging in what appears at times to be parallel parent and adolescent treatments. Nevertheless, I agree with them that there are moments when confidential information can be legitimately if briefly shared to help contain the representational capacity of the dyad.

One can assert – if needed – the integrity of the frame both to patients and to external parties. It does not have to be expressed in hostile fashion, just firmly and clearly. Most deontological codes contain articles which can be used to justify refusal so that most of the time, this is sufficient to push back the wish of third-parties to intrude. Nonetheless, as noted already, no explicit statement on the part of the analyst may be needed, as can be seen from clinical examples in the literature, if the request coming from a third-party can be associated to as a disavowed part of the patient. Third-parties may unwittingly play a part in the patient's internal struggle. As Hinshelwood (2003) has cogently pointed out, at times the analyst *can be being enlisted to play the needed part* of constraining authority when the patient's self-control over feared violent impulses is slipping; whereas at the same time - paradoxically - the analyst may minimize danger, having become befuddled by the patient's projections and *failing* to act appropriately. *Confidentiality is not so much an ethical matter as a clinical one, the final arbiter of ethical decisions being faithfulness to clinical considerations to the best of the clinician's theoretical understanding.* Whereas the word "secret" come from *secernere*, which means "to set apart", confidentiality comes from *com* ("together", "with") and *fidere*, meaning to "have confidence in". The natural movement of confidentiality, unless resisted by conflict, is relational sharing. There are moments, such as in supervision, where the dyad's boundaries need to temporarily enlarge *to allow triangulation of the analytic listening-instrument.* Viewed in this way, *the ethical criterion for disclosure becomes: will it further the analytic listening and thus the treatment, or is it for unrelated purposes which disrupt this listening?*

We are not supposed to "know"

Let us reiterate: the analytic offer is not to play advocate for the patient's perceived interests with respect to insurance contracts, educational institutions, legal proceedings, workman compensation boards, divorce arrangements or any other third-party interaction. The analytic offer is more complex and more trying, which is why it necessitates intensive training: to listen in an impartial manner to all the contending forces within the patient's mind as Strachey (1969/1934) invited us to do. Advocacy for one force over another is more likely to distort evenly suspended attention, thereby distorting the psychoanalytic situation. As they are trying to figure out how to handle third-party requests for information about treatments, analysts often evince concern about deontological obligations to their professional regulatory bodies, a source of stress unknown to the first generations of analysts but which is a frequent "foreign body" in modern psychoanalytic practice. These organizations have the mandate of protecting the public in the context of a substantial array of different psychotherapeutic approaches. Consequently, it is perhaps not surprising that their "quality of practice" guidelines inflict violence on the psychoanalytic framework. Therein the challenge for psychoanalytic practitioners: how to transcribe a specifically psychoanalytic ethical sensibility into language shareable with regulators whose theoretical references can be appreciably different?

Some references for lesson three

Forrester, J. 2003. Trust, confidentiality, and the possibility of psychoanalysis. In *Confidentiality: Ethical Perspectives and Clinical Dilemmas*, edited by C. Levin, A. Furlong & M. K. O'Neil, 19–27. Hillsdale, New Jersey: Analytic Press.

Furlong, A. 2003. The why of sharing and not the what: Confidentiality and analytic purpose. In *Confidentiality: Ethical Perspectives and Clinical Dilemmas*, edited by C. Levin, A. Furlong & M. K. O'Neil, 39–49. Hillsdale, New Jersey: The Analytic Press.

Furlong, A. 2005. Confidentiality With Respect to Third Parties: A Psychoanalytic View. *International Journal of Psychoanalysis* 86:375–394.

Glancy, G., Patel, M., & Borooah, M. 2022. Participation as an Expert in Cases Involving the Production of Mental Health Records in Canadian Courts. *International Journal of Risk and Recovery* 5(1):44–52. https://doi.org/10.59703/ijrr.v5i1.44-51.

Hinshelwood, R. D. 2003. A psychoanalytic perspective on confidentiality: The divided mind in treatment. In *Confidential Relationships. Psychoanalytic, Ethical, and Legal Contexts*, 31–51. Amsterdam/New York: Editions Rodopi.

Macdonald, R. 1999. Law, justice and community: The way ahead. From an address delivered April 17, 1999 at the symposium, *Law, Justice and Community*, held at then Faculty of Law at Dalhousie University, Halifax, Nova Scotia.

Novick, K. K. & Novick, J. 2013. Concurrent Work with Parents of Adolescent Patients. *Psychoanalytic Study of the Child* 67:103–136.

Strachey, J. 1969/1934. The Nature of the Therapeutic Action of Psychoanalysis. *International Journal of Psychoanalysis* 50:275–292.

Stone, A. A., & Maccourt, D. C. (2008). Ethics in Forensic Psychiatry: Re-Imagining the Wasteland after 25 Years. *The Journal of Psychiatry & Law*, 36(4), 617–643. https://doi.org/10.1177/009318530803600406

Lesson #4: The safety of third-parties is usually better addressed as a clinical decision

Confidentiality is not only for the individual patient's benefit

Since the original Tarasoff rulings, unfortunately widely misunderstood by mental health professionals, regulatory bodies have frequently required that patients be warned at the beginning of any treatment, including psychoanalysis, that confidentiality will be waived if they are deemed dangerous to themselves, to others, and particularly to the security of children. The 1976 Tarasoff decision declared: "The protective privilege ends where the public peril begins". Some jurisdictions provide that confidentiality *may* be waived in such circumstances, an essential difference which restores the clinician's responsibility to carefully assess the clinical situation before proceeding to a non-psychoanalytic "action". The doctrine of public safety as part of a psychotherapist's "obligation to society" has, however, so insinuated itself into the training of future therapists that even psychoanalysts are prone to uncritical submission. We have all been told at some point in our professional lives that we are obliged to "warn third parties of imminent danger". Unfortunately, this is not the lesson of the original Tarasoff tragedy where the young Poddar, a student in Berkeley, knifed his fellow student, Tarasoff, to death after his therapist had threatened to hospitalize him and warned the police that Poddar might be dangerous to her. This warning mobilized university police to interview Poddar. Though the police did not find him imminently dangerous, the breach in confidentiality precipitated his dropping out of treatment. When he committed the murder, he had not seen his therapist for weeks.

While the Tarasoff rulings were handed out with the best of intentions and with the aim of protecting the life of potential innocent victims, it remains a matter of debate as to how successful they have been in their original intent. Since the Tarasoff case, research has continued to confirm that third-party warnings are ineffective in averting violence. Disastrous consequences for children and adults have occurred after hasty reporting in accordance with legal requirements. Research has also revealed that knowing that therapists might feel obliged to trigger third-party warnings, women and children at risk have been avoiding telling their therapists about their exposure to domestic violence. Donald Bersoff (2014), former president of the American Psychological Association, and author of all four editions of *Ethical Conflicts in Psychology*, concluded that "*Tarasoff* is bad law, bad social science, and bad social policy". Bersoff's contributions are part of a fifty-year history (which cannot realistically be summarized here) of analysis and debate about the value of mandatory reporting for potentially dangerous psychotherapy patients. Even before the Tarasoff murder, many prominent mental health experts had expressed the belief that to reveal confidential information under circumstances where violence was imminent was neither a breach of trust nor unethical. Moreover, psychotherapists had revealed in earlier surveys that they would consider a wide array of options in managing the risks of danger to others, including hospitalization, warnings, more frequent therapy sessions, starting or increasing medication, and/or close monitoring. Their approach was already similar to management of an acutely suicidal patient, *with the emphasis on concern for the patient*. As Slovenko (1998) has stated: "imposing control where self-control breaks down is not a breach of trust when it is not deceptive. And it is not necessary to be deceptive".

My lesson for the framework was to realize that much regulatory thinking about the safety of other people who might be harmed by a disgruntled or mentally ill patient erroneously views the ethical challenge as weighing a "public good" of safety against an "individual right" to treatment. This way of putting the problem is misleading, inciting feelings of conflicting allegiances and primitive anguish about legal reprisals in the therapist, which can be extremely difficult to rationally dissipate. Neglected is the fact that good psychoanalytic/psychotherapeutic work is itself a contribution to the public good, that it saves and transforms lives, ultimately facilitating patients in adding their unique vitalities to collective life. Lawyers do not lose track of the importance of their professional services both to individuals and to society. Slovenko's book length study found that when violence is committed, individuals have often never been in psychotherapy, or to have dropped out. A related complication to the regulatory expectations since Tarasoff was pointed out by Bollas and Sundelson but it had already been stressed by forensic ethics experts, such as Alan Stone: these articles in professional deontological codes seem to invite a role conflict, which is itself expressly discouraged by these same codes. The containment of the analyst's mind may be the first to weaken when a crisis in a patient's therapy is viewed as a conflict of the interest of the one against another or others. This seems to have been the case for Poddar's university psychologist who was struggling with a serious family conflict at the time and with a sharp difference of opinion among his superiors about what course of action to follow. Hinshelwood has noted that "breaking confidentiality is not just a technical obstruction to our method. It produces violent feelings, and overwhelming experiences for our patients; as well as for us as analysts". See Agyapong et al (2009) for a dispiriting more recent account of the abortion of treatment aim occasioned by the confusion between public good and individual treatment seeking. The anxiety stirred up in the treating psychiatrists about a man admitting to criminal sexual acts is such that their case report is completely buried by an assessment of relevant articles in the Irish, Australian, British, and American criminal codes. A formal report was made to relevant social authorities, there was insufficient evidence to charge him, but the individual in question refused further cooperation with the investigation. Conclusion: clinical care aborted and societal gain indeterminant.

The analyst's state of mind as container

As a professional community, we have to be careful not to be swept up by a "disclosure industry" (Bollas) where public persecutory anxiety about violence and sexual abuse can lead to identification with the abusive figure, enacted through politically correct and defensive "reporting". When psychoanalysts are examining this issue with their own patients or, frequently, in their supervisions and intervisions, a careful study of the containing capacity of the psychotherapeutic dyad - that is, patient and psychotherapist together - is primary. Hindsight reveals how vulnerable Poddar was, unlike other Berkeley students, as an Indian immigrant of the Dalit, or "Untouchable" class, a group so low that they are considered beneath the four castes that make up the Hindu system. The cultural shock for Poddar must have been enormous and with a diagnosis of paranoid schizophrenia, his psyche was clearly overwhelmed. The relevant question should be clinical: is the current treatment plan adequate to *protect the patient* from a violent acting out? The goal of a psychoanalytic treatment is not to have the patient end up destroying his life by hurting another or hurting himself. It is misleading to speak of the alternative as waged between the patient and others. The respective interests are in fact congruent, not divergent. Ferocity is not only dangerous to other people: *it is equally disastrous to the patient* by virtue of concomitant treatment failure, legal repercussions, alienation from family and community, deep despair and regret over the often-irreparable consequences of his actions, and potential suicide.

Some references for lesson four

Agyapong V. I. O., Kirrane R., & Bangaru R. 2009. Medical confidentiality versus disclosure: Ethical and legal dilemmas. *Journal of Forensic and Legal Medicine* 16(2):93–96. https://doi.org/10.1016/j.jflm.2008.08.007

Bersoff, D. N. 1976. Therapists as Protectors and Policemen: New Roles as a Result of Tarasoff? *Professional Psychology* 7(3):267–273.

Bersoff, D. N. 2014. Protecting Victims of Violent Patients While Protecting Confidentiality. *The American Psychologist* 69(5): 461–467. https://doi.org/10.1037/a0037198

Blum, D. 1986. *Bad Karma: A True Story of Obsession and Murder*. New York: Atheneum.

Buckner, F. & Firestone, M. 2000. "Where the Public Peril Begins". 25 Years after Tarasoff. *The Journal of Legal Medicine* 21(2):187–222. https://doi.org/10.1080/01947640050074698

Furlong, A. 2005. Cadre et confidentialité. *Filigrane* 14(2):62–76.

Sheppard, G. 2015. A landmark decision for counsellors in Canada. https://www.ccpaaccp.ca/wp-content/uploads/2015/05/NOE.Landmark-Decision-with-Implications-for-Counsellors-in-Canada.pdf Consulted November 4, 2024.

Slovenko, R. 1998. *Psychotherapy and Confidentiality: Testimonial Privileged Communication, Breach of Confidentiality, and Reporting Duties*. Springfield, Illinois: Charles C Thomas.

Tarasoff v. *Regents of the University of California*, 17 Cal. 3d 425, 551 P.2d 334, 131 Cal. Rptr. 14 (Cal. 1976).

Lesson #5: The inherent ethical uncertainty about whether psychoanalysts should seek permission to present or publish patients' clinical material

There are legal situations, Quebec Court of Appeal Judge Yves-Marie Morissette, once wrote that "are not self-solving because they involve genuine factual or legal indeterminacy". He continued that a solution in these cases is rarely "ever amenable to apodictic reasoning", that is, it rarely can be clearly established and beyond doubt. The International Psychoanalytical Association's Report on Confidentiality arrived at a similar conclusion regarding the question of seeking "informed" consent from patients for the use of clinical material in their analyst's presentations or publications. Having reviewed the sizable literature for and against seeking consent, the Committee decided "there is no universal, fail-safe procedure which can be recommended as the best way to protect the analysand when sharing clinical material with colleagues". This conclusion was reached not only because of the diversity of theoretical points of view in contemporary psychoanalysis which each entail an – at least partial – concomitant set of ethics on the matter, some pushing the idea of "co-construction" or of the "jointly constructed psychoanalytic field" to the point of inviting the patient to become co-author in publications. Others have given up the very idea of resorting to clinical material in publications because it is experienced as such a betrayal of the patient's intimacy. For the Confidentiality

Committee, there remains the real possibility of unresolvable conflict between competing needs or views.

The IPA Confidentiality Committee's conclusion echoed that expressed already twenty-five years ago, by Glen Gabbard and Paul Williams, then Joint Editors-in-chief of the *International Journal of Psychoanalysis*. The dilemma of professional use of clinical material goes back, of course, to the dawn of psychoanalysis but it had become more acute. The two editors were facing a new and concerted ethos amongst medical journals which rejected disguise in clinical accounts as unscientific and risking leading readers to spurious deductions. The guideline was that informed consent must always be obtained from patients whose material is referred to in professional sharing. Gabbard and Williams lent their voices to challenge the suitability of these guidelines for analytic writing. As we had occasion to emphasize earlier in this chapter, the ethical requirement of confidentiality in the psychoanalytic sense of the term arises primarily from within psychoanalytic practice, not from laws or ethical codes external to psychoanalysis. Gabbard and Williams contended that the method of preserving confidentiality had to be left in the hands of individual psychoanalytic authors whose choices needed to be founded on clinical considerations. They made a number of suggestions which remain pertinent, and which we will come back to, about how to optimally treat the problem. For the moment, though, let us review the pros and cons that various authors have brought to our attention.

In favour of disguise

Most of the clinical accounts in our psychoanalytic literature have relied up until now on disguise to protect patients' identities.

Against disguise

It can introduce distortions which lead readers astray about the facts of the case. It does not protect the patient that much, since patients may still recognize themselves and feel hurt or otherwise dismayed either by the portrait of themselves or the fact that they were not asked. Moreover, the clinical material selected as the subject of a presentation is always to some extent a construction created by the analyst. This observation makes the sharing of clinical material with peers or supervisors both a professional necessity and a constant call to scientific modesty.

In favour of informed consent

The protection of the analyst from legal recourse by the patient is a major argument in favour of informed consent, though it is not the only one. Many analysts feel that the patient has a moral right to know and they point out that if the patient's permission has not been obtained, the analyst will feel that he or she has committed a betrayal of the patient's trust. Asking permission offers patients the possibility of blocking publication, yet in so doing, they may have the impression of having damaged their analyst. Nevertheless, there are those who refute the idea that psychoanalysis should be a special case, separate from general standards of professional care where respect for the patient's autonomy is the norm.

Against informed consent

While a patient's consent to a breach in confidentiality may render it permissible from a non-psychoanalytic viewpoint, such a breach may remain ethically compromising in the eyes of many analysts, who would feel that the patient cannot always know at the time how the transference has affected his giving consent. Moreover, there is a strong resistance on the part of many authors to involving the patient in the project of publication or presentation, eloquently expressed in some of the sources provided in the references. A long-term student of confidentiality issues recently raised her scruples about the pretense of co-writing with patients about their treatment as a way of dealing with potential accusations of betrayal: "it stretches the concept of co-construction to a clinical breaking point". Asking for consent always destabilizes the analytic relationship to some extent by introducing the enigma of the analyst's desire: why me? Why does the analyst want to share this specific material? The disguise itself can raise questions for the patient. There is documentation of patients' feeling manipulated and dismayed by the process of being asked to consent. We simply cannot know everything that we may be unconsciously communicating when we write about or orally present our analysands to others. And we cannot reliably predict what the impact on them will be, either immediately or long afterwards, of discovering that their analyst has written about them, whether their permission has been obtained or not. Another reservation about informed consent according to Grier is the recognition that, legally, patients are in no way bound to the consent they have given. They can apparently rescind their consent at a later date, even after publication. A redoubtable implication of the multiple arguments against informed consent is the effect it might have on the clinical material available henceforth in the literature. Certainly, fewer clinical vignettes will submitted for publication, with a possible bias of theoretical explication narrowing those that are.

What about fictionalization?

There are authors who have decided to fictionalize their clinical presentations as a way around the dilemmas enumerated above. Some have even published avowedly fictional cases as a way of communicating psychoanalytic concepts. This strategy can be quite effective though it probably lacks the ingenuity of real unconscious expression and one has no way of measuring the impact on their "fictions" of unconscious biases on the part of the authors themselves.

Disguising the author

Since internet search by author's name is the easiest and most common access patients and others have to publications which may contain private information, Gabbard proposed that one way to protect confidentiality was to publish or present anonymously or with a pseudonym. Though this would effectively solve the quandary about asking patient permission, most analysts are reluctant to give up the narcissistic, or economic career, benefits that go with publishing under one's name. When there are multiple authors, one can avoid identifying the individual source of clinical material, substantially reducing the chance that a patient's identity will be revealed. As mentioned at the beginning of this book, I have taken the route of using disguise in clinical examples from my role as supervisor or from peer intervisions, thus combining two of Gabbard's suggestions: disguising both author and patient.

What about anonymization?

The *International Journal of Psychoanalysis* (*IJP*), and other psychoanalytic journals, have recently initiated a substantial "ethical shift". Henceforth, the *IJP* will not expect authors to seek patient consent for submission to the Journal, though authors who feel obliged to seek consent still can. Official policy is that *anonymization*, viewed as a stronger term than disguise is primary, and de rigueur. Future authors will be required to declare that all steps have been taken to prevent the possibility of their patient being recognized by any third-party, and – so far as is possible – patients should also not be able to recognize themselves. The current editor of IJP, Francis Grier explains, that "in the process of writing the paper, the author needs to move to a position where that patient is no longer in him/herself the core of the focus, but instead becomes an exemplar". Grier argues that the new policy encourages analysts to transition properly to the "position of author, where they are now writing not so much about the patient but about an analytic experience that the author reckons will be useful to other analysts". One suggested version of anonymization is the use of clinical vignettes constructed from the material of several patients thus making individual patients less recognizable, a suggestion Gabbard made years ago. The problem with anonymization, similar to that of fictionalization – though it may not be insurmountable – is loss of detail: it is the uncanny play on detail which makes unconscious derivatives so riveting. At the beginning of Freud's 1909 Case of Obsessional Neurosis, he notes that "the intelligibility of material" "depends for its coherence precisely upon the small details of real life". As Ogden put it in a recent publication: "Each situation I shall describe is specific to a moment in analysis created by a particular analyst and a particular patient and would not occur in an analysis conducted by any other analytic pair".

Creating a community of concern

"Because of these limitations in our capacity to be confident about our particular ethical choices, in addition to our ethical responsibility as individual practitioners we are proposing a *community-of-concern approach* ... in which safeguards are introduced at several points in the development and presentation of clinical material, and responsibility for their effectiveness is held by all involved" (Added emphasis, Report of the IPA Confidentiality Committee). The aim is to foster a culture of confidentiality in which protection of the patient´s privacy and dignity becomes a paramount concern at every point in the development, sharing, and presentation of clinical material.

Consultation with colleagues about one's plan to present or publish using patient clinical material is strongly advised. Research has shown that analysts are not always aware of the impact of the counter-transferential roots of their choosing to share their clinical work in a professionally competitive setting, nor are they always attuned to the patients' negative responses to being asked. We simply cannot know everything that we may be unconsciously communicating when we write about or orally present our analysands to others. One or more peers can help flush out self-deception. It is also known that indiscretions can occur unexpectedly when analysts reply off the cuff to audience questions, or discuss a case in a social setting. Nevertheless, as I argued earlier in this chapter, there are situations (usually supervisory or forms of intervision) of sharing which do not to my way of thinking betray the patient's trust because they are much needed spaces to enhance the therapeutic couple's grasp of their unconscious interactions.

Some references for lesson five

Ackerman, S. 2018. (How) Can We Write about Our Patients? *Journal of the American Psychoanalytic Association* 66:59–81.
Agyapong V. I. O., Kirrane R., & Bangaru R. 2009. Medical confidentiality versus disclosure: Ethical and legal dilemmas. *Journal of Forensic and Legal Medicine* 16(2), 93–96. https://doi.org/10.1016/j.jflm.2008.08.007
Anonymous. 2013. "Sibling Violence, Trauma, and Reality": The Analysand Writes Back. *Canadian Journal of Psychoanalysis* 21:44–50.
Barrett, D. & Miller, J. 2024. Cultivating a Culture of Concern Regarding Confidentiality in Writing about Child and Adolescent Psychoanalysis. *Psychoanalytic Study of the Child* 77:1–6.
Furlong, A. 1998a. Should We or shouldn't We? Some Aspects of the Confidentiality of Clinical Reporting and Dossier Access. *International Journal of Psychoanalysis* 79: 727–739.
Furlong, A. 1998b. L'histoire de cas: histoire de qui? *Trans* 10:106–118.
Furlong, A. 2005. Cadre et confidentialité. *Filigrane* 14(2):62–76.
Furlong, A. 2006. Further Reflections on the Impact of Clinical Writing on Patients. *International Journal of Psychoanalysis* 87:747–768.
Gabbard, G. O. 1997. Case Histories and "confidentiality. *International Journal of Psychoanalysis* 78:820–821.
Gabbard, G. O. 2000. Disguise or Consent? Problems and Recommendations Concerning the Publication and Presentation of Clinical Material. *International Journal of Psychoanalysis* 81:1071–1086.

Grier, F. 2023. *Editorial. International Journal of Psychoanalysis* 104:981–985.

International Psychoanalytical Association. 2018. Report of IPA Confidentiality Committee.

Kantrowitz, J. L. 2006. *Writing about Patients. Responsibilities, Risks, and Ramifications.* New York: Other Press.

Kanwal, G. 2024. To Reveal or Not to Reveal, That Is the Wrong Question: Thoughts About Clinical Writing in Psychoanalysis. *Psychoanalytic Quarterly* 93:135–156.

Lafarge, L. 2024. What We Do, What We Say, What We Don't Say: Confidentiality In The Publication Of Clinical Writing. *The Psychoanalytic Quarterly* 93(1):77–103. https://doi.org/10.1080/00332828.2024.2316219

Lear, J. 2003. Confidentiality as a virtue. In *Confidentiality: Ethical Perspectives and Clinical Dilemmas*, edited by C. Levin, A. Furlong & M. K. O'Neil, 3–18. New York: Routledge.

Lemma, A. 2023. Writing and Intimate Privacy. *Journal of the American Psychoanalytic Association* 71:1041–1045.

Levin, C. 2000. The Siege of Psychotherapeutic Space: Psychoanalysis in the Age of Transparency. *Canadian Journal of Psychoanalysis* 9:187–215.

Morissette, Y.-M. 2000. Deux ou trois choses que je sais d'elle (la rationalité juridique). *McGill Law Journal* 45:591–605. Consulted November 7, 2924. https://canlii.ca/t/2pgb

Ogden, T. H. 2024. Ontological Psychoanalysis in Clinical Practice. *The Psychoanalytic Quarterly* 93(1):13–31. https://doi.org/10.1080/00332828.2024.2314776

Robertson, B. M. 2013a. Sibling Violence, Trauma, and Reality: A Clinical Report. *Canadian Journal of Psychoanalysis* 21:35–43.

Robertson, B. M. 2013b. The Analyst's Pain: An Aspect of Clinical Writing and Publication. *International Psychoanalytic Association panel Prague* 2013.

Sheppard, G. 2015. A landmark decision for counsellors in Canada. https://www.ccpaaccp.ca/wp-content/uploads/2015/05/NOE.Landmark-Decision-with-Implications-for-Counsellors-in-Canada.pdf Consulted November 4, 2024.

Slovenko, R. 1998. *Psychotherapy and Confidentiality: Testimonial Privileged Communication, Breach of Confidentiality, and Reporting Duties.* Springfield, Illinois: Charles C Thomas.

Stein, M. H. 1988b. Writing about Psychoanalysis: II. Analysts Who Write, Patients Who Read. *Journal of the American Psychoanalytic Association* 36:393–408.

Stimmel, B. 2013. The Conundrum of Confidentiality. *Canadian Journal of Psychoanalysis* 21(1):84–106.

Stimmel, B. 2024. Episode 163: Secrets Kept and Secrets Told: the Analyst's Responsibility with Barbara Stimmel. IPA Off the Couch. July 14. https://ipaoffthecouch.org/2024/07/14/episode-163-secrets-kept-and-secrets-told-the-analysts-responsibility-with- barbarastimmel-phd-new-york/

Note

1 Though I cannot find the exact reference, C. Bollas has had the same intuition regarding the pertinence of this legal principle to the protection of psychoanalytic work.

Chapter 7

Concluding notes

Despite from the outset restricting the thematic boundaries of this monograph to aspects of the framework the author has found challenging, we have constantly been at the fringe of broad questions of psychoanalytic theory and practice. Analysts and their patients have been modifying the framework since Freud first instituted it, as he himself gave them cause to follow. They have been doing this because of practical considerations or to widen the scope of analytic theory to new populations or because of the psychic limitations of one or the other partner to the analytic project. Though the moniker *putting the frame to work* is probably mine, evidence has been presented to show that the concept is not foreign to most analysts. In communicating the advantages of putting contested parts of the frame "to work", that is, by offering them the same analytic attention as the patient's discourse, this monograph has omitted many contributions, and scarcely developed others (for example, Ferenczi, Roussillon, Ferro, and Green). To keep the text readable and brief, only a handful of authors have been cited to persuade the reader of the widespread adherence to the idea, though it may have been couched in different terms, of welcoming the opportunity of putting the frame to work. The movement in the literature from viewing acting out as purely pathological to seeing its useful communicative aspects is consonant with this general positioning.

Borrowing from Laplanche's description of his own career as studying so closely the sequences of inspired insights, inconsistencies, and regressions in the Freudian oeuvre – applying the Freudian method to the Freudian corpus – that he made it "creak" (grincer), I have evoked the image and sound of "groaning" in the framework, as in the sound of wood responding to changes in air pressure or load, as metaphor for occasional strain as an integral part of the setting's ongoing "being". Once the framework has been set up, it can be expected to groan sooner or later. *It is in this benevolent expectation of "trouble" as an inherent part of the therapeutic couple's getting to more deeply know each other that starkly distinguishes the psychoanalytic frame from that emulated by professional regulatory bodies.*

The rub was, and remains, to distinguish which alterations in either the external or the internal frame deepen and broaden the reach of psychoanalytic treatment, and which weaken the dyad's ability to notice and analyse repudiated parts of the self. In perusing the literature, we have found that the agreement about putting the frame to

DOI: 10.4324/9781003527459-8

work fractures when clinical examples are perused in some detail since analysts from different parts of the world and from alternate theoretical backgrounds have quite different views of therapeutic action and their role as clinicians in achieving it. Major theoretical differences have been revealed in the apprehension of what it means to the dyad and in what manner it factors into therapeutic progress. Some have argued for the frame's flexibility, encouraging "adaptation" to patients' psychic limitations, while others insist that the frame is a "third", not to be manipulated by either party without due study of the unconscious resistances potentially in play. Like Boesky (2015), we welcome the theoretical pluralism that has so enriched our literature. What remains constant among working analysts regardless of "school" of origin is a commitment to making meaning. Thus, we must be prepared for, and even encourage, our peers to query our particular approach to the problems we have encountered. Is our personal theory both internally coherent and defensible in others' eyes? Have we gone as far as we could enlarging the capacity to feel and think of particular patients given their psychic structure and the time and commitment they have made to the work? Are some frames of reference incommensurable with our own?

The present monograph hopes to help beginners in *constructing* (and for more experienced therapists, in *tinkering with)* a workable frame without recourse to a one-size-fits-all. *The ultimate usefulness of theory is its generation of new psychic receptors for the thoughtful clinician.* The personal stance in this monograph has been in favour of a strong frame, of the expectation of its inevitable breaches or failures (perpetrated by either the patient or the analyst), and of the fertile opportunities thereby offered to discern and elaborate hidden longings and frustrations. The French analyst, Raymond Cahn, espoused a view similar to our own when he argued in 2008 that:

> If the absence of the gaze of the other [in the classical disposition of couch and chair] is often an important factor in the unfolding of the process, it can also occasionally constitute an obstacle. In any case, whether the setup includes [being able to look at the analyst] or not, the essential clearly appears elsewhere, transcending the alternative of lying down or sitting. [What counts], regardless of the chosen framework, is the psychoanalytic manner or lack of it with which the therapist greets and utilizes patient material. Even better: *the frame itself can become the place for process to unfold and thus render psychoanalytic a number of interventions which up to now have been considered purely psychotherapeutic.*
>
> (emphasis added, 15)

One cannot study framework issues without including the analyst's internal framework, that is, his or her understanding of what might constitute an analytic "benefit". Without a rather clearly developed analytic offer, and concomitant setting in mind, two pitfalls can occur: on the one hand, by fetishizing the framework, or, on the other, by losing track of its underlying purpose. The latter, as conceived here, is to enlarge the ego's capacity to tolerate and elaborate repressed and split off remnants of the past and present, as well as to constructively meet strong affect, inner turmoil and uncertainty in the current relationship with the therapist and others. In this book psychoanalysis "proper" has not been set apart from psychoanalytically oriented psychotherapy. That structural change is possible in both types of work, *especially if undertaken by fully trained psychoanalysts,* is now taken for granted by many. Of the various terms authors have used to describe the analyst's setup, our personal preference is for the term "framework" precisely because it contains the word "work", in continuity with several classical Freudian concepts (such as "dream-work", the "work of mourning", and others). A similar view of the setting has been expressed by Parsons (2000, 59): "there is work involved in sustaining it. There is a sense of tension. . . Keeping oneself attuned to the realm of psychic reality rather than ordinary reality requires a particular sort of effort".The psychic work of both parties in the analytic relationship is required before it can become what Donnet called an "analysing situation".

The comprehension of the analytic process valued in this book is not one of mutual recognition and symmetry, goals considered at least partially if not completely illusory in the context of inherently divided subjects. It starts with accepting that one does not know, cannot quickly know, the hidden springs of vitality and destruction in patients when we first meet. How could it be otherwise if we harken to Freud's foundational discovery of resistance as an obstacle and fulcrum of analytic work? For many years my colleague Jacques Mauger (most recently in 2025) has reiterated that "the practice of psychoanalysis is inseparable from a taking into account of resistance to psychoanalysis" (1). In fact "it is where it is resisting that there can actually be a chance of having analysis" (7) (There is a word play of meanings for "ça" in the original French which can stand for "this", "there", it" and "id").

The words of Jacques André (André & Simpson, 2006) were meant to shock: "*You can't have an analysis between people who understand each other (get along) (s'entendent)*" (564). In using the French verb "s'entendre", André plays with the condensation in French of two meanings: to hear each other and to get along with each other. Agreement and understanding between the protagonists in the analytic situation –unconscious or not – signals, in André's view, more of a hindrance to the analytic process than the mark of its dynamic (566). Such a vision of the analytic couple seems counterintuitive unless one bears in mind the Freudian vision of the radical otherness of unconscious life. As we opined in the company of Laurence Kahn at the beginning of this book, the psychoanalytic method has as task to make room for the "uninvited stowaway" within the psychic envelope, that of our patients as well as of ourselves. Glitches in the framework may reveal a stowaway or two. In this way of looking at our work, *the psychoanalytic setting cannot be a place of zero tolerance; rather it must provide for insult and duress.* Both the analyst's mental attitude and his or her setting is only *ideally invariant,* that is invariance is an ideal not always a fact, subject as Ferro pointed out to oscillations, such that it is "*continuously disturbed and continuously refound*" (2002/2021, original emphasis, 122).

It would be unconscionable to expect less experienced psychoanalytic clinicians to meet their new patients "without memory or desire", if one Bionian piece of advice were taken at face value. A unique preparedness in the clinician's mind and manner is conducive to eliciting the patient's cooperation in the setup. Alongside the "evenly hovering attention" counselled by Freud (1912), the "analytic offer" benefits from an equally "floating theorization" (de Mijolla-Mellor, 1998) to thicken and anchor that listening. Since more rides on the "personal equation" (https://en.wikipedia.org/wiki/Personal_equation) in our field than in other fields of study, not only does training have to include a good personal analysis, it also means that a universal and manualized framework becomes an impossibility. Ironically, the dream of being able to offer "personalized treatments", such as in the increasing competence of oncologists to adjust cancer protocols to the genetic profile of their patients' illnesses, has the risk of normative, manualized, implications in our field. Every psychoanalytic framework derives necessarily, and ethically, from a personal distillation of theory and experience.

Consequently, we set great store by the analyst's capacity to introduce the framework, to adequately present it, to inhabit it in the initial interviews, and to listen carefully for the way in which patients understand and respond to it. Emphasis has been laid on the usefulness of a time for comprehending separated from a time for conclusion in patients' consent to this unusual treatment relationship. Equally important has been the possibility of intellectualizing consent in "telling" patients what analysis is instead of "showing" them by the quality of the clinician's listening. A conception of our role as a presence deliberately partially "absentified" to facilitate the analyst's thinking from a different place than in transference (and countertransference) projections, and to survive as an object used by the patient in bringing alive meaningful or missing aspects of past objects, has found expression in our intellection of the setting. The reader is referred to Chapter 1 for a detailed description of the present author's *usual range of frameworks* (note the plural) and her manner of introducing it or them. Only one detail will be mentioned here as illustration of the specificity of our approach: our treatment of payment where written invoices are not given to patients nor are receipts prepared in advance. The tradition of presenting a monthly bill to patients, either by hand or in the mail, deprives in our view the therapeutic couple of fertile transferential and countertransferential information. Without a tangible piece of paper with a written sum on it to rein in their unconscious dynamics, patients are as liable to overpay as to underpay. The absence of a tangible bill increases the malleability of the payment gesture whereas a tangible bill forcloses this expressivity.

A repeated thread in this book is the belief that *the genius of the Freudian framework is – generally speaking – as a receptive organ, empowering the dyad to sense phenomena which could otherwise easily slip by unperceived in "real" life. The metaphor is that of sensor more than of picture frame.* In the consulting room, inadvertently and unexpectedly, overdetermined investment of aspects of the setup can emerge "ultra-clearly", as in the perceptually enhanced quality of dream elements which Freud unraveled as nodal points for multiple lines of latent thinking. An analogy was made with the search for the Higgs Bosons sub-atomic particle which was theorized long before it was confirmed in observation, thanks to the special "container" of the highest-energy particle collider in the world and to an incredible number of experimental repetitions. Even then, the existence of this particle can only be demonstrated from monitoring its decay into other elements. In analogous fashion, the psychic stowaways of human beings can similarly remain invisible or overlooked in ordinary life before being inferred from their offshoots in speech or behaviour in the specialized setting created by Freud.

The psychoanalytic framework, compared to the settings cultivated by other psychotherapeutic approaches, is just as "unnatural" and "constructed" as a particle collider. A "very peculiar activity", in the words of Caper (1992, 287). Thus, as intimated earlier, it is not by making the patient feel "comfortable" and "understood" when he or she first meets the analyst that the conditions for observation are inherently propitious. *We interpret the notion of benevolent neutrality as a certain "hollowing out" of the analyst's presence, a partial self-effacement, but not emotional distance, to leave space for the patient's spontaneous expression.* In contrast to alternate approaches to psychological distress, the psychoanalytic situation puts the patient somewhat off kilter, a delicate posture which takes training and experience to optimally manage. If things go well, both parties to the initial interviews submit to a certain duress as unconscious anxiety is mobilized which may take time to deconstruct.

In Chapter 3, we saw that "some of the most complex and fateful analytic work can take place in the early stages of treatment before an analytic process has fully deepened or matured" (Stern, 2009, 647). This observation helps us to understand *what a strain on both parties the beginning of treatment can be*, an insight we owe to Bion (1979) who theorized the unleashing of an "emotional storm" though – weirdly – this event can easily be overlooked or defended against by both parties. Lack of awareness of this initial storm can lead to the patient's premature flight from treatment or to the unconscious creation by the clinical pair of an ongoing blind spot in their work together. Though Freud warned of the panic and confusion that the "fire" of unconscious transference can bring to an ongoing "theatre" of analytic treatment (Freud, 1914), I do not know of a passage in his work wherein he addresses the intangible storm which may break out right at the beginning of treatment. Yet, the unconscious anxieties stirred up in the two protagonists at the inception of their relationship are not accidental, nor are they something to be avoided. *Implausible though it may seem, this state of disequilibrium is the vital hallmark of a psychoanalytic framework and methodology.* From the vantage point espoused here, initial interviews receive the same analytic attention and attitude as those that follow, so there is not a before and an after commencement of treatment. Whereas for psychotherapists inspired by other theoretical orientations, the "treatment" phase is envisaged as initiated *after* a preliminary evaluative interview, and after the framework has been explained to patients.

Collective psychoanalytic experience confirms empirical research: informed consent, despite the precautions of contemporary ethical guidelines, can be neither "informed subjectively" nor stable over time. Yet until recently the matter has received little theoretical curiosity among us, surprising given that one might think that the notion of unconscious determinism would lead analysts to be more suspicious of the cursory manner in which many of us apparently deal with patients' consent. A distinction was advanced between the notions of "consent" and "assent" to psychoanalytic treatment. The first term was used to designate acquiescence based on intellectual understanding whereas the latter referred to more bittersweet acceptance of the setting after the patient has struggled with doubt and ambivalence in negotiating breaches of it. Our thinking has benefited from inspired insights into the "psychoanalysis of the frame" by Latin American authors. On the one hand, there have been the Barangers (Baranger, Baranger, & Mom, 1983; Maldonado, 2022) with their notion of "bastion" as tenacious phantasy, shameful but crucial to the patient's psychic equilibrium, deposited in the setting where it remains invisible. It is only when the setting is disturbed revealing the existence of a hidden bastion that analyst and patient can have a crack at analysing and dismantling it. On the other hand, there has been Bleger's similar insight into the frame's role as depository of the most primitive part of the personality. Bleger (1967) added that "there are *two settings*: one which is proposed and maintained by the psychoanalyst, and accepted consciously by the patient, and another, that of the 'phantom world' into which the patient projects" (233, original emphasis). The astuteness of these intuitions affords fresh vantage points concerning behaviour that could easily be reductively dismissed as "resistance". Or perhaps these additions to psychoanalytic theory could be said to reveal resistance in all its vital regressive and progressive polyphony. These and other considerations mentioned in this book inform a belief in a tensile ethics specific to analytic purpose with preoccupation for a truly intra-psychically informed assent to the disruptiveness of the analytic project. Occasionally renewable, such assent preserves the inherent tension and strangeness of the analytic frame. Tact and timing are crucial. Though it may take a while for the patient to be able to hear the following delicate inquiry into the impact of his or her analyst's absence, Boesky has intuitively sensed the shadow cast by the two-setting problem: "Do you think it would sound weird to think that this upcoming interruption in our work might evoke some worries for you?" (2015, 68).

We found it useful to introduce a distinction between *informed consenting and good enough assenting*. While the patient needs to have access to a certain amount of information about the analytic setting to *consent* to beginning treatment, deeper *assent* will come through the insight about himself in the form of the working through of unexpected emotional responses to aspects (usually disruptive) of the frame and of the person of the analyst. Can there be – at least with certain patients – an *illusion of informed consent* insofar as the operating assumptions of the framework consciously or unconsciously assumed by the patient are not necessarily identical to those held by the analyst? Psychologically naïve patients are not at first in the position of sharing our psychoanalytic assumptions about the value of the framework we propose to them, nor may they have any idea of the unconscious "flags" burning within them until they stumble upon them in the course of treatment. We are, nevertheless, discomforted by the position taken by analysts who believe that the unconscious precludes adequately informed consent. Not being aware of certain responses to the analyst and to the setting complexifies the process of consent but does not negate it, particularly if the analyst remains attuned to signs of the patient's unconscious ambivalence. If the analyst merely "recommends" an analytic treatment with a list of requirements, and awaits a global agreement, is there not a chance that the analyst is substituting her thinking for that of the patient?

In this matter, Freud cannot serve as much of a guide. Other than treating the initial frame of mind and setup, Freud wrote little about other aspects of the frame, such as conflicts of interest, confidentiality, informed consent, third party payment, record-keeping, and related administrative offshoots of clinical work. The concern about proper technique among second-generation analysts may have inadvertently externalized the issue of consent and displaced it onto to evaluations of patient analysibility, thus bypassing the patient's self-reflective participation in the decision. In this book, we have demonstrated that the risks of negative outcomes in analysis are unlikely to be alleviated by the informed consent guidelines so far developed by legal scholars and professional regulatory bodies. We argued for continued dialogue between evolving case law and legal theory and psychoanalytic practice and theory as mutually enriching, but were adamant that attempts to bind them together, or – as was more common in the past – to impose the law on top of psychoanalytic ethics, should be avoided. The law cannot prescribe "best practice" though it can integrate – or at least dialogue with – contemporary scientific (psychoanalysis is considered here as a scientific study of the unconscious) consensus. Like it or not, components of drive remain resolutely non-subjective, experienced but not mastered by the ego, possibly "owned-up to" but never completely owned.

In Chapter 4, the analytic offer was seen as risking becoming meaningless if patients are not yet curious about the irrationality of their symptoms. The request for treatment implies a pledge for the future, and the wish for help to overcome internal obstacles to that wished-for future, which can make the offer of, and assent to, a psychoanalytic framework a shared identificatory project for achieving a more integrated and energetic inner life. Paradoxically, resistance to the psychoanalytic setting can lodge within the analyst who shies away from the deep engagement required to kept alive the patient's hope for a more satisfying future, under the guise of "recognizing" and "adapting" to patients' ambivalence about accepting a setting more likely to make that goal reachable. The analytic offer was viewed as preceding the patient's arrival as a strategy and "posture" rather than as a fixed position. We stressed the temporality of an "identificatory project" inherent in the offer of psychoanalytic treatment responsive to a wish for a better future rendered possible by a more integrated self. The therapist's *desire to analyse* presented to the patient as an *offer to analyse* is not necessarily supportive or reassuring to the ego of the patient, but it carries with it a real hope for internal transformation. This offer cannot be "co-created" in the customary sense because it has to *start* with the analytically oriented therapist and it has to *withstand* the patient's necessary (and welcome for observation) attempts to turn it into something else, more narcissistically rewarding or libidinally satisfying. If the necessary dependency of the human subject on a psychic passage through the other is fully appreciated, we are led to concur with Aulagnier that there is an unavoidable violence of interpretation inherent in the psychoanalytic offer. We illustrated with reference to Rothstein's engaging series of articles on how he brings patients into a subjectively appropriable analysing situation. His work shows how *the symbolizing capacities of the analytic situation can be paradoxically instigated or restored through the analyst's momentary twisting of the frame.*

Sometimes, there is no apparent "emotional storm" in the initial interviews when patients present whose ways of thinking are strictly "operational", that is factual in a concrete sense without double meanings and capacity for imaginative play. I have recently come across an "old" article of Mariela Aisenstein (1998) whose work with psychosomatic patients led her to stress an aspect of the analytic offer particular to these cases which most analysts can easily generalize to other psychic configurations:

> [T]hey require a unique labour of approach where a "well tempered seduction" in the psychoanalyst participates with something of the order of an anticipatory illusion of shared pleasure in mental functioning.
>
> (31)

Like other analysts referred to in this book, Aisenstein emphasized the importance of a *theoretical container* in the analyst ("powerful theoretical convictions" (39) in her words) which precedes the patient's request and informs its reception for both parties.

We scrutinized a rather typical disparity between regulatory body deontology and the ethics of a psychoanalytic framework. The notion of our work as an "offer" rather than a "constraint" allowed the author wiggle room vis-à-vis the local Order of Psychologists' legitimate concern about the potential for abuse of patient consent for financial gain without having to resort to the distraction of written contracts as patient protection. Langs wrote about the classical framework as a structural "provision". The idea of "providing" is close to mine of "offering". It is there to be used. "Establishing, managing, rectifying, and analysing infringements on the frame constitute a major group of relatively unrecognized and consistently crucial interventions" (1979, 12).

We have had several occasions to refer to Ogden's (1992) thoughtful considerations of the frame. For instance, he proposes (1996) the couch to patients as *an arrangement useful to him, the analyst, thus making it a petition in the name of the analyst's ability to pursue analytic goals, not an imposition thrust upon the patient.* In this interesting twist of perspective, Odgen asks for the patient's consent to him, the analyst, being out of sight of the patient. I also liked Odgen's recent suggestion of the term "style" over "the theory-stiffened term technique" to designate the manner of developing one's own way of being an analyst (2024, 20). The word "style" rather than "technique" has the advantage of pointing to a "personal factor" in the individual analyst's refinement of the framework. However, it has the disadvantage of potentially being reduced (I am not saying Odgen is implying this but others might read it this way) to an aesthetic or comfort choice, rather than posited as a way of working imbued with the analyst's theory of therapeutic action and which can be critically evaluated by peers for misunderstood countertransference shortcomings.

This is not the place to review the extensive literature beginning in the seventies of inquiry into a widespread decline in psychoanalytic practice. Compared to the period when the idealization of psychoanalysis could lead patients and analysts to disillusionment or mutual alienation, the risk today may be a fading of hope on both sides for help from psychoanalysis as anything more than a benign encounter between two well-meaning individuals. I have argued that *less experienced therapists assume they understand what their patients are saying.* They accept the manifest content of hackneyed phrases that have lost their mystery and mislead the therapist into believing that they come from a place of insight. The therapist makes the mistake of not tarrying to expand and decorticate them, whereas there can be a stupendous store of overlooked associations hidden in the banal crevasses of the ordinary speech patients bring to the consulting room. Some time was spent in Chapter 4 examining the *acquirable art of conveying non-confronting curiosity.* All the evidence suggests that for a psychoanalytic process to engage, the analytic offer and the framework accompanying it have to go out on a limb; they have to be already there to hear the patient in an out-of-the-ordinary way. This is related to resistance, to the inevitable violence of interpretation attached to bringing into the relationship what has been disavowed or ignored by the ego. Thus, we reiterate conceptualizing the analytic setting is an *identificatory offer not an imposition; it is an invitation for the future, or more accurately, an offer to join the patient's quest to look forward to a better psychic future.* It is not a *push* towards the future. There is a qualitative and temporal distinction between viewing one's personal therapy project as a "treatment" to expunge bothersome symptoms, presumably leaving the rest of the personality intact, and as a project in alliance with the therapist to move forward towards transformative ego-ideals.

In the vexing challenge of handling missed sessions, theme of Chapter 5, it is clarifying to think in terms of a double causality: there is the causality of material reality (stalled vehicle, cancelled metro train, sick child, broken leg, etc.) and there is the causality of a transference wish. Since the two are intertwined, they are not easily teased apart for separate appreciation. Several short vignettes were shared to demonstrate that this work cannot be done at a distance, such as in a text or an email. Even a phone conversation might be inadequate. *The "operation of elaboration" needs to be inhabited and handled with kid gloves.* Detective stories have taught us the crucial prohibition against disturbing the scene of a crime before the investigation has been completed. The missed session is similar; it is important not to disturb the "scene of the symptom" until the dyad can pour over it together. Hence the importance of learning to wait before reacting, especially when there is no objective emergency, since the reaction can so easily muddle the "scene" by introducing foreign elements of the therapist's anxiety, reproach, or call to order.

The break in the frame brought about by a missed session can be intersubjectively complex and emotionally violent. The missed session brings an intrinsic or incipient threat to treatment which seems to spur the undertrained or inexperienced therapist to act out in rapid tit for tat, instead of offering noncommittal containment until the dyad has the time to examine the situation together. There is a world of difference between technical rigidity and thoughtful resolve. It is better to suspend judgement until the dyad has the time to reflect; this negative capability (the capacity to tolerate not knowing for a time) is easier to preserve if one is persuaded of the rewards of an unhurried attention to particulars. Some time was devoted to discussion of the payment gesture related to missed sessions as "representation" of the absent, eclipsed, or left out parts of the psyche.

The last Chapter 6 summarized thirty odd years of concern and reflection about confidentiality in psychoanalytic work. What does it mean specifically for us? Does it conflict with obligations towards third parties? Has it been overly concretized in some cases? Has it been too readily diluted in others? What honour is there to a method which announces the limits of confidentiality before even initiating an analytic relationship? Are we unconcerned about the broader integrity of psychotherapy practiced by non-analysts as long as our ivory towers remain untouched? Do our professional associations leave individual analysts to their own devices when it comes to defending and thinking about confidentiality? Can we publish clinical material without asking patients permission to do so? How might such permission-seeking alter work with these patients or distort the array of clinical accounts to be shared in the literature? The author presented her view of confidentiality as a skin rather than a lock, a protected "confiding" beyond manifest speech instead of secret sharing of particular content and defined by analytic purpose rather than external pressure. The notion of *deliberative process* was introduced as a potentially powerful legal shield for confidentiality in psychoanalysis.

Though lifelong learning through peer supervision, seminars, and reading has to be an ethical requirement of every psychoanalyst's career, a jarring aspect of contemporary continuing education requirements is the expectation that references be made to "recent" work, that is, within the past decade. The bizarre implication of this requirement is that our work has to keep up with the latest empirical evidence or politically correct bestseller. However, the unconscious is empathically neither up to date nor politically correct. I consciously end this book, therefore, with a "really old" reference to the work of the French psychoanalyst, Georges Favez, which anticipates central premises argued in previous chapters and which, incidentally, I only stumbled across on the verge of submitting this manuscript to the publisher. In 1958, Favez gave a conference "About contestation", in which he argued that the patient's contestation of analysis and of his/her analyst, variously understood as objection/resistance/protest/challenge, was a universal expression of our struggle to recognize or disown the reappearance of the child's helplessness. It is this contestation which saves the analysis, Favez felt, because through it "can come out, can bring me the ego subject, out of its fainting away, out of its sleep" (35).

Favez makes the same point Laurence Kahn will make a generation later that "it is to be able to meet the unexpected that one must be prepared, and not to be able to anticipate everything. One never knows, in truth, how an analysis will unfold" (40–41). Anticipating our concerns with the topic of missed sessions and our notion of the frame as an identificatory offer rather than an authoritarian constraint, he stated that it is the question of money that often brings contestation to the forefront between analysand and analyst. It can, however, deteriorate into "a test of strength", a situation he cautions us to avoid. "The subject's sincerity, which is immediately put into question by money, is more important in the moment as well as throughout the analysis than the money he gives or does not give. We must not abuse our privileged position in this regard" (42). In a very modern "bi-personal" musing, he asks if the most important question is whether observed contestations are offshoots of the analyst's way of doing things which until now he, the analyst, has only rationalized? (42). In every case, Favez viewed contestation as always significant and signifying.

> One cannot spare the analysand from contestation. Without it, he or she will not be able to tell what has been at stake for them in their analysis. And it is contestation, finally, which restores the unity of their personality and saves it. *Contestation can do this, every time good use is made of it.*
>
> (added emphasis, 43)

In this quote, Favez seems to be anticipating Winnicott's concept of the use of the object and Roussillon's (2015) reflections on the analyst as malleable medium. I was also surprised to find Favez making a distinction similar to the one made in this book about the psychic labour separating assent and consent in psychoanalysis when he claimed at the end of this article: "Thus analysis can be … *attestation* after having been *contestation*" (emphasis added, 43). My notion of putting the frame to work relates to the patient's (or the analyst's) unconscious contestation of commitment to what it means to be in analysis. And Favez's article independently asserted the truth discovered by the Barangers and by Bleger (also "old" references) that patient protest against reality constraints, hidden and then uncovered by analytic work, can be the most alive and vital part of the patient's libidinal and narcissistic economy: recrimination, cry to be heard, refusal to give up on something unconsciously believed to be essential to the self. *It is because it matters that we must try to deal with it clearly, adroitly, and compassionately.*

References

André, J. & Simpson, R. B. 2006. The Misunderstanding (Le Malentendu). *Psychoanalytic Quarterly* 75:557–581.

Baranger, M., Baranger, W., & Mom, J. 1983. Process and Non-Process in Analytic Work. *International Journal of Psychoanalysis* 64:1–15.

Bion, W. R. 1979. Making the best of a bad job. In *Clinical seminars and Four Papers*, 247–257, edited by W. R. Bion & F. Bion. Abingdon, UK: Fleetwood Press, 1987.

Bleger, J. 1967. Psycho-analysis of the psychoanalytic frame. In *Symbiosis and ambiguity: a psychoanalytic study*, 1–13, trans. S. Rogers and edited by J. Churcher & L. Bleger. London: Routledge, 2013. https://doi.org/10.4324/9781003252252-1

Boesky, D. 2015. Action and the Analyst's Responsibility: Commentary on Greenberg. *Journal of the American Psychoanalytic Association* 63:65–83.

Caper, R. 1992. Does Psychoanalysis Heal? a Contribution to the Theory of Psychoanalytic Technique. *International Journal of Psychoanalysis* 73:283–292.

Donnet, J.-L. 2001. From the Fundamental Rule to the Analysing Situation. *International Journal of Psychoanalysis* 82:129–140. Trans Andrew Weller.

De Mijolla-Mellor, S. 1998. *Penser la psychose. Une lecture de l'oeuvre de Piera Aulagnier*, Paris, Dunod.

Favez, G. 1958. De la contestation (about contestation). In *Psychanalyste, où est-tu?* 33–43. Montreal: L'Harmattan, 1999.

Ferro, A. 2002. *In the Analyst's Consulting Room*. Translated by P. Slotkin. Hove, UK: Routledge, 2021.

Freud, S. 1914. Remembering, repeating and working-through. *Standard Edition* 12: 147–156.

Langs, R. 1979. Interventions in the Bipersonal Field. *Contemporary Psychoanalysis* 15:1–54.

Maldonado, J. L. 2022. Madeleine and Willy Baranger's Contribution to Psychoanalysis. *International Journal of Psychoanalysis* 103:872–889.

Mauger, J. 2025. L'avenir d'une resistance. Presentation made to the *Siciéty psychanalytique de Montréal* on March 12, 2025.

Ogden, T. H. 1992. Comments on Transference and Countertransference in the Initial Analytic Meeting. *Psychoanalytic Inquiry* 12:225–247.

Ogden, T. H. 1996. Reconsidering Three Aspects of Psychoanalytic Technique. *International Journal of Psychoanalysis* 77:883–899.

Ogden, T. H. 2024. Ontological Psychoanalysis in Clinical Practice. *The Psychoanalytic Quarterly* 93(1):13–31.

Parsons, M. 2000. Psychic reality, negation, and the analytic setting. In *The dove that vanishes, the dove that returns*. London: Routledge, 59–75.

Roussillon, R. 2015. An Introduction to the Work on Primary Symbolization. *International Journal of Psychoanalysis* 96:583–594.

Stern, S. 2009. Session Frequency and the Definition of Psychoanalysis. *Psychoanalytic Dialogues* 19:639–655.

Index

work 65, 67; with a psychotic patient
66–67, 69–70; as refusal 66, 82, 84; as
renewable 77, 79; as resistance 72, 79;
risk of patient misunderstanding 66,
68; template of 125–126; unconscious
perception of analyst, patient 72; as
unique to particular analyst 71–72;
See also assent; beginning of treatment;
professional regulation
initiating psychoanalysis 77–78
instant of the glance 41; *See also* moment
of concluding; time for understanding;
time of conclusion
institutional setting 1–2, 4, 44, 108–110,
121, 128–130
internal analytic setting 21–23, 54
internal frame/analytic mind/analytic
attitude *See* analytic offer
*International Journal of Psychoanalysis
(IJP)* 141, 143
International Psychoanalytical Association
(IPA) 44, 117–118; Report of the
IPA Confidentiality Committee
144; Working Party on Initiating
Psychoanalysis (WPIP) 36, 64, 77
intervention compared to interpretation
54–55
intrinsic factors 3, 22, 45, 91

Jaffee vs. Redmond 127, 128, 131
Joseph, B. 10*n*3, 58

Kahn, L. 18, 77, 91, 148, 156
Kantrowitz, J. L. 145
Kanwal, G. 145
Kattlove, S. 78
Kirshner, L. 77
Kite, J. 26, 78
Klein, M. 10*n*3, 91, 107, 108
Kohut, H. 68
Krueger, D. 32

Lacan, J. 24, 25, 40–41, 68, 72, 73, 100,
111, 113; demand 94–95; desire 94–95;
ego as place of alienation 60*n*2; need
94–95; psychic experience, division of
47
Lafarge, L. 145
Langs, R. 25, 26, 153
Laplanche, J. 2, 5, 19, 21, 24, 26, 40, 49,
64, 68, 84*n*7, 92, 103, 104
Lear, J. 67

Lemma, A. 145
Letarte, P. 8–10, 15–17, 21–23, 27, 45, 46,
53–56
Levin, C. 43, 130, 133, 145
Levine, A. 45–47
Lew, R. 32
Lidz. C.W. 85*n*10
Lipton, S. D. 22, 58, 99
listening: benevolently neutral 134–135; to
manifest content 66, 91; psychoanalytic
29, 90
listening to listening 26
Little, M. I. 17, 63
logical time 40; *See also* time for
understanding; time of conclusion
Lohser, B. 108

Macdonald, R. 133, 137
"making" *vs.* "finding" analysands 103
Manzano, J. J. 5, 22–23, 47, 48, 92
Marleau, I. 120
Masson, J. M. 97
May, U. 69
microdots 98, 114; *See also* Colombo
Miller, J. M. 7
Mills, R. 128
Milner, M. 14
Minow, M. 130
missed session: anguish for the analyst 111;
circulation of money 108; consent and
assent 110; contingency, role of 114;
co-signed written contracts 117–123;
external circumstances 113; fantacized
payment 108; gesture of payment 108;
mutative interpretation 107; payment
for 69, 108–111; representation of
155; symbolic markers 109; symbolic
payments, child 109; tangible bill 115
misunderstanding 68, 84*n*5, 113, 118–119;
confidentiality in psychoanalytic work
131; frame 66; usefulness of 119
moment of concluding 41
Morissette, Y.-M. 140, 145
Morris, H. 78
Moss, D. 78
mutative interpretation 107

negative capability 91, 114, 115, 155
negotiation of frame, relational approaches
48–50
Newton, P. M. 108
non-process 5; *See also* process

Nordmo, M. 90
not knowing *See* subject-supposed-to-know
not zero tolerance 8–10, 17, 148; *See also* benevolent expectation of trouble
Novick, K. K. and J. 135, 137

Office of Science, US Department of Energy 18
Ogden, T. H. 6, 18, 27, 56, 72, 78–79, 93, 104, 116, 143, 145, 153
O'Neill, P. 79
overdetermination as epistemological problem 37

paradox, the role of 19, 23, 52, 55, 59, 77, 78, 83–84, 103, 110, 152–153
Parsons, M. 21, 22, 148
Patel, M. 137
payment: as incest interdiction 110; institutional settings 108–110; lack of 110; for missed session 69, 108–111; as part of analytic offer 90; receipts 31, 115–116, 149; as wish for analysis 96; *See also* gesture of payment; symbolic markers
perplexity about oneself as indication for psychoanalytic approach 39
personal equation, the: in handling the frame 6; in preferred theory 6
phantasy, temporality of 101
Polubinskaya, S. V. 130
Pontalis, J.-B. 23
Popova, M. 1
Poulin, B. 118–120
process 3, 43, 45–46, 65–66, 76–77, 120, 131–133, 155; *See also* frame, when "groaning"; informed consent; non-process
professional novel 2
professional regulation 1, 4, 63, 81, 123, 136, 146, 152
psychic posture, analyst 90, 99, 104*n*1; *See also* analytic offer
psychic stowaways 18–21, 37, 91, 150
psychoanalysis 1–2; consent and assent 65–68; and current realities of marketplace 44; emotional difficulty for analyst 20; informed consent (*see* informed consent); lay analysts 123*n*2
psychoanalytically-oriented psychotherapy 3, 6, 19, 25, 41, 56, 65, 115, 120, 148; *See also* psychotherapy *vs.* psychoanalysis
psychoanalytic community 24, 71
psychoanalytic setting 8–10; disruption to 41–43; emotional storm 19, 64, 77, 150, 153; first interview 64, 77–83; four quadrants 22; out-of-ordinariness of 18–21; professional presentation, analysts 73; psychic stowaways 18–21; reformulation of 54–60; zero tolerance 8–10
psychoanalytic site/psychoanalytic situation 5, 19, 46, 56, 69, 72, 79, 84*n*7, 92, 136, 150
psychoanalytic thinking 13, 20, 72
psychotherapy *vs.* psychoanalysis 22, 31, 53
publication of clinical material *See* clinical writing

Quebec Order of Psychologists (OPQ) 118–119

Raney, J. 31
Rangell, L. 76
receipts as part of framework 31, 115–116, 149
reformulation of setting 54–60; bringing aggressivity into setting 56; internal setting 56–57; interventions by analyst 54–55; restoring the setting 56
register of neurotic functioning 25
regulatory bodies *See* professional regulation
Reid, W. 8, 21, 23–25
Reith, B. 63, 64, 78, 102
relational approaches to the framework 46–48
remoralization 90
resistance: in the analyst 72; in the patient 99, 102–103; as withdrawal of consent 79
Ridel, L. 100
Robertson, B. M. 144
Rothstein, A. 64, 102–104, 153
Roussillon, R. 3, 21, 23, 24, 157
R. vs Mills 128, 130

Saketopoulou, A. 84*n*7
Saks, E. 71–73, 79, 80
Saucier, J. 110

For Product Safety Concerns and Information please contact our EU
representative GPSR@taylorandfrancis.com
Taylor & Francis Verlag GmbH, Kaufingerstraße 24, 80331 München, Germany

www.ingramcontent.com/pod-product-compliance
Lightning Source LLC
Chambersburg PA
CBHW070343270326
41926CB00017B/3965

9 7 8 1 0 3 2 8 6 4 1 9 8